Cooking Up Memories

A Rockhurst High School
Heritage Cookbook

Rockhurst High School serves the greater Kansas City area by educating Ignatian leaders, Men for Others, in the Roman Catholic, Jesuit college preparatory tradition.

In the spirit of Ignatius Loyola, its goal is for the formation of the whole person within a diverse and disciplined environment, as one who is open to growth, strives for academic excellence, is religious, loving and committed to justice through service.

Rockhurst High School
9301 State Line Road
Kansas City, Missouri 64114
www.rockhursths.edu

To order copies send a check for $24.95 per book plus $3 shipping per book to
Heritage Cookbook
Rockhurst High School
9301 State Line Road
Kansas City, Missouri 64114

Or order online at www.rockhursths.edu

Table of Contents

The Rockettes

This book is a fundraising project for the Rockette Student Assistance Fund. The Rockette group was founded in 2004 by and for Rockhurst Alumni Moms.

The purpose of the Rockettes is twofold: Social and Service. Through our social events (potluck dinners, Masses, etc) Alumni Moms have a means by which to maintain and strengthen the many friendships we made while our sons were students at Rockhurst. In our Service, we have created the Rockette Fund which is available to assist students in covering expenses related to their Rockhurst experience, such as books, retreat fees and special needs. The fund is administered through requests to the Rockhurst Administration and anonymity is maintained.

As Mothers we see the positive impact that Rockhurst had on our sons, and our wish is that every boy who attends Rockhurst will have the opportunity to fully enjoy every aspect of the experience. Every Rockhurst Alumni Mom is a Rockette and every Rockhurst boy is our son.

By purchasing this book, you are helping make the Rockhurst experience attainable for more young men. Thank you for supporting this project!

In the time I have been in Kansas City I have had the pleasure of meeting so many wonderful people. During my tenure it has been a privilege to oversee the final phase of our Millennium Plan. The Loyola Center will benefit our young men for many generations. I am truly grateful to those committed to making Rockhurst High School the exceptional place it is today.

- Rev. Terrence A. Baum, S.J., President

This cookbook speaks volumes of the rich and diverse community I have experienced at Rockhurst High School over the past 29 years. Often we gather "around the table" to celebrate our work, our hopes and dreams. Splendid dishes are the result of the blend of diverse ingredients. In the same way, the diverse Rockhurst community working together for common values and a common purpose has brought us all to this moment in our history. Enjoy these recipes. Savor the moment. The best is yet to come.

- Larry E. Ruby, Principal

Hawklet Heritage

HAWKLET HERITAGE

Rockhurst alumnus Michael Stacy (2003) researched and wrote the information on the backs of each section divider page (like this one.) His brief summaries lend a historical perspective and remind us of events and topics influencing Rockhurst families during these decades.

1900s

National:

Innovation cruised along - at the pace of a Model T - and flew by - like the first airplane - during the first decade of the 20th century. Henry Ford's "Tin Lizzie" made the automobile affordable for the masses rather than a novelty item enjoyed exclusively by the wealthy. Brothers Orville and Wilbur Wright, meanwhile, completed the first successful airplane flight in Kitty Hawk, North Carolina in 1903. The duo of Max Planck and Albert Einstein forever complicated physics classes for future generations of Hawklets, as Planck formulated his quantum theory in 1901 and Einstein followed with his theory of relativity in 1905. The decade was an important one for a couple of America's favorite pastimes: 1903 marked the birth of both the World Series and silent movies.

Local:

The world's focus turned, at least briefly, to Missouri at the turn of the century, as Kansas City's cross-state neighbor St. Louis hosted the 1904 World's Fair and Olympic Summer Games. Across the state, Kansas City was also making a name for itself. The most populous city between its eastern Missouri neighbor and the West Coast at the time, Kansas City welcomed its first steel-frame skyscraper, the RA Long building, and opened the gates to Swope Park zoo during the decade.

Cooking Up Memories:
Gathering the Ingredients

Members of the Rockhurst community were asked to submit their favorite recipes for this book. We make no claim that these are original recipes (except where noted), only delicious! Recipes were tested and selected by our committees, a process we thoroughly enjoyed. Thanks to all who assisted with this sweet and savory task!

Similarly, alumni, parents, faculty, staff and students were asked to send in stories of their Rockhurst experiences. These made for delightful reading! Some alums responded to a questionnaire, asking for favorite teachers and subjects, memories of favorite times and other specific info. Their answers are scattered through the pages of the book, in the blue boxes. The person submitting the story is solely responsible for the validity of the information or recollection.

Our Heritage Committee spent many hours poring through scrapbooks and old newspapers and yearbooks to glean information for the blue "heritage" boxes on the following pages. Although every attempt was made to be accurate, we regret any errors the reader may note. We hope you enjoy reading the heritage sections as much as we enjoyed compiling it.

In addition, there are several longer pieces, as well as national and local historical information, on the following pages. Credit for these go to the writers and researchers noted, who are also responsible for the accuracy of the information.

In keeping with the "heritage" theme of the book, Rockhurst sons and grandsons of contributors are included with recipes and stores. Since we could not anticipate enrollment of future Hawklets, listings were limited to alumni and current students as the book was being completed. Thus, the Class of 2010, the current freshmen as we go to press, is the last class to be included. Not coincidentally, they are the 100-year class for RHS, which, as you will learn in the following pages, was chartered in 1910.

Enjoy the journey through 100 years of Rockhurst and nearly 400 recipes!

Rockhurst High School - from the beginning

The future Saint Ignatius of Loyola was born in 1491 in Spain. His early education was spotty, but by age 33, determined to become a priest, he began studying Latin, a requirement for priests. His initial studies were with students half his age in Barcelona. Later he continued his academic pursuits in Latin grammar and literature, philosophy and theology at the University of Paris. He received his degree at age 44, becoming known as "Master Ignatius of Loyola" and at age 46 he finally professed his vows as a priest.

While in Paris, Ignatius studied with a group of men and eventually six of them decided to take vows of chastity and poverty. They placed themselves at the disposal of the Pope to serve in whatever capacity he needed them. They were not a real order or congregation, just a small group banded together, dedicated to service. In order to legally teach about God at that time, the new priests needed the Pope's official approval. In 1539, they sought and received Pope Paul III's approval to form a community and in 1540 they were officially designated Societatis Jesu, in Latin, or Society of Jesus.

Ignatius was selected as their leader. Within 15 years, the Society grew from 8 to 1000 members, with houses and colleges throughout Europe, Brazil and Japan. Initially, teaching was not in the plans for the Society. They went where the Pope needed their service. But by 1548, Ignatius had opened schools in Italy, Portugal, Netherlands, Spain, Germany and Italy, mainly intended to educate new Jesuit recruits. Then leaders in Sicily asked Ignatius to open a school for lay men as well as Jesuits and it soon became evident to Ignatius that opening schools was the best way to achieve the mission of Ad Majorem Dei Gloriam (for the Greater Glory of God). In addition, schools served to educate both clergy and lay faithful and to stem the decline of the Church due to the Reformation.

From there, Jesuit schools and universities spread throughout Europe and the world. In the New World 22 universities were founded or taken over by the Jesuits in the 19th century. By the 21st century, there were 28 universities and 46 high schools in the United States. In 1908, Reverend Michael P. Dowling, S.J., wrote to his superiors that he had selected a site for a Jesuit school to be built in Kansas City, Missouri. He called the area at 52nd and Troost "Rockhurst" because the grounds were stony and a nearby grove of trees inspired him to use the term "hurst."

The school was officially chartered by the State of Missouri on August 30, 1910 and on September 15, 1914, the new school year began with 42 students under the direction of three Jesuit faculty. The school's original prospectus defined the education and purpose of the "Academy" of Rockhurst College: "to turn out young men whose mental faculties have been so developed and formed that they may successfully enter upon the immediate preparation of any career." This was accomplished by offering a course of classical studies with equal emphasis on moral formation and religious instruction, noting "it is men who are to be trained, not mere minds."

The "Academy" of Rockhurst College became Rockhurst High School in 1923, though it remained as part of the original corporation that included both the college and the high school. In 1962, Rockhurst High School became a new and separate corporation and moved to its present site at 9301 State Line Road. The Robert C. Greenlease family became the high school's principal benefactor and the name "Greenlease Memorial" was added to the school's official title and the new 13-acre campus was dedicated to the Sacred Heart of Jesus. Since that time, Rockhurst High School has continued to grow in status and reputation.

Today the school includes a student body of over 1,000 young men, each dedicating himself to the noble objectives of becoming a man of competence, conscience, and compassion. The school features a comprehensive curriculum that focuses on the arts and sciences, extensive co-curricular activities, a wide variety of spiritual programs and numerous special interest clubs. Rockhurst High School's motto is "Men for Others," which challenges every member of the school community to strive to reach his or her highest potential for the greater Glory of God, as first set forth by Ignatius back in the 1500s.

The Rockhurst Hawklets have won thousands of scholastic honors, dozens of state sports titles, and have consistently contributed positively to the Kansas City community through their work as students and alumni.Campus expansion and improvements over the past two decades have further added to the resources available to faculty and students. The Rose Theatre was opened in 1990 and houses a main performing center, lower-level classrooms, vocal and instrumental music rooms, a "Black Box Theatre" for smaller productions, and the McGee Reception Hall. A new Learning Resource Center, Library, journalism area, speech and debate classrooms, and refurbishment of the annex building called Xavier Hall (formerly the Jesuit residence) were also completed at that time.

The most comprehensive overhaul of the campus occurred in 1998, as a response to the recommendations made in the institution's "Millennium Master Plan" crafted in the early 1990s. The total number of classrooms was increased from 37 to 50, with the addition of approximately 31,000 square feet of space. New science laboratories and computer classrooms were added. The gymnasium was enlarged and provided with new seating. A new worship space, the John and Laura Sullivan, Sr., Chapel of the Sacred Heart was constructed, along with new administrative spaces for Admissions, Development, the Principal and the President. Virtually the entire facility was renovated to provide new heating and air-conditioning. The Barry Student Commons reclaimed outdoor space to create a gathering area for students, enhanced by a new bookstore, the Rock Shop, and direct access to a variety of student services including Counselors, College Placement, Pastoral Office and Dean of Students.

In 2002, an extensive renovation and expansion of the Dasta Memorial Stadium was completed. This work included a state-of-the-art artificial grass surface and a larger field for football, tournament soccer, lacrosse and intramural sports. A new facility was built to provide "home" seating for nearly 5000 persons with new restroom facilities, Rock Shop, concessions and storage. A 400-meter eight-lane track with additional facilities for field events completed the renovation. A new baseball/soccer field was built a year later just south of the main school building. In 2007, the school completed the Millennium Master Plan work by building the Loyola Center. It includes an activities complex with a second gymnasium, along with adjacent new classrooms, a choral room and administrative spaces.

As the school approaches its centennial year in 2010, Rockhurst High School has renewed its commitment to excellence. Today's "Men for Others" carry on a proud tradition forged by thousands of alumni before them, a heritage that distinguishes them as the leaders of tomorrow for the Greater Glory of God. A.M.D.G.

Two Who Make a Difference

Mission statements are, in truth, nothing more than a recitation of words. It takes administrators, clergy, students, parents, and, of course, teachers to execute the kind of plan envisioned by Rev. Michael Dowling in 1908. And in the universe of teachers who have honored the mission statement that the Rockhurst visionaries embraced so many years ago, one is hard pressed to find anyone more passionate about this goal than two faculty members who joined the school on the same day in August 1971.

It was then that Rockhurst added two energetic, passionate, but quite young educators named Ron Geldhof and Steve Ryan. And it would be only a modest exaggeration to say that on that day, this school was changed in a very significant way. Thirty-six years later, they are still holding true to Father Dowling's mission. While many know their level of seniority, what most may not appreciate is how these two teachers arrived at one destination in two different ways. In 1971 Ryan was the product of a Kansas City family, having grown up in midtown Kansas City, 73rd and Walnut. His father was a dentist. His family attended St. Elizabeth's parish. His high school of choice was Rockhurst. He played football and in 1958 was the Defensive Captain -- under Al Davis, of course.

Geldhof, on the other hand, was raised in a small town in southeastern Kansas, in a place called Frontenac. Sixty years ago this small Italian community was a railroad boom town. Geldhof's father worked for the Kansas City Southern Railroad. When Ron was in fourth grade his father was laid off. If the railroad was firing, not hiring, as it was at that time, then job prospects in southeast Kansas were bleak. So his family picked up and moved to Kansas City. Geldhof's school of choice was not Rockhurst, but rather its biggest rival, De La Salle. His sport of choice -- soccer.

Collectively, they have more college and post-graduate degrees than most college professors, from four different institutions of higher learning. In the course of their years they coached state champions and helped their students in countless ways. But it's the impact on the school's academic standards that remains their most compelling legacy.

One of Geldhof's first students, Keith Connor, class of 1976, had this to say about his passion: "Mr. Geldhof gave much to us in the classroom and outside. I was one of those who was with him on the soccer fields for four winters and on the tennis courts in the spring as well as having him as a Phys-Chem teacher as a freshman and a chemistry teacher junior year. I credit the background he provided me with allowing me to cruise through my first college "weed-out" course in chemistry at Notre Dame. In addition, he helped many of us further our enjoyment of two lifetime sports. I still play tennis regularly with four members of the first Rockhurst state championship team."

Steve Ryan's impact was no different. One of the students he taught in year two was Jay Reardon. "I will never forget the first day of my biology class freshman year with Mr. Steve Ryan. There stood this very large athletic man and most of us were a little intimidated by him at first. When one of my classmates started to test the limits, Mr. Ryan walked right next to him and slammed down his open hand on top of the portable lab table. Not only could you hear a pin drop in that classroom, but when Mr. Ryan lifted his hand off of the table, there was a perfect imprint of his entire hand permanently embedded in the table top.

Needless to say, he had our full attention the rest of that year. His imprint may still be there, for all I know. He would probably be embarrassed to hear that story now, but he commanded a respect that carried forward for seemingly his entire career at the school. He later coached me my junior and senior years in track when we were back to back state champions. He probably influenced me more than anyone in those years, next to my parents."

Reverend Dowling, it seems, would be proud.

- Matt Keenan, Sons Connor, 2007; Tom, 2009

There are thousands of Rockhurst alumni, and each has a story worth telling.
Future governors, captains of industry, musicians, priests, military men, scientists, authors,
teachers, sports figures and extraordinary citizens have all graced these halls.
We can not know or tell all the stories, but here is ...

One Rockhurst Story

In the sports world, one would be hard pressed to find a rags-to-riches story more compelling than that of Kurt Warner. In four years his football career went from grocery store clerk in Cedar Falls, Iowa while playing arena football to Super Bowl MVP. But in the world of television sports broadcasting, there is a story that would make the Kurt Warner fairytale seem like an exercise in underachievement. That story has not been fully told. Until now.

Some 25 years ago the Rockhurst freshman class included one Brian Sexton. He loved football, but his talents did not match his passion, which landed him on the "B" team where he labored in relative obscurity. He stuck with it and in his senior year something quite remarkable happened. Rockhurst won its first state title under Coach Tony Severino, beating Hazelwood Central at Arrowhead Stadium. The defensive MVP? Brian Sexton. If our story ended there it would be good, not great. But Brian had grander dreams. He wanted to be a football announcer. An NFL announcer.

In pursuit of his dream job, he graduated from the KU Journalism school and headed to the one place that offered him a job: KKOY in Chanute, Kansas. Chanute, for the geographically challenged, is not at the end of the earth. But you can see it from there. He was a salesman first, a radio play-by-play guy second. The only team in that part of the world was the Chanute Blue Comets. He did it all --- football, basketball, volleyball and baseball, mowed the lawn at the station and even blacktopped the parking lot.

In 1992 a larger venue called him. Wichita. He worked for an AM/FM combo just emerging from bankruptcy - meaning no listeners and less money. The gig included an AM sports talk program. But Brian spent too much time focusing on the talking and less time on the selling. As a consequence, he found himself in the general manager's office after 9 months on the job. He was fired, and the non-compete clause precluded him from selling advertising or talking on another station in the market for six months.

So he worked as a glorified daytime janitor, then double dipped at a Stroud's just opening in Wichita. He bartended and waited tables six days a week. His non-compete ended on November 30, 1993, a day that was noteworthy for another reason: that was the day the NFL awarded their 30th franchise, to Jacksonville, Florida. On Christmas Eve the station's general manager called him. Sexton remembers: "He asked me a question that I thought was simply rhetorical...did I want to move to Florida? He told me that the group that owned the stations I was working for owned a group in Jacksonville and were going to get the rights to the new NFL franchise. They needed good salespeople who knew sports and there might be a place for me in the pre-game show. All I had to do was meet my sales goals for the next six months and I would be in Florida." On June 21, 1994, he was driving his Ford Escort to Jacksonville.

There he flourished. One thing led to another and he became their Sports Director. Before he knew it, he was meeting with the GM and the Jaguars, who wondered if he would be willing to host the Tom Coughlin Show in the fall of 1994. They didn't have a play-by-play guy yet and Sexton was on the short list. He remembers: "My dreams were coming true. Less than a year after pushing a broom and slinging chicken in Wichita to keep the dream alive I was suddenly hosting an NFL coach's radio show in a beautiful restaurant overlooking the intercoastal waterway."

He continued: "A few weeks into the show the coach and I had formed a nice on-air relationship and the show was a hit in the ratings. I got a call one Thursday that the Jaguars' owner was going to sit in on the show that night. I quickly called my mother to ask her to light a Novena candle for me. She obliged, as any mother would. The show went well as usual and the next Thursday I got a call asking for an audition tape. 'For what?' 'To be the Jaguars' NFL announcer' he said."

Now it would be an understatement to say that this job opening had some competition. Some of the best and brightest college announcers from the southeastern part of the country were salivating for a shot at this dream job. Here is where it gets interesting. Brian didn't have any tapes of other games and they told him there wasn't enough time for him to do a demo at a local game. So Brian searched his earthly possessions and found one tape. A game he called back in the days of working in southeast Kansas: the Erie Red Devils and Oswego Indians… Kansas Class 1A 8-man high school football. The game where Sexton drove to Erie and climbed the water tower next to the football field in a driving rainstorm to hang his radio antenna. They don't have press boxes in southeast Kansas, you see. "I stood in a crow's nest atop a telephone pole and called the play-by-play on a glorified CB radio. I did the play-by-play and the color analysis. I hosted the pre-game, half-time and post-game shows, kept my own stats and read my own commercials live. That was my showcase." It was like showing up at a parade of vintage Mercedes in a Ford Pinto. No matter. He had no choice.

But Brian trusted his instincts. He knew the team owner didn't earn the NFL franchise by being stupid. Sexton's talent, enthusiasm, work ethic, and dare I say - cojones -- bubbled over in that demo tape. And when the sun set on the next day, the Jacksonville Jaguars had their first play-by-play announcer. He was, quite simply, the youngest radio play-by-play man the NFL had ever seen. And over the intervening years, he's witnessed an NFL team and stadium built from the ground up, traveled the country and became the face of the team. All the while never forgetting those lessons learned at Rockhurst High School or his modest beginnings at KKOY.

Kurt Warner can't touch this story.   *- Matt Keenan*

Appetizers AND Beverages

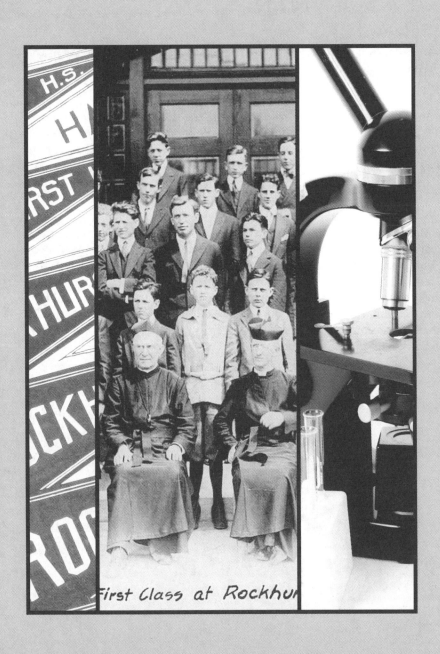

First Class at Rockhur

1910s

National:

A couple of sinking ships made an indelible impact on the decade. The supposedly unsinkable Titanic went down in the North Atlantic midway through its inaugural voyage in 1912, and torpedoes from German U-Boats sunk the Lusitania off the coast of Britain in 1915. Back in the United States, the first self-service grocery store opened in 1916, likely selling Oreo cookies (the American favorites were introduced in 1912). The decade saw the birth of the Boy Scouts of America, an organization that has provided the opportunity for many Hawklets to become Eagles. Sadly, many of those same boys were forced to grow up quickly as, on the heels of the Lusitania's sinking, the U.S. entered World War I and instituted a draft in 1917.

Local:

The man behind the Magic Kingdom got his start in Kansas City during the century's second decade. Fourteen year-old Walt Disney enrolled in classes at the Kansas City Art Institute in 1915, marking the only formal art training for the creator of Mickey Mouse and crew. Another innovative artistic mind took root in Kansas City around the same time, as Joyce Hall came to town in 1914 and started a company known worldwide today for its ability to brighten any occasion - Hallmark Cards. The decade marked the beginning of the end for the police department's horse patrol; the police began using cars in 1913, a year before Kansas City's Union Station first opened its doors.

Chipotle Shrimp Wontons

Olive oil for pan

16-ounce package wonton wrappers

1 pound shrimp, cooked, peeled, coarsely chopped

1 yellow bell pepper, roasted, peeled, chopped

1 red bell pepper, roasted, peeled, chopped

½ cup chopped fresh cilantro

8 ounces Manchego cheese or Fontina or German Bianco cheese

1 chipotle pepper in adobe sauce, drained, finely chopped

Sprinkle of Old Bay seasoning

Garlic salt to taste

2 tablespoons picante sauce

Wontons and filling may be prepared separately in advance and assembled just before baking. Preheat oven to 350 degrees. Brush mini muffin cups with olive oil. Press one wonton wrapper into each cup. Bake about 10 minutes, until tops are golden brown. Remove from oven and cool slightly, place on baking sheet.

In large bowl, combine remaining ingredients. Fill wontons with shrimp mixture and bake 7-10 minutes or until cheese is melted. Makes 30.

Patty Gound
Sons Ryan, 2003; Matthew, 2007

I have been taking these to Rockhurst Gift Gathering parties since 2000!

The first President of Rockhurst High was the Rev. Michael P. Dowling, S.J. from 1914-1915. He was followed by Rev. Aloysius A. Breen, S.J., 1915-1918 and Rev. John A. Weiand, S.J., 1918-1924.

Rockhurst's first Principal was Rev. Aloysius A. Breen, S.J., 1914-1915. He was succeeded by Rev. R.A. Henneman, S.J., 1915-1916 and Rev. Patrick F. Harvey, S.J., 1916-1920.

Sausage Cups

1 pound mild pork sausage

1¼ cups grated cheddar cheese

1¼ cups grated Monterey Jack cheese

1 cup prepared ranch dressing

2.25-ounce can sliced black olives, drained

¼ teaspoon ground red pepper

16-ounce package wonton wrappers

Preheat oven to 350 degrees. Cook sausage and drain thoroughly. Combine sausage with cheeses, ranch dressing, olives and red pepper, set aside. Lightly grease muffin tins. Press one wonton into each cup and bake for 5 minutes. Remove wontons from tins and place on baking sheet. Fill each wonton cup with sausage mixture. Bake an additional 10 minutes until bubbly.

Yvette Miceli
Husband Joseph, 1978

I took these to the October 2005 Rockette gathering as a recipe "testing". They were a big hit. They can be frozen after filling. Bake from frozen state, adding just a minute or two to baking time. Watch closely. The filling can even be put into purchased mini phyllo cups. Great make-ahead appetizer!   - Jan Flanagan

French Chestnuts

1 jar chestnuts (not water chestnuts)

½ pound good quality thick sliced bacon

3 tablespoons pure maple syrup

Wrap each chestnut with a half slice of bacon, secure with a toothpick. Put wrapped chestnuts in a skillet and fry until bacon is crisp on all sides. Drain well on paper towels, then place on serving platter. Drizzle syrup over. Serve warm.

Alison Flowers
RHS Faculty member

This calls for the real nut. The key is to use good quality ingredients for a delicious result.

Crunchy Phyllo Spinach Squares

12 sheets frozen phyllo dough (18x14-inch rectangles), thawed

½ cup unsalted butter, melted

2 (12-ounce) packages frozen spinach soufflé, thawed

8-ounce can water chestnuts, drained, finely chopped

Arrange 6 sheets of phyllo dough in bottom of a 15x20x1-inch baking sheet, brushing melted butter between each sheet. Allow edges of dough to overlap sides of pan. Spread spinach soufflé evenly over dough. Sprinkle with chopped water chestnuts. Top with remaining sheets of phyllo dough, brushing melted butter between sheets. Score gently through all 6 top layers of phyllo, making 48 squares or diamonds. Bake at 400 degrees for 30 minutes, until golden brown. Cool slightly. Cut through all layers. Serve warm or at room temperature. Makes 48 appetizers.

Katherine Huerter
Husband Dan, 1971; Son Andrew, 2002

This has been in my recipe repertoire for years. It was featured in a collection of my recipes in the Come Into My Kitchen column in the Kansas City Star in 1991.

Brie-Pecan Quesadillas

3 ounces Brie cheese, chopped (about ¼ cup)

2 (8- or 9-inch) flour tortillas

2 tablespoons toasted chopped pecans or walnuts

2 tablespoons chopped fresh Italian parsley

¼ cup sour cream

Parsley sprigs for garnish

Tip: put Brie in freezer for 30 minutes to make it easier to chop. Sprinkle half the cheese on half of each tortilla. Top with nuts and chopped parsley. Fold each tortilla in half, pressing gently. In a lightly greased skillet, cook quesadillas over medium heat, turning once, until lightly browned, about 2 or 3 minutes. Cut quesadillas into wedges with pizza roller. Top each wedge with a dollop of sour cream. Garnish with parsley. Serves 4.

Wendy Zecy
Sons Kit, 2003; Connor, 2007; Cameron, 2009

When I went to Rockhurst (1947-1951), an entrance exam was taken for admission and about 100 were accepted. Those 100 were divided into four classes, with the top 25 scores on the entrance exam assigned to the A class, the next 25 to B, the next 25 to C and the bottom 25 to D. Each class had its own room. Teachers, rather than students, moved from classroom to classroom. At the end of each quarter the classes were reshuffled based on overall class rank, with the top 25 in A, the next 25 in B, etc. Your rank in each subject, and your overall class rank were posted on the bulletin board in the activities room for all to see. This proved to be a great incentive to study.

- Ken Fligg, 1951

Bobo-licious

Prepared thin pizza crust, such as Boboli

Olive oil

4 ounces grated mozzarella cheese

Large Granny Smith apple, cored but not peeled, very thinly sliced

½ teaspoon cinnamon or more, to taste

4 ounces crumbled blue cheese

Preheat oven to 450 degrees. Brush pizza crust with olive oil. Sprinkle with mozzarella, then cover with apple slices. Sprinkle cinnamon over apples, top with blue cheese. Bake about 8 minutes, until cheese melts. Cut into wedges and serve.

Jan Flanagan
Husband Jim, 1971; Sons Bryan, 2002; Sean, 2004; Kevin, 2007

My friend Jodie Barnes served this before a Christmas gathering of dear friends. We loved it.

Swiss Curry Crab Rounds

1 cup mayonnaise

2 cloves garlic, minced, or 1 teaspoon garlic powder

1 teaspoon curry powder

½ teaspoon salt

2 tablespoons lemon juice

1 tablespoon finely chopped onion

2 cups grated Swiss cheese

1 can crabmeat

2 tubes Hungry Jack "flaky" biscuits

Dill weed for garnish

Mix together first eight ingredients. Peel each biscuit apart into 3 pieces, place on baking sheet. Add spoonful of crab mixture to top of each biscuit piece. Sprinkle tops with dill weed. Bake at 375 degrees about 10 minutes, until biscuits are golden brown at edges. Makes 48.

Polly Mandl
Husband Richard, 1978; Son Ryan, 2006

In the summer of 1962 a number of us from the future class of 1964 spent our days at the Ward Parkway Country Club pool, looking up the hill watching the completion of the new Rockhurst High School on State Line.
That swimming pool is long gone, replaced by a tall office building. Some of the friends are also gone, others retired or nearing. Over time almost everything changes. My last child will be in the class of 2010. Thank God the Rock is still there, better than ever!

- Thomas R. Mura, 1964

1953 swim team: Arens, Delaney, Waterman, Alderman, Anderson, Brewster, Walters, Grimsley. (No first names listed.)

- yearbook

Artichoke Bruschetta

15 ounces ricotta cheese

1 package Good Seasons salad dressing dry mix

1 baguette loaf, cut into ¼-inch slices

2 tablespoons olive oil plus additional for brushing

1 cup artichoke hearts, drained, chopped

1 cup diced fresh tomato

¼ cup finely chopped onion

¼ cup chopped fresh basil or ½ teaspoon dry basil

3 cloves garlic, crushed

1½ tablespoons balsamic vinegar

½ teaspoon black pepper

freshly grated Parmesan cheese to taste

Mix ricotta and Good Seasons dry mix, refrigerate one hour. Meanwhile, place baguette slices on baking sheet. Brush each slice with olive oil. Bake at 450 degrees for 5 minutes or until golden. Cool.

Mix together all remaining ingredients except Parmesan, set aside. Spread one tablespoon ricotta mixture on each baguette slice. Spoon one heaping tablespoon artichoke mixture on top of ricotta. Arrange on platter. Sprinkle Parmesan over all. Makes 2 dozen.

Pam Cowan
Son Alex, 2008

Ciabatta Appetizer

One loaf ciabatta bread, sliced horizontally

Basil/garlic pesto

3-4 ripe tomatoes, including yellow if available

1 pound fresh mozzarella

Fresh basil leaves

Place ciabatta cut side up under broiler until slightly toasted, remove. Slather on pesto, cover with sliced tomatoes and top with thin slices of mozzarella. Place under broiler until the cheese is bubbly and slightly browned. Sprinkle on hand-torn basil. Cut into 2-inch squares and serve warm.

Pat O'Byrne, 1975

Caponata

2 medium eggplants, cut into 1-inch pieces, drained well

½ cup olive oil

2 onions, chopped

28-ounce can Italian plum tomatoes

1 cup sliced celery

2 ounces capers, rinsed

2 tablespoons sugar

4 tablespoons wine vinegar

Salt and pepper to taste

Sauté eggplant in oil over high heat for about 10 minutes, or until soft and browned. Remove from skillet with slotted spoon and set aside. In same skillet, sauté onions, adding more oil if necessary. When onions are golden, add tomatoes and celery. Simmer about 15 minutes or until celery is tender. Add capers and cooked eggplant.

In small saucepan, dissolve sugar in vinegar, add salt and pepper. Heat slightly. Pour mixture over vegetables. Cover and simmer over low heat about 20 minutes, stirring occasionally. Serves 4-6.

Michelle Nemmers
Son John, 2008

This is good warm or cold.

Asparagus Spears Wrapped in Proscuitto

30 pieces thin asparagus

15 thinly sliced proscuitto strips

1 carton boursin herb cheese (such as Alouette)

Trim off bottom portions of asparagus. Blanch spears about 2 minutes, set aside to cool slightly. Cut each piece of proscuitto in half. Spread a thick layer of boursin cheese on proscuitto, place asparagus at one end of proscuitto and roll up. Serve slightly warm. Can be made ahead, refrigerated and then warmed about 1 minute in microwave before serving.

Joan Jones
Son Spencer, 2006

JE Dunn was awarded the contract for the new RHS at 92nd & State Line, to open in Fall 1962. Father Maurice Van Ackeren, SJ, reported that the completed facility would cost in the range of $2.1 million, including landscaping, site, equipment and a residence hall for the 35 Jesuit faculty members. Half of that amount was donated by Robert & Virginia Greenlease, who donated much more over the years. The new campus was planned for 900 students.

Oven-Style Poppers

12 fresh jalapeno peppers, halved lengthwise, stems, seeds and membranes removed

16 ounces cream cheese, softened

1½ cups Monterey Jack, co-jack or pepper jack cheese

½ teaspoon ground cumin

½ teaspoon cayenne pepper or to taste

2 large eggs

2 tablespoons milk

8 teaspoons Cajun-style seasoned salt (like Emeril's Original Essence), divided

1 cup panko crumbs or fine dry bread crumbs

½ cup flour

Preheat oven to 350 degrees. Lightly oil baking sheet and set aside. In one bowl, beat together cream cheese, Monterey Jack cheese, cumin and cayenne. In separate bowl, beat eggs and milk and 2 teaspoons of seasoned salt. In a shallow dish, combine crumbs and 4 teaspoons seasoned salt. In another dish, combine flour and remaining 2 teaspoons seasoned salt.

Spread 1 tablespoon cheese mixture into each pepper half. Dredge pepper halves in flour, then dip in egg mixture, then dredge in crumbs, pressing to coat. If desired, repeat this process. Place peppers cut side up on baking sheet and bake until filling is runny and crust is golden, about 30 minutes. Do not overbake or filling will run out of peppers.

Kathy Huerter
Husband Dan, 1971; Son Drew, 2002

These freeze well, so making a double batch to have some now and freeze others for later is a win-win situation. If baking from frozen state, increase baking time slightly.

Father Mario Purcelli was infamous. He taught Latin 3 and 4 to Caesar before teaching at RHS! I usually spent more time on other subjects and was not prepared in Latin. I lived in fear of being called upon to translate, but I noticed he never called on students who had their hands up. So one day when I was really unprepared, I raised my hand when he asked who would translate. Well, he called on me. I was stunned. Before I could engage my brain, my lips moved and I blurted "You can't call on me, I had my hand up." Well, what happened next was not pretty. But the lessons learned about being prepared served me well, both in the Navy and in business.

- Capt. Tom Spink, USN (Ret), 1963 (first graduating class from the current location)

Chicken Satay with Peanut Sauce

1 pound boneless chicken breasts

Marinade:

6 tablespoons vegetable oil

4 tablespoons soy sauce

4 tablespoons lime juice

1-inch piece ginger root, freshly peeled and chopped

1 teaspoon Chinese-style chili sauce

2 tablespoons chopped fresh cilantro

Peanut Sauce:

2 tablespoons smooth peanut butter

2 tablespoons soy sauce

1 teaspoon vegetable oil

2 green onions, chopped

2 cloves garlic

2 tablespoons fresh lime juice

1 tablespoon brown sugar

Red chile sauce to taste, optional

Garnishes: sesame seeds, red pepper strips, pea pods

Put chicken in a ziplock bag. Put all marinade ingredients in food processor or blender and process until smooth. Pour over chicken. Marinate in refrigerator 3-4 hours or overnight.

Put all peanut sauce ingredients in same processor and process until well blended. Add a little water if too thick. Pour into bowl, cover and set aside until ready to use.

Remove chicken from marinade, drain. Grill or broil chicken until done. Slice into strips or cut into cubes. Put on skewers, if desired. Sprinkle with sesame seeds and garnish with strips of red pepper or steamed pea pods. Serve with peanut sauce.

Pat Shealy
Sons John, 2007; Westly, 2010

Chicken Wings

5 pound bag chicken wings

½ cup butter

2 packages dry Good Season's Italian Dressing Mix

12 ounces Durkee's Red Hot Sauce

Put chicken wings in single layer on foil-lined cookie sheet. Bake at 350 degrees for 30 minutes. While wings are baking, in saucepan melt butter, add dressing mix and hot sauce. Simmer for about 5 minutes. Drain fat from wings, brush with sauce, and continue baking an additional 30 minutes. Serves 10.

Pam Cowan
Son Alex, 2008

Spicy Baked Shrimp

1 cup olive oil

4 tablespoons Cajun or Creole seasoning, or to taste

4 tablespoons fresh lemon juice

4 tablespoons chopped fresh parsley

2 tablespoons honey

2 tablespoons soy sauce

Dash cayenne pepper

2½ pounds large uncooked shrimp, shelled, deveined

Combine all ingredients except shrimp in a 9x13-inch baking dish. Add shrimp and toss to coat. Refrigerate at least 2 hours or overnight. Bake at 450 degrees or until shrimp are cooked, about 8 minutes. Stir occasionally. Transfer to serving platter and garnish with lemon.

Patti Gound
Sons Ryan, 2003; Matthew, 2007

First year coach Steve Ryan took the golf team to state where they won!

- 1991 yearbook

Soccer was a winter sport when I was at RHS. We played on a field behind the gym that was built on rock. The field was either icy or when it thawed, muddy as could be. The ball would get so thickly covered with mud that when you'd kick it, it would be like kicking a medicine ball. It would be so heavy it would only move about 6 feet.

- Jim Flanagan, 1971
Sons Bryan, 2002;
Sean, 2004;
Kevin, 2007

Marinated Shrimp

2 pounds cooked shrimp, peeled, tails off

2 cans quartered artichokes, drained

3 jars button mushrooms, drained

2 cloves garlic, minced

Marinade:

¾ cup olive oil

2 tablespoons tarragon vinegar

1½ teaspoons dry mustard

2 tablespoons sugar

1½ teaspoons salt

1 teaspoon pepper

Combine shrimp, artichokes, mushrooms and garlic in a large bowl. Whisk marinade ingredients together and pour over shrimp. Mix together well. Marinate overnight in refrigerator. Transfer to serving bowl.

Mary Jo Barton
Sons Brett, 2005; Scott, 2007

Salami Crisps

24 paper-thin slices (4-inch rounds) Genoa salami (¼ pound)

Position oven racks in upper and lower thirds of oven and preheat oven to 325 degrees. Arrange salami slices in single layer on 2 large baking sheets lined with parchment paper. Bake, switching oven positions of baking sheets halfway through baking time, until edges are crisp and beginning to curl, 10-12 minutes. Transfer slices to wire rack to cool. They will crisp as they cool.

Kathy Huerter
Husband Dan, 1971; Son Andrew, 2002

Men really like these. I serve a big basket of them when we entertain outside.

It was the spring of 1970. I was a junior at all-girls school Loretto. I was a dancer and in Rockhurst's play Brigadoon, directed by Jerry Stark. We were let go from practice early so I went out to the parking lot and waited with my good friend Johnny Bowen. Back then they had a paper drive contest and the juniors were filling their truck. I asked Johnny who this one particular guy was and said I thought he was cute. I made John swear he wouldn't say anything and he didn't. He just kept showing up at my house with his good buddy Jake Schloegel. Jake asked me out, we married in 1976 and have two sons who graduated from Rockhurst and we still support Rockhurst.

- Debby Schloegel
Husband Jake, 1971
Sons Peter, 2001;
Charlie, 2002

Bacon Crisps

½ cup freshly grated
Parmesan cheese

1 pound sliced bacon,
cut in half

1 sleeve Waverly Wafers or
other buttery rectangular
cracker

Preheat oven to 350 degrees. Place 1 teaspoon cheese on each
cracker and wrap tightly with a strip of bacon. Place wrapped
crackers on broiler rack on a baking sheet and bake 40 minutes,
until bacon is done. Do not turn. Drain on paper towels. Serve
hot or at room temperature.

Karen Stacy
Son Patrick, 2006

*These can be frozen after baking and reheated for 5 minutes at 350
degrees.*

Bacon Roll-Ups

½ cup butter, melted

⅓ cup water

2 cups Pepperidge Farm
Herb Stuffing

1 cup Parmesan cheese

2 (10-ounce) packages frozen
chopped spinach, cooked,
drained well

½ pound R.B. Rice hot
sausage

2 pounds bacon

Stir together butter, water and stuffing mix. Add Parmesan,
spinach and sausage, mix well. Chill for one hour. Shape into
1-inch balls. Cut bacon strips into thirds, wrap each piece
around a ball and secure with a toothpick. Place on foil-lined
baking sheets and freeze. Transfer to ziplock bags. Thaw and
use as needed. When ready to cook, bake thawed balls 35-45
minutes at 375 degrees. Makes 4 dozen.

Donna Tulipana
Son Joe, 2008

A great make-ahead appetizer.

*Inter-class competition
in fundraising events
was fierce in 1965, my
freshman year, and the
paper drive was a biggie.
Each class would have a
semi-trailer to fill.
One of my classmates had
a connection that scored
us tons of old phone
books, but we had to pick
them up before the trailers
were set on the north lot.
And we had to keep our
windfall secret from the
other classes. I got my
father to agree to store
"a few papers" in a large
shed at the back of our
property. Within a few
weeks, a steady stream
of farm trucks,
station wagons and
sedans (all driven by
people with learner's
permits) had filled the
shed to the rafters. Then
came time to move it all to
the trailers at school.
The resulting traffic jam
had a pretty negative
effect on my dad's lawn.
But we did win the paper
drive competition! We
were on our third filled
trailer when the drive
ended, raising over
$20,000 (in 1965 dollars.)
That eased my dad's pain
a little.*

- Mark Caffrey, 1969
Son Charlie, 2004

Prosciutto and Gruyère Pinwheels

⅓ cup (about 3 ounces) finely grated Gruyère cheese

4 teaspoons chopped fresh sage or basil leaves

1 puff pastry sheet, thawed

1 large egg, lightly beaten

2 ounces thinly sliced prosciutto

Combine Gruyère with sage or basil in bowl. Arrange pastry sheet on a lightly floured surface with short side facing you. Cut in half crosswise. Arrange half of sheet with a long side facing you, brush edge of far side with a little egg. Arrange half of prosciutto evenly on top of pastry, avoiding egg-brushed edge. Top with half the cheese/herb mixture.

Starting with side nearest you, roll pastry jelly-roll fashion. Wrap in plastic wrap. Make another log with remaining ingredients. Chill logs, seam side down until firm, at least 3 hours and up to 3 days.

Preheat oven to 400 degrees. Lightly grease 2 large baking sheets. Cut logs crosswise into ½-inch thick pinwheels and arrange, cut sides down, 1 inch apart on baking sheets. Bake 14-16 minutes or until golden. Cool slightly and serve. Makes 20-30.

Mimi O'Laughlin
Husband Brian, 1975
Sons Matthew, 2001; Thomas, 2007; John, 2010

Stuffed Mushrooms

8-ounce package cream cheese

2 tablespoons Lipton onion soup mix

3 slices bacon, fried crisp

30 mushroom caps, washed, dried

Mix cream cheese, soup mix and bacon. Stuff mushroom caps and broil until heated through.

Kathleen Clement
Sons Christopher, 1999; Andrew, 2003

These always fly off the plate!

The present cafeteria is like a royal dining hall compared to the 1933 cafeteria. It was in the basement, with stone walls and a concrete floor. In 1934 & 1935, I worked in the cafeteria clearing tables and scraping dishes for 35 cents an hour. Not too bad a wage for the times, but we were paid in tokens only good in the cafeteria. Ernie, the operator was making a profit on our wages. If you were caught selling the tokens, you were fired. But the food was good and 35 cents an hour was some income during the Depression.

- James Flanagan, 1937
Sons Jim, 1971;
Terry, 1975

Pine Nut Pesto Cheesecake

Crust:

½ cup Italian breadcrumbs

2 tablespoons grated Romano cheese

1 tablespoon toasted pine nuts

2 tablespoons melted butter

Filling:

16 ounces cream cheese

1 cup sour cream

½ cup freshly grated Romano cheese

3 eggs

¼ cup chopped pine nuts, toasted

3 tablespoons chopped fresh basil

2-3 tablespoons chopped green onions

1 garlic clove, finely minced

¼ teaspoon white pepper

½ teaspoon fresh cracked peppercorns

⅛ teaspoon salt

To prepare crust, grease a 9-inch springform pan. Combine breadcrumbs, cheese, nuts and butter, press into bottom of pan, set aside.

For filling, beat cream cheese until smooth. Add sour cream and cheese, beat until smooth. At low speed, add eggs, then nuts, basil, green onions, garlic, peppers and salt. Pour filling into crust. Bake at 375 degrees for 30 minutes or until set. Let cool. Refrigerate for 3 hours or overnight, then remove sides from pan. Garnish with additional pine nuts and fresh herbs.

Carolyn Sturgeon
Son Joe, 2005

We built the Senior class Homecoming float at my house. It was to be an engineering marvel… a giant projector that actually had WORKING reels (yep-it had a motor inside it!) The wood beams we used to hold up the reels were the trickiest part of the contraption and I remember how proud we were when we finally achieved what we thought was a true design feat. We worked hard and pulled at least a couple of all nighters. For some reason on the day to transport the float to school we got the idea to use side streets to get there. About three blocks from school we had a nasty encounter with a low hanging tree branch and there went our reels. By the time we got to school, wires were strewn about and our hopes of a major float victory were dashed. I remember that our "tech team" (they weren't called that then, by the way) did the best they could to get "Humpty Dumpty" back together again, but we ended up with reels that had a wicked wobble.

- Peter Brown, 1976
Sons Chris, 2000;
Kevin, 2003;
Scott, 2010

Cheddar Chutney Cheesecake

40 ounces cream cheese	1 cup chopped pecans
4 eggs	1 teaspoon sherry
⅔ cup grated onion	
1 teaspoon cayenne pepper	Topping:
1 cup mango chutney (Major Grey's)	1 cup mango chutney
	1 cup chopped pecans
1½ cups grated sharp cheddar cheese	

Preheat oven to 325 degrees. Blend all cheesecake ingredients in mixer until smooth. Pack in an 8-inch springform pan. Mix topping ingredients, swirl over top. Bake in water bath for 1 hour or until center is set. Serve with red and green apple wedges. Serves 35-40 as part of a cocktail buffet.

Lon and Marcia Lane, The Catering Company
Sons Lon IV, 2002; Stewart, 2004

This is a Catering Company original recipe. We serve it with apples and fried wonton crisps.

Warm Brie with Gingered Onions

¼ cup butter	Juice of one lemon or lime
3 onions, sliced thin	2-3 teaspoons finely chopped crystallized ginger
1 cup good-quality apricot jelly	1 wheel Brie
1 teaspoon red pepper flakes	

Melt butter in skillet, sauté onions on low heat until golden, 15-20 minutes. Add jelly, pepper flakes, lemon or lime juice and ginger. Heat through. Heat Brie in oven or microwave until it is warm and softened. Place on serving dish, pour onion mixture over.

Maraline Hayob
Son David, 2000

Raspberry Appetizer

2 cups shredded cheddar cheese

6-8 green onions, finely chopped

1 cup slivered almonds

4 tablespoons mayonnaise (or more if mixture is too thick)

Fresh raspberries

Place a sheet of plastic wrap into and over sides of a 9-inch pie pan. Mix all ingredients but raspberries and press into pan. Refrigerate overnight. Flip upside down onto serving plate and garnish with raspberries. Serve with crackers.

Sally O'Neill
Sons Patrick, 2002; Peter, 2008

Pecan-Crusted Artichoke and Cheese Spread

¼ cup butter, divided

1 medium onion, diced

2 garlic cloves, minced

4 cups coarsely chopped fresh spinach

14-ounce can artichoke hearts, drained, chopped

8 ounces cream cheese, cut into cubes

½ cup mayonnaise

¾ cup shredded Parmesan cheese

8-ounce package 4-cheese Country Casserole Recipe Blend shredded cheese

⅔ cup chopped pecans

½ cup herb seasoned stuffing

Pita chips or French bread

Melt 3 tablespoons butter in a large skillet, add onion and garlic and sauté until tender. Add spinach and cook over medium heat, stirring often, about 3 minutes. Add artichoke hearts, cream cheese, mayonnaise, Parmesan and 4-cheese blend, stirring until cheese melts. Spoon into greased 2-quart baking dish. Bake at 350 degrees for 20 minutes, stir gently. Combine remaining 1 tablespoon butter, pecans and stuffing mix, tossing until blended. Sprinkle over top of cheese dish, bake 15 more minutes. Serve with pita chips or bread slices. Makes 15-20 appetizer servings.

Wendy Zecy
Sons Kit, 2003; Connor, 2007; Cameron, 2009

It was the Cross Country awards ceremony 2003, and this would be my last time cheering on the team and my son Andrew Bly, who would be a senior next year. My Army Reserve Medical unit was put on active duty orders to be sent to Afghanistan in March 2004 for one year. I was very honored when Coach Dierks and the other coaches and team paid tribute to me at the ceremony. It was a moment of happiness and sadness that I'll always remember and cherish.

- Terri Bly

1994 - Kairos retreats begin at RHS.

Hot Reuben Spread

8-ounce package sauerkraut

½ pound sliced corned beef, chopped

8 ounces shredded Swiss cheese

8 ounces shredded cheddar cheese

1 cup mayonnaise

1 package sliced cocktail rye bread

Drain and rinse sauerkraut. Mix all ingredients except bread. Spoon into a 9x13-inch baking dish. Bake at 350 degrees for 30 minutes. Toast rye bread just before serving. Spread Reuben mixture on toasted bread.

Kate Link
Sons Paul, 2002; Joe, 2004; Michael, 2006

BLT Spread

1 cup mayonnaise

2 (8-ounce) packages cream cheese, softened

1½ teaspoons pepper

1 cup shredded lettuce

1½ cups cooked, crumbled bacon

½ cup chopped tomatoes

¼ cup chopped green onions, tops included

¾ cup shredded cheddar cheese

Lavosh or bagel chips

Combine mayonnaise, cream cheese and pepper, mix until smooth. Spread onto bottom of 9-inch pie pan. Layer with lettuce, bacon, tomatoes, green onions and cheese. Serve with lavosh or bagel chips. The mayonnaise mixture can be made ahead and tightly covered with plastic wrap. Add toppings just before serving.

Tina Gaughan
Husband Mike, 1977; Son Danny, 2005

This is a great, easy appetizer. It was served at a senior (class of 2005) gift gathering party for the auction.

Holiday Dip

1 cup hot water

½ cup sundried tomatoes

8 ounces cream cheese, softened

½ cup pesto

4-ounce log goat cheese

Pour a cup of very hot water over sundried tomatoes and let them sit for 30 minutes, then drain and snip into small pieces. Spread cream cheese in bottom of a pie plate or oven-proof serving dish. Drizzle pesto over top, crumble goat cheese over. Sprinkle top with sundried tomatoes. Cover and bake at 350 degrees about 15 minutes. Serve with crackers, toasted baguette slices or bagel chips.

Lynne Knott
Son Keaton, 2007

The colors in this dip make it perfect for the Christmas holidays, but it is great all year.

Cheese and Olive Spread

4 ounces garlic-and-herb spreadable cheese (such as Alouette)

4 ounces crumbled feta cheese

¼ cup chopped kalamata olives

2 tablespoons chopped fresh parsley

1 tablespoon balsamic vinegar

1 tablespoon olive oil

Combine all ingredients and mix well. Serve with bagel or pita chips or crackers.

Jan Flanagan
Husband Jim, 1971; Sons Bryan, 2002; Sean, 2004; Kevin, 2007

The first day of freshman year, I was in the main hallway talking with my cross country coach Mr. Mike Dierks about practice that afternoon. Suddenly Father Mark Daues (whom I had never met), came up behind me, grabbed my leg and arm and lifted me above his head shouting, "I'm Mr. Dierks' bodyguard! You mess with him, you mess with me!" He proceeded to carry me down the main hall above his head while all the upperclassmen cheered. Definitely my "Welcome to Rockhurst" moment.

- Matthew Harris, 2002

Gorgonzola Fondue

1 clove garlic, halved

1 cup whipping cream

1 cup dry white wine

½ cup chicken broth

2 tablespoons cornstarch

8 ounces Italian-made Gorgonzola cheese or any high-quality blue cheese (with high fat content), crumbled

Dash ground white pepper

Dipping selections:

Dark rye or pumpernickel bread cubes

French baguette cubes

Asparagus spears, cooked until crisp-tender

New potatoes, cooked and halved

Seedless grapes

Apple chunks

Pear chunks

Strawberries

Rub bottom of heavy medium saucepan with halved garlic, discard garlic. Add whipping cream and wine. Bring to boil. Meanwhile, stir together broth and cornstarch until combined, then stir into cream mixture. Cook and stir until slightly thickened and bubbling. Gradually add cheese; stir until cheese is melted. Stir in white pepper. Pour hot mixture into fondue pot; place over very low heat on fondue burner. Serves 10-12.

Wendy Zecy
Sons Kit, 2003; Connor, 2007; Cameron, 2009

Gorgonzola Dip

4 ounces Gorgonzola, softened

8 ounces cream cheese, softened

1 tablespoon ranch dip dry seasoning mix

¼ teaspoon dried chopped chives

¼ cup coarsely chopped toasted walnuts

Combine all ingredients with an electric mixer, refrigerate. Serve with crackers or crudités.

Julie Schorgl
Husband Daniel, 1981; son Bryan, 2008

If (deceased) former principal Tom Murphy had a favorite class, it had to be Liturgy and Worship. This class trains and forms students in the art and history of liturgical worship, particularly Catholic worship. The class thrives to this day and is responsible for the most inspiring, holy and community driven liturgies the school has ever experienced. One day, walking through the empty Pesci Atrium after such a service, I caught myself saying "What did you think of that one, Tom?"

- Larry Ruby, RHS Principal

Spicy Thai Peanut Dip

½ cup smooth peanut butter

4 tablespoons soy sauce
(preferably low sodium)

3 tablespoons white vinegar

1 tablespoon sugar

¼ teaspoon cayenne pepper

3 cloves fresh garlic, minced
or crushed

4 green onions, minced

Whisk all ingredients until creamy. Serve with fresh vegetables like baby carrots, celery sticks, sliced cucumber, bell peppers, fresh sugar snap peas and peeled, julienned jicama. The peas and jicama are especially good and worth the extra effort! Serves 20-plus.

Melinda O'Brien
Sons Kyle 2005, Evan 2008

A sure hit at any party! Easy to make with ingredients always on hand.

Hot Crab Dip

12 ounces cream cheese,
softened

1 can crabmeat

¼ cup slivered almonds

½ teaspoon horseradish

½ teaspoon salt

¼ teaspoon pepper

1 tablespoon sherry

2 tablespoons finely grated
onion

Mix all ingredients. Spray a small baking dish with cooking spray. Add crab mixture and bake, covered, at 375 degrees for 15 minutes. Serve hot with thin wheat crackers.

Mary LeCluyse
Husband Paul, 1967; Son John, 2008

The first Alumni 3-on-3 Basketball tournament (in 1991) showed the old guys have still got it. After a Mass offered by Father Gregg Grovensburg, 1976, 26 teams competed. The winning team in the "competitive" division was composed of John Sweeney, 1975, Mark Teahan, 1978, and Bryan Wilkerson, 1978. The "recreational" division sported co-champions. The Gasser team included Jim Grasser, 1969, Mike Kopp, 1975, and Tim Quinlan, 1975. The Car Hops were Steve Hughes, 1970, Tom Bosilevac, 1971, and Greg Stockbauer, 1971.

Pomegranate-Avocado Salsa with Spiced Chips

Chips:

1 teaspoon paprika

¾ teaspoon ground cumin

½ teaspoon salt

½ teaspoon sugar

½ teaspoon garlic powder

½ teaspoon onion powder

12 (6-inch) corn tortillas, each cut into 8 wedges

Cooking spray

Salsa:

1⅓ cups peeled, diced avocado (about 2)

3 tablespoons fresh lime juice

2 cups clementine sections (about 6 clementines)

1 cup pomegranate seeds (1 medium pomegranate)

½ cup thinly sliced green onions

½ cup minced fresh cilantro

2 tablespoons honey

½ teaspoon salt

1 jalapeno pepper, seeded, minced

Chips: Preheat oven to 500 degrees. Combine paprika, cumin, salt, sugar, garlic powder and onion powder in a small bowl. Arrange tortilla wedges in a single layer on 2 baking sheets; coat with cooking spray. Bake for 5 minutes. Turn wedges over, coat with cooking spray. Sprinkle paprika mixture evenly over wedges. Bake an additional 2 minutes or until lightly browned. Remove from oven, cool completely. Bake the chips up to a day ahead, and store at room temperature in a ziplock bag.

Salsa: Combine avocado and lime juice in a medium bowl; toss gently to coat. Add remaining ingredients, toss gently to combine. Serve salsa with chips.

Mary Jo Strauss
Sons Ben, 2007; Jason, 2009

This jewel-toned dip makes the most of seasonal fruit. If clementines are unavailable, substitute tangerines. Salsa may be prepared a day ahead, minus the avocado. Add avocado shortly before serving to keep the avocado green. Salsa is also good with purchased chips.

Imitation Ceviche

1 pound shrimp, chopped

1 cup lime juice

½ cup zesty Italian dressing

1 red pepper, chopped

2 tablespoons cilantro

4 green onions, chopped

Dash of Worcestershire sauce

Pinch of oregano

3 avocados, chopped

Combine all ingredients except avocados. Refrigerate overnight. Before serving drain any excess liquid and add avocados. Serve with tortilla chips. Serves 20.

Mary Jo Barton
Sons Brett, 2005; Scott, 2007

Texas Caviar

2 cans black-eyed peas

1 can yellow hominy

1 can white hominy

1 cup chopped cilantro

2 cloves garlic, chopped

1 can drained Rotel
(tomatoes and chilies)

1 chopped red pepper

1 chopped green pepper

1 chopped yellow pepper,
optional

8 ounces (about) "lite" zesty
Italian dressing

Rinse and drain black-eyed peas and hominy. Add cilantro, garlic and vegetables. Cover with lite zesty Italian dressing and toss. (Go easy on the dressing or it gets soggy). Prepare a few hours ahead to allow flavors to develop.

Gerri Sopyla
RHS Counselor

The 4th annual Mother-Son Banquet was held in April 1985 at the Gold Buffet in North Kansas City. Reservations were $12 per person. Helen Cooke and Kathy Donnelly co-chaired the popular event.

The bike club was in its 2nd year. Members organized trips and rode to Lake Pomona, Lawrence, Kansas, the Renaissance Festival and Lake Jacomo.

- 1982 yearbook.

Cool Gazpacho Dip with Pita Chips

Pita bread

1 clove garlic

2 tablespoons snipped cilantro

8 ounces cream cheese, softened

¼ cup sour cream

½ cup shredded sharp white cheddar cheese

1 tomato, chopped

2 green onions, sliced

⅓ cup cucumber, peeled, chopped

Preheat oven to 400 degrees. Cut pita into 8 triangles. Bake 8-10 minutes or until crisp. Mix garlic, cilantro, cream cheese, sour cream and cheddar. Spread into bottom of a chilled serving dish. Sprinkle chopped tomato, onion and cucumber over cheese mixture. Serve with pita chips.

Joan Jones
Son Spencer, 2006

Guacamole with Roasted Corn and Black Beans

1 cup frozen or fresh corn

3 tablespoons oil, divided

2 large avocados, ½-inch dice

1 large tomato, ¼-inch dice

¼ cup chopped cilantro

2 tablespoons minced red onion

1 teaspoon chopped jalapeno

1 teaspoon minced garlic

2 tablespoons lime juice

1 teaspoon cider vinegar

1 teaspoon kosher salt

¼ teaspoon cumin

15-ounce can black beans, drained

In a frying pan over medium-high heat, "roast" corn in 1 tablespoon oil, stirring constantly until golden, about 5 minutes. Cool. In a large bowl, fold together avocado, tomato, cilantro, onion, jalapeno, and garlic. Stir in lime juice, vinegar, salt and cumin. Add remaining 2 tablespoons oil, roasted corn and black beans. Adjust seasonings. Add more lime juice and oil if needed. Serve with tortilla chips.

Sarah Jurcyk
Sons Jordan, 2006; Seth, 2008

Roasted Corn Salsa

2 (16-ounce) bags frozen corn

1 large red pepper, cored, ¼-inch dice

1 large green pepper, cored, ¼-inch dice

¼ cup olive oil

2 Roma tomatoes, ¼-inch dice

16-ounce can black beans, drained, rinsed

16-ounce can red beans, drained, rinsed

6 Serrano peppers, seeded, finely diced

2 banana peppers, seeded, finely diced

1 bunch cilantro, rinsed, finely minced

2 tablespoons ground oregano leaves (preferably Mexican)

2 tablespoons garlic powder

¼ cup balsamic vinegar

Preheat oven to 350 degrees. Place frozen corn and diced red and green peppers in a large bowl. Mix with olive oil until corn and peppers are well coated. Spread corn and pepper mixture onto 2 ungreased cookie sheets and place in oven. Bake for 45 minutes, turning occasionally with a spatula to ensure even browning. Remove from oven and cool to room temperature. Place corn mixture in a large bowl and add remaining ingredients. Mix thoroughly, cover bowl and refrigerate until ready to serve. Serve with tortilla chips as an appetizer or use as a topping for tacos, fajitas or burritos. Salsa can be kept 2-3 days refrigerated.

Note: For a spicier mix, add 2-4 jalapeno peppers, seeded and diced. For a milder flavor, only use half the peppers.

Michael Prater
Husband of Laurie Prater, RHS Faculty member

Every HOT August, Coach Tony Severino would hold two football practices a day. After each first practice of the day, my son David would round up 4-8 guys who either didn't have a car or who lived too far away to drive back and forth, and bring them to our Overland Park home. In would walk these great big, dripping with sweat, exhausted, adorable guys, usually carrying a bagged lunch. They would head to our lower level, gulp down their lunches and lay out on the carpet or floor enjoying the air conditioning for a short while before time to head back for the second practice. The room would smell a little rank, and sometimes there was a spot or two, but it was such a pleasure to have all of them.

- Beverly Hynes
Sons Chris, 1995;
David, 1995

Rockhurst Tailgate Dip

2 cans black-eyed peas, drained

2 cans white shoepeg corn

1 large green pepper, chopped

1½ bunches green onion, chopped

1 or 2 ripe avocados, chopped

4-ounce can chopped jalapenos, with juice, to taste

16-ounce bottle zesty Italian dressing

Mix all ingredients and serve with tortilla chips. Use more or less of the jalapenos as your taste buds desire.

Jan Carter
Son Sean, 2007

This was a favorite at the parents' tailgating barbecue parties before football games at Rockhurst.

Crunchy Corn Dip

2 (8-ounce) packages cream cheese

1 red pepper, chopped

4-ounce can chopped black olives

4-ounce can chopped green chilies

11-ounce can corn, drained

1 package of Hidden Valley Ranch Original dressing packet

Mix all ingredients together and chill 2 or more hours. Serve with tortilla chips.

Debi Hudson
Former RHS Staff member

This was enjoyed at a faculty "Five Minutes of Fun" gathering after school.

Mexican Spinach Dip

16-ounce package chopped frozen spinach

8 ounces cream cheese, cut into cubes

2 cups chunky salsa, hot or mild

2 cups shredded Monterey Jack cheese

Cook spinach according to package directions, drain. Stir together all ingredients in an oven-proof pan or a crockpot. Heat until melted. (Can be baked, microwaved or heated in crockpot.) Serve with tortilla chips.

Joyce Romine
Nephews Bryan Flanagan, 2002; Sean, 2004; Kevin, 2007

Salsa Bean Dip

2 (8-ounce) packages cream cheese, room temperature

16-ounce can corn, drained

½ teaspoon ground cumin

10-ounce can hot Rotel (tomatoes and chilies)

2-3 cups shredded cheddar cheese

1 onion, chopped

Salt to taste

½ green pepper, chopped

Small can chopped green chilies, optional

15-ounce can black beans, drained, rinsed

With electric mixer, combine cream cheese and Rotel. Dip will be very wet. Add onion, green pepper, black beans and corn. Add cumin and stir with rubber spatula. Fold in 2 cups cheese. If dip is not thick enough, add more cheese as desired. Taste, add salt or green chilies as desired. Can also add another can of beans or corn.

Josephine Nigro
Sons Michael, 2001; John-Paul, 2003

1981-82 Mother's Club events included a freshmen mothers coffee, hosted by Gail Lembeck and Jane Cook; Wine and Cheese welcome for freshman and alumni moms, hosted by Marilyn Schudy and Kay Dolson; Getting to Know You hosted by Kelly Perkins, Sandie Vader and Pat Dunlay; All About College hosted by Betty Keim and Jackie Mayer; a Christmas Tea for grandmothers of students hosted by Patty Garbeff; Sale-O-Rama, chaired by Mary Gillis, co-chaired by Pat Whittaker, Kay Burke and Jean Honan; Day of Recollection, hosted by Alma Clarke and the Mother-Son dinner at the Plaza Inn hosted by the Mother's Club Board.

Soccer was a winter
sport when we were
at Rockhurst.
We played in every type
of condition, including
sheets of solid ice.
In the early 70s there
was no Gore-Tex or fancy
winter sweat suits
(at least not in Brookside),
so our garb usually
consisted of long
underwear or sweat
pants, stocking hats,
gloves and baggies
around our feet to keep
them warm. I also
remember that our home
field which was in
Leawood Park
(Al Davis would never
let us use his football
field), sloped uphill on the
North end.

- Mark Fitzpatrick, 1974
Sons Tim, 2002;
John, 2008

Signing Day Dip

16 ounces mayonnaise

8 ounces sour cream

3-ounce can real bacon bits

2 tablespoons chopped fresh onion

1 teaspoon Accent

1 tablespoon sugar

2 tablespoons Parmesan cheese

8 ounces shredded mozzarella cheese

Mix all ingredients. Serve chilled. May be prepared day ahead. Serve with crackers or vegetables.

Donna Mandl
Sons Mark 1996; T.J. 1999

I was given this recipe from a Hungry Boys cookbook and asked to bring it to a luncheon after Football Signing Day in February, 1999. My son was one of those signing that day, becoming a Bearcat. We've served it ever since, with fond memories.

Artichoke and Sundried Tomato Hot Dip

½ cup sundried tomatoes, coarsely chopped

¼ cup shredded Parmesan cheese

½ cup sour cream

½ cup mayonnaise

8 ounces shredded Swiss cheese

14-ounce can artichoke hearts, drained, chopped

¼ teaspoon garlic powder

¼ teaspoon hot pepper sauce

Soften sundried tomatoes by covering with very hot water for 10 minutes. Drain. Heat oven to 350 degrees. Stir all ingredients together. Spoon into shallow oven-proof bowl. Bake about 25 minutes, until edges are very lightly browned. Serve with crackers or pita chips.

Valerie Caffrey
Son Charlie, 2004

Kahlua Fruit Dip

16 ounces cream cheese, softened

2⅓ cups non-dairy whipped topping

1½ cups brown sugar

2 cups sour cream

⅔ cup Kahlua, optional

⅔ cup chopped pecans

Fruit to dip: strawberries, cantaloupe slices, apple wedges, etc

In large bowl, combine cream cheese, whipped topping, brown sugar, sour cream and Kahlua. Cover and refrigerate overnight. Just before serving, stir and top with pecans.

Mary Long
Sons Chris, 1998; Bradford, 2003

I served this at a brunch at my home for outgoing and incoming Mothers Club Board members in 1998.

Cranberry Chutney

¾ cup sugar

1 cup water

12-ounce package fresh cranberries

1 cup peeled, diced apples

½ cup cider vinegar

½ cup golden raisins

½ teaspoon cinnamon

¼ teaspoon ground ginger

¼ teaspoon ground allspice

⅛ teaspoon ground cloves

1 teaspoon fresh orange zest

In a medium saucepan combine sugar and water, bring mixture to boil over medium heat. Add remaining ingredients. Bring to a boil and simmer over medium heat for 20 minutes, breaking up some of the cranberries. Cool slightly and pour into jars or containers. Keep in refrigerator. Serve over cream cheese for a great appetizer. Also good served with turkey and pork.

Catherine Moussa
Son Alex VanMaren, 2007

Chocolate Chip Cheese Ball

8 ounces cream cheese, softened

½ cup butter, softened (no substitutions)

¼ teaspoon vanilla

¾ cup powdered sugar

2 tablespoons brown sugar

¾ cup mini chocolate chips

¾ cup chopped pecans

Beat cream cheese, butter and vanilla until fluffy. Gradually add both sugars, beat until well combined. Stir in chocolate chips and pecans. Cover and refrigerate at least 2 hours. Shape into a ball. Serve with graham crackers or vanilla wafers.

Rose Dorlac & Jim Bevan
Grandson Dennis Ogle, 2009

Cheese Ball

2 (8-ounce) packages cream cheese

8-ounce can crushed pineapple, drained

2 tablespoons minced green pepper

2 tablespoons minced onion

1 tablespoon seasoned salt

Chopped pecans

Mix all ingredients except pecans. Form into 2 balls. Roll in pecans.

Kathleen Callahan
Son Connor, 2008

This is great to make ahead and freeze. Pull out when you need an appetizer or if someone just stops by.

Parmesan Cheese Ball

2 (8-ounce) packages cream cheese

⅔ cup Parmesan cheese

1 small onion, finely chopped

1 tablespoon milk

½ teaspoon salt

¼ teaspoon pepper

¼ teaspoon garlic powder

⅔ cup chopped walnuts or other nuts

Mix all ingredients (or leave nuts out.) Roll in coarsely ground nuts.

Catherine Moussa
Son Alex VanMaren, 2007

Cheese Crackers

4 tablespoons butter, room temperature

1 cup freshly grated Romano cheese

¾ teaspoon coarsely ground peppercorns, black or mixed

¼ teaspoon white pepper

12 tablespoons flour

2-4 tablespoons whole milk

Blend butter and cheese. Add peppercorns, then flour. Stir in milk until dough holds together. Shape into a long log, wrap in plastic wrap and chill. Slice ¼-inch thick and bake on ungreased cookie sheet for 15 minutes at 375 degrees. Cool. Makes 24-30 crackers.

Carolyn Sturgeon
Son Joe, 2005

Citrus Pecans

1 egg white

2 cups pecan halves

½ cup firmly packed light brown sugar

2 teaspoons orange zest

2 tablespoons orange juice

½ teaspoon salt

¼ teaspoon ground cinnamon

Whisk egg whites in medium bowl until frothy. Toss in pecans. In a large bowl, stir together brown sugar, orange zest and juice, salt and cinnamon. Add pecans, toss. Drain well. Spray baking sheet with cooking spray, line with aluminum foil. Place pecans on baking sheet in single layer. Bake at 325 degrees, stirring occasionally, 20-25 minutes.

These were served at Mr. Chris Elmore's history class for parents and received a solid grade "A".

Peppy Cocktail Nuts

4 tablespoons butter

1 tablespoon Worcestershire sauce

2 teaspoons hot pepper sauce

1 tablespoon McCormick Salad Supreme Seasoning

1 teaspoon salt

½ teaspoon garlic salt

¼ teaspoon black pepper

1 pound walnut or pecan halves

In a large pan, melt butter and add Worcestershire, pepper sauce, McCormick seasoning, salt, garlic salt and pepper. Stir until blended, then fold in nuts, toss to coat well. Cook, covered, over low heat for 20 minutes. Stir occasionally. Cool and drain on paper towels. Store in an airtight container. Makes 4½ cups.

Kathy Huerter
Husband Dan, 1971; Son Drew, 2002

Salted Pecans

2 cups pecan halves

3 tablespoons butter, melted

1 envelope dry onion soup mix

Coat pecans with butter, spread on baking sheet. Bake at 300 degrees for 20 minutes, stirring occasionally. Add soup mix, stir. Dry on paper towels.

Annie Osborn
Son Scott Miller, 2007

Party Mix

15-ounce box Cheerios

12-ounce box Corn Chex

12-ounce box Rice Chex

12-ounce box Wheat Chex

2 (12-ounce) bags pretzels

2 (16-ounce) jars dry roasted peanuts

¾ cup margarine

¾ cup vegetable oil

1 tablespoon celery salt

1 teaspoon garlic powder

1 tablespoon onion salt

2 tablespoons Worcestershire

Mix cereals, pretzels and peanuts together and divide into 2 large roasting pans. Melt margarine in a small pan, stir in oil, celery salt, garlic powder, onion salt and Worcestershire. Pour half of mixture over each cereal mixture, stir to coat. Bake at 250 degrees for about 1½ hours, stirring every 15 minutes.

Steve Ryan
RHS Faculty member

Al Davis became the golf coach my junior year. My senior year we were at the State tournament just outside St. Louis. The first day was rained out, so we had to play 36 holes the second day. My Rockhurst graduation was that night. I had planned to fly to KC, but with 36 holes to play there was no chance to make the flight. Coach Davis knew this. He called KMOX radio in St. Louis. The station manager was a Rockhurst guy. Davis asked if they would send the station traffic helicopter to pick me up… which they did! Picked me up right in front of the first tee and took me to a helipad at a hospital near the airport where he had arranged for a Jesuit priest from DeSmet to pick me up and take me to the airport! If not for Al Davis' deep care and concern for his players I would have missed my graduation. I thanked him every time I saw him until his death. He was a wonderful man.

- John S. Howell, Sr., 1978

Crisp Cracker Snack Mix

5 cups rice/corn chex cereal (Crispix)

5 cups white cheddar snack crackers (Cheez-Its)

1 cup small pretzels

1 cup cashews

1 tablespoon vegetable oil

4 teaspoons lemon juice

2 tablespoons Worcestershire sauce

1 teaspoon celery salt

1 teaspoon garlic salt

1 teaspoon onion salt

1 teaspoon garlic powder

1 teaspoon onion powder

Combine cereal, crackers, pretzels and cashews in a large mixing bowl. In a small bowl, combine remaining ingredients, mixing well. Pour seasonings over cereal mixture, stir gently until evenly coated. Pour into a large baking pan. Bake at 250 degrees for 45 minutes, stirring every 15 minutes. Spread on paper towels to cool. Store in an airtight container. Makes 12 cups.

Kathy Huerter
Husband Dan, 1971; Son Drew, 2002

Microwave Party Mix

1 bag small pretzels

1 box Wheat Thins

1 box Cheez-Its

¾ cup oil

1 envelope Hidden Valley Ranch dressing

1 tablespoon dill weed

½ tablespoon lemon pepper

½ tablespoon garlic salt

Mix first 3 ingredients together in a brown paper bag. Whisk remaining ingredients together, then pour over pretzel mixture in bag. Fold or seal top of bag. Turn bag until it is oily all over. (That's how you know it is well mixed.) Leave in bag and microwave on high 1 minute. Cool and serve.

Judie Scanlon
RHS Special Events Coordinator
Sons Steve, 1988; Kerry, 1994

Mr. Bernie Kreikemeier passed away December 1, 2006 from Neurofibromatosis Type II, a genetic disease which causes fibroid tumors to grow on the neck and brain. Coach K was part of Rockhurst for 18 years, as a computer and accounting teacher and a coach for basketball and baseball. His memorial service was held in the Rose Theater at RHS, and mourners filled the theater to overflowing. His teams past and present lined the stairways as an honorary guard· while mourners expressed condolences to his wife Mary and their family.

Baked Olives

4 cups mixed olives
(kalamata, green, etc)

6 cloves garlic, crushed

½ teaspoon crushed red
pepper flakes

2 tablespoons olive oil

1 teaspoon kosher salt

Drain olives, place in glass 8-inch oven-proof dish. Add remaining ingredients, mix well. Cover tightly with foil. Bake 30 minutes at 350 degrees. Serve at room temperature.

Stephen Stock
RHS Faculty member

French Hot Chocolate

5 (1-ounce) squares Baker's
chocolate or other good
chocolate

1 cup water

1½ cups sugar

Pinch of salt

8 ounces heavy cream

Milk

In a heavy pan melt chocolate in water, stirring until thick. Add sugar and salt, bring to a boil. Boil for 6 minutes. The mixture should be a thick fudge syrup. Cover and cool. Whip cream and blend with the syrup. Keep covered in refrigerator.

To make a cup of hot chocolate: heat enough milk to fill a mug to almost boiling and pour it over a heaping tablespoon of chocolate mixture and stir. Use more if you like it sweeter.

Sarah Jurcyk
Sons Jordan, 2006; Seth, 2008

Homemade Irish Cream

1 pint whipping cream

1 can sweetened condensed milk

3 tablespoons caramel sauce

2 tablespoons chocolate syrup (Hershey's)

1 cup good whiskey

Mix or blend ingredients together. Place in a plastic container and refrigerate or freeze.

Julie & Paul Schleicher, 1978
Son Thomas, 2009

Plan Ahead Amaretto

4 cups sugar

4 cups water

3 ounces pure almond extract

1 quart apricot brandy

½ gallon vodka (cheap kind)

Boil sugar and water, cool. Add remaining ingredients, bottle, cap and age 3 months or longer. The longer, the better.

Ann Marie Scahill
Son Michael, 2009

Rockhurst Cosmo

For each cosmo:

½ part vodka

¼ part blue curacao

⅛ part lime juice

⅛ part white cranberry juice or more, to taste

Be sure to use blue curacao to get that Rockhurst color! Mix all ingredients and serve.

Paul Ptasnik
RHS Faculty member

Margaritas

12-ounce can frozen limeade

12-ounce can beer

1½ juice cans water

1 juice can minus
2 tablespoons tequila

2 tablespoons triple sec

Mix all ingredients in pitcher. Serve over cubed or crushed ice.

Kate Link
Sons Paul 2002; Joe 2004; Michael, 2006

Sangria

2 quarts Zinfandel

¼ cup brandy

⅛ cup Cointreau

1 pint orange juice

½ cups lemon juice

¼ cup superfine sugar

6-12 ice cubes

1 pint chilled club soda

1 orange, thinly sliced

1 lemon, thinly sliced

Thoroughly chill all ingredients. Pour wine, brandy and Cointreau into a large punch bowl. Stir orange and lemon juice with the sugar until sugar has dissolved. Add to bowl and stir to blend. Add ice cubes and soda and garnish with fruit slices. Serve in 4-ounce punch glasses or wine glasses. Can multiply this recipe for more servings. Can make this the day before without club soda and add it just prior to serving. Serves 20-25.

Maraline Hayob
Son David, 2000

Berry Spritzer

Fresh berries (such as blackberries, raspberries, blueberries)

Corn syrup

Zest of 1 lime

Sparkling water or lemonade or iced tea

Mint leaves for garnish

Thread fresh berries onto 6-inch wooden skewers. (Use single type of berry or mixed.) Freeze 1 hour. Dip rims of tall glasses into corn syrup, then lime zest. Place a frozen berry skewer in each glass, then pour beverage over skewer into glass. Garnish each skewer with a mint sprig. Serve cold.

Jan Flanagan
Husband Jim, 1971; Sons Bryan, 2002; Sean, 2004; Kevin, 2007

Eagle Scout Punch

46-ounce can pineapple juice

6-ounce can frozen lemonade

2 quarts cranberry juice

1 quart ginger ale

Chill all ingredients. Mix, adding ginger ale just before serving.

Barbara Mashburn
Sons Bill, 2000; Robert, 2001

Mint Tea

6 sprigs fresh mint

3 tea bags

4 cups boiling water, divided

1 cup sugar

½ cup lemon juice

3-4 cups cold water

Steep mint and tea bags in 2 cups boiling water for 15 minutes. Combine sugar and lemon juice in large bowl, add 2 cups boiling water and steep 15 minutes. Combine 2 mixtures and add 3-4 cups cold water. Chill in refrigerator. Serve over ice.

Annie Osborn
Son Scott Miller, 2007

Cabaret '73 was the theme of the spring fundraiser with dancing to the Warren Durrett orchestra. Committee members were Mrs. Eugene Vandenboom, Mrs. William Reichmeier, Mrs. Donald Williams.

Every year the yearbook would take a picture of all the Eagle Scouts at Rockhurst.
We are the proud parents of 5 Eagle Scout sons, all of whom graduated from Rockhurst: William, 1970; Terence, 1974; Gregory, 1978; twins Kevin and John, 1985. Grandson Benjamin, 2007, is also an Eagle Scout.

- Mary Elizabeth & Harold Heiman

Hot Tea Punch

6 cups water

¾ cup sugar

2 cinnamon sticks

8 whole cloves

5 teabags

1½ cups orange juice

⅓ cup fresh lemon juice

Bring first 4 ingredients to boil in heavy large saucepan over high heat, stirring until sugar dissolves. Boil 6 minutes. Remove from heat. Add teabags. Cover and let steep 10 minutes. Discard teabags. Add orange and lemon juices to punch. (Can be prepared 1 day ahead. Cover and refrigerate. Reheat before continuing.) Using slotted spoon, remove whole spices. Serve hot. Makes 6 cups.

Carrie McCausland
Son Stuart, 2007

Indian Spiced Tea

4 cups water

1 cinnamon stick

1 teaspoon fennel seed

8 whole cloves

¼ teaspoon ground ginger

1 teaspoon cardamom seeds

3 teabags

1 cup milk

3 tablespoons honey

Bring water, cinnamon stick, fennel seed, cloves, ginger and cardamom to a boil; simmer for 10 minutes. Add teabags and steep off heat for 30 minutes. Strain mixture. Add milk and honey. Reheat until honey dissolves and tea is hot. Serve immediately or refrigerate and heat by the cup in the microwave.

Sarah Jurcyk
Sons Jordan, 2006; Seth, 2008

*December, 1977.
We were on the top floor south taking our sophomore English final for Mr. Mike Kelly when the fire alarm went off. Mr. Kelly said it was a prank and continued with the exam. We quickly began smelling smoke, so he closed the door. A few moments later, Mr. Mike McWilliams, the Vice Principal, knocked on our door and told us to get out - the wrestling mats just below our room were on fire!*

*- Rick Bishop, 1979
Son Sean, 2008*

The most fun I ever had at Rockhurst was being in the Spring musical.

- David Chartrand, 1971

Praline Coffee

¼ cup ground coffee	3 cups water
2 tablespoons coarsely ground pecans	1 cup skim milk
3-inch cinnamon stick, plus additional for garnish	1½ teaspoons brown sugar
	⅛ teaspoon vanilla, butter and nut flavoring

Combine first 3 ingredients in basket of drip coffee maker or percolator. Fill pot to 3 cup mark with water. Prepare coffee according to manufacturer's instructions. In a small pan, combine milk and brown sugar and heat until sugar dissolves. Stir in flavoring. Pour ¾ cup coffee into mugs. Pour ¼ cup milk mixture into each mug, stir well. Garnish each cup with a cinnamon stick, if desired. Makes 4 cups.

*Linda Dro
Son Justin, 1997*

Cappuccino

2 cups black coffee	1½ ounces brandy
2 cups milk	1½ ounces crème de cacao
1 tablespoon sugar	Whipped cream, sweetened
1 tablespoon cocoa	4 cinnamon sticks

Heat first six ingredients to a boil. Pour into 4 cups. Top with sweetened whipped cream and a cinnamon stick.

*Kate Link
Sons Paul, 2002; Joe, 2004; Michael, 2006*

Bread AND Breakfast

BREAD AND BREAKFAST

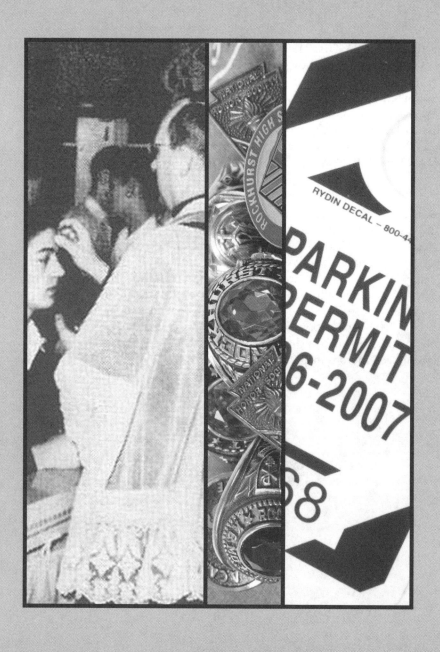

1920s

National:

The 1920s roared in like, well, the 20s. The Roaring 20s, renowned as one of the most colorful decades in American history, saw speakeasies spring up and flapper dresses come en vogue. Talking movies were introduced in 1923, and the first-ever Academy Awards followed soon thereafter, in 1929. The sort of high school curriculum now commonplace in classrooms nationwide sparked serious controversy in 1925, as the teaching of evolution in a Tennessee high school led to the Scopes Monkey Trial. The decade ended as ominously as it had begun auspiciously; the crash of the American stock market on "Black Tuesday," October 29, 1929, marked the beginning of the Great Depression.

Local:

The 1920s was a decade of successful starts for several Kansas City institutions. The Negro National Baseball League was founded in 1920, and the Monarchs, one of the league's flagship franchises, won the first Negro Leagues World Series in 1924. Around the same time, a little-known downtown haberdasher was selected by political boss Tom Pendergast to run for Jackson County Eastern Judge. Harry Truman won that election, the first of many he would win in an illustrious political career that carried him all the way from Independence to the White House. The Liberty Memorial was dedicated in 1921 before a crowd estimated over 100,000 people. Soon thereafter, the first retail stores on the Country Club Plaza opened their doors in 1922, and the shopping district held the first of its now-famous Christmas lighting ceremonies in 1925.

Baguette

1 cup whole milk	1 package active dry yeast
2 teaspoons butter	4 cups flour
2 teaspoons sugar	Olive oil
2 teaspoons salt	1 egg white, beaten
1 cup water at room temperature	Options: fresh herbs, olives, sundried tomatoes, etc.

Bring milk to a simmer. Add butter, sugar and salt. Add water, cool mixture to lukewarm. Place in food processor or bowl, add yeast. Beat in flour until soft dough forms. Knead on floured surface until smooth and elastic, about 10 minutes. Place in bowl coated with olive oil. Turn to coat all sides. Cover with plastic and let rise in warm place or refrigerate for use the next day. Allow to rise 1 hour or remove from refrigerator and let rise about 45 minutes.

Divide dough in half. Form each into a rustic 15x2-inch rope by rolling between hands. Place on parchment paper-lined baking sheet. Cover with tea towel. Let rise about 30 minutes. Brush with beaten egg white. Preheat oven to 500 degrees. When ready to bake spray oven with water to create steam. (Careful!) Immediately place bread in oven. Bake 10 minutes. Reduce oven temperature to 400 degrees, bake about 30 minutes longer.

Variations: Add flavorings such as thyme and chopped kalamata olives or oregano and diced sundried tomatoes. The herbs can be added when mixing the dough. Larger ingredients should be kneaded in after the first rising as follows: Flatten dough on work surface. Sprinkle ¼ of ingredient over half of dough and fold other half over and punch down to seal. Repeat this process three times with remaining ingredients. Allow to rise 15 minutes then form loaves as directed.

Karen Reintjes McLeese
Father Robert Reintjes, 1945

Crescent Dinner Rolls

1 package regular yeast	3 large eggs
½ cup water, 110-120 degrees	½ cup sugar
½ cup butter	½ teaspoon salt
1 cup half & half or whole milk	5 cups flour
	Unsalted butter, melted

Proof yeast in water for five minutes. Melt butter in saucepan, add milk, warm. (Do not let milk get too hot or it will kill the yeast when added.) In mixer, beat eggs and sugar. Add salt, then milk mixture. Add yeast mixture. Gradually add flour. Refrigerate overnight or for up to two days.

Roll out ¼ of the cold dough on floured table, brush with unsalted butter. Cut into eight wedges and roll up into crescents. Place rolls on ungreased cookie sheet and cover with dry towel. Let rise in warm oven (200 degrees) for 30-60 minutes or overnight at room temperature. Bake for 10 minutes at 400 degrees. Makes 32 rolls.

Carolyn Sturgeon
Son Joe, 2005

Blueberry Jam

8 cups blueberries, divided	1 cup sugar or honey
3 tablespoons lemon juice	½ teaspoon cinnamon

Purée 4 cups blueberries. Add in 4 cups whole blueberries. Add remaining ingredients and boil vigorously until thickened, stirring very often, about 30 minutes. Skim foam. Test on a frozen plate: if jam runs slowly, it is done.

Ann Marie Scahill
Son Michael, 2009

The first Sale-O-Rama was during my year as president of the Mothers Club. The day we opened the sale to the public, a woman came to the sale in a blue coat. When she left, after spending $1.50 for 2 small items, she was wearing our most expensive item, a vicuna (fur) coat priced at $50. After she walked out, Father Purcelli, who was taking money along with me, said, "Why didn't you stop that woman?" I turned to him and said, "You have the collar, why didn't you stop her?" That's when we hired an off-duty policeman.

- Maryhelen VanDyke
Husband Joe, 1940;
Sons Mike, 1996;
Jim, 1972

Pecan Coffee Rolls

Dough:

1 package (2½ teaspoons) active dry yeast

¼ cup lukewarm water (should feel tepid on the wrist)

1½ tablespoons sugar

1 teaspoon salt

2 eggs

⅓ cup cold milk

6 tablespoons butter, softened

3¼ cups flour

Topping:

¾ cup brown sugar

6 tablespoons butter

¾ cup chopped pecans

¼ cup orange juice

1 teaspoon vanilla

Soften yeast in warm water for 5-10 minutes. Add sugar and salt. Add eggs, milk and butter. Begin stirring in flour. Add about 2 cups flour and stir until soft dough forms. Knead on floured surface adding flour as necessary until soft, elastic dough is formed. Place in a bowl that has been greased with oil or butter. Turn dough over and let rise for 1-1½ hours in a warm place (or refrigerate at this point for up to 3 days.) Punch down dough and let rest a few minutes.

Combine all topping ingredients and place in bottom of well-greased 9- or 10-inch baking dish or springform pan with tight fitting bottom. If using a springform pan, first wrap heavy duty foil around outside of pan. Roll dough into approximately 1½-inch balls and place on top of sugar mixture. Let rise until doubled about 1 hour. Bake in a preheated 350-degree oven for 25-30 minutes.

Karen Reintjes McLeese
Father Robert Reintjes, 1945

The year was 1941. The class was freshman algebra in Sedgwick Hall, Room 1C (faced Troost) taught by Mr. O'Brien, then a Jesuit scholastic. As a thunderstorm moved through the area, a deafening explosion interrupted class. The flagpole just outside the window had been struck by lightening and the concrete base exploded, disintegrating. When the class next met, Mr. O'Brien came with a detailed explanation of what we had witnessed. Apparently the discharge of energy from the lightening bolt was so strong it caused the metal reinforcing bars imbedded in the base to instantly become hot enough to obliterate the concrete… Mr. O'Brien's algebra served me well, and years later I encountered him once again. This time I was a med student at Creighton and answered an ad looking for tutors. I was hired by my former Rockhurst teacher to tutor histology.

- Raymond J. Caffrey, 1945

Povitica Bread
(Croatian Nut Bread)

The 1987 Sale-O was chaired by Jan Knopke, assisted by Yolanda Knox, Paula Thomas, Betty Conway and Carol Fallucco.

Bread:

1 package dry yeast

½ cup warm water

2 cups lukewarm milk

½ cup sugar

½ cup butter, melted

2 eggs, beaten

6 cups flour

Filling:

1 pound English walnuts or pecans

2 cups sugar

1½ cups milk, scalded

½ cup butter

4 eggs, beaten

½ cup white raisins, optional

Bread: Dissolve yeast in about ½ cup warm water. Set aside and let proof. Put lukewarm milk in a large bowl, then add yeast. Stir in sugar, salt, butter and eggs. Add flour gradually, stirring with a wooden spoon until smooth. Add enough flour to make a soft dough that can be kneaded. Knead well. Dough will be smooth but not sticky. Place in a greased bowl. Place a towel over bowl and keep in a warm place. Let rise until light and doubled in size, about 1 hour. Roll out dough on a floured cotton sheet covering a table. Should roll out to about 48x66 inches. Traditionally it is stretched with your hands but I have better luck rolling it out with a rolling pin.

Filling: Grind nuts finely in a food processor. Add sugar to nuts and mix thoroughly in a large mixing bowl. In a sauce pan, bring milk to scalding and then add butter to melt. Stir in nut mixture and beaten eggs. Simmer over low heat. Do not cook too much or it will be too thick to spread over dough.

Spread nut filling over entire dough. Sprinkle raisins over filling on dough. Cut dough into 3 equal parts. Roll up each section as you would for a jellyroll. Hold up an edge of the sheet and let dough roll together. Coil each section into a loaf shape. Put into a greased 9x12-inch loaf pan. Bake at 350 degrees for about 1 hour. Brush top of loaf with an egg wash if you like.

Dottie Evans Ruby
Husband Larry Ruby, RHS Principal

This is my Mom's (Mary Sackuvich Evans) Povitica Bread

Greek Christmas Bread

1 cup sugar

½ cup butter

5 eggs, well beaten

Zest of 2 lemons

3 yeast packets

1½ cups scalded milk, cooled to lukewarm

6½ cups bread flour, divided

½ teaspoon salt

1 beaten egg

Cream sugar and butter. Add eggs and lemon zest. Dissolve yeast in lukewarm milk and add to butter and sugar mixture. Add 2½ cups flour and salt, mix well. Cover and let rise in a warm spot until doubled in bulk. Add remaining flour to sponge. Do not add more flour than necessary to keep the dough from sticking when turned out on a floured board. Knead dough for about 7 minutes, or until smooth and glossy.

Form into loaves or rolls of any shape. Traditionally, Greek Christmas bread is made into braided loaves. Cut off 3 pieces of dough the size of oranges. Roll into long sausage shapes and braid together. Fold ends underneath the braids. Cover and set in a warm place until double in bulk. Brush with beaten egg and bake in a greased pan or baking sheet at 350 degrees until loaves are brown, about 20-25 minutes for rolls, 25-30 minutes for braided bread.

Susan Jianas
Sons Matt, 2004; Michael, 2007

I remember helping to paint Tom Norman's classroom over one weekend with Dave Starke and Mark Beauchamp and a few others. We were in his junior theology class and the walls were two gawdawful tones of olive green. We decided to surprise him with a freshly painted classroom. After getting permission, we settled in all weekend without his knowing and painted the room with two tones of light/dark blue with a red racing stripe through the middle. I'm pretty sure he liked the colors, but I'm even more certain that the fact we wanted to do it for him at all was the best part.

- Brian J. Soher, 1985

Chipotle Corn Bread

1 cup yellow cornmeal

1 cup flour

¼ cup sugar

2 teaspoons baking powder

1 teaspoon baking soda

1 teaspoon salt

1 cup corn, drained well

1 cup grated Monterey Jack cheese

1 cup buttermilk

3 eggs

6 tablespoons butter, melted

2 tablespoons minced, seeded, canned chipotle chilies

Preheat oven to 375 degrees. Grease a 9x5-inch loaf pan. Mix first 6 ingredients in large bowl. Stir in corn and cheese. Whisk buttermilk, eggs, butter and chipotle chilies in medium bowl. Add buttermilk mixture to dry ingredients, stir until blended. Spoon batter into prepared pan. Bake bread until tester comes out clean from center, about 35 minutes. Cool in pan on rack 15 minutes. Turn bread out onto rack. Cool completely.

Shari Webb
Sons Adam, 2003; Cameron, 2005

After a frustrating loss in Columbia to the Hickman Kewpies, Coach Jerry Culver had our bus head to the McDonald's on Providence Street. He had called ahead and placed a big order for our tired and hungry team. Our bus pulled up to the McDonald's drive through window and asked for 120 Big Macs, 60 orders of fries and 60 large drinks. Bag after bag came parading through the bus window. At least for a moment our loss was forgotten.

- Rick Bishop, 1979
Son Sean, 2008

Byrne Clan Soda Bread

2 cups sugar

½ teaspoon salt

1 teaspoon baking soda

¼ teaspoon baking powder

5 cups flour

½ cup butter

2 cups raisins

3 eggs

1½ cups buttermilk

Mix sugar, salt, baking soda, baking powder and flour. Sift together. Add butter to dry ingredients. Add raisins. Whip eggs slightly, add to buttermilk. Stir into flour mixture until smooth. Pour into greased iron skillet. Bake at 350 degrees for 1 hour and 15 minutes.

Rev. Luke Byrne, S.J.
Former RHS President

Chocolate Chip Zucchini Bread

¾ cup sugar

3 tablespoons vegetable oil

2 large eggs

1 cup applesauce

½ cup whole wheat flour

1½ cups flour

2 tablespoons unsweetened cocoa

1¼ teaspoons baking soda

1 teaspoon ground cinnamon

¼ teaspoon salt

1½ cups finely shredded zucchini

½ cup semisweet mini chocolate chips

Cooking spray

Preheat oven to 350 degrees. In a large bowl, beat sugar, oil and eggs with a mixer at low speed until well blended. Stir in applesauce. Combine flours, cocoa, baking soda and salt, stirring well with whisk. Add flour mixture to sugar mixture, beating just until moist. Stir in zucchini and chocolate chips. Spoon into 9x5-inch loaf pan coated with cooking spray. Bake at 350 degrees for 1 hour or until a wooden pick inserted in the center comes out clean. Cool in pan 10 minutes on a wire rack and remove from pan. Makes 16 servings.

Anne Rhoades
Sons Charles, 1998; Chris, 2005; Dan, 2007

Autumn Apple Bread

¼ cup shortening

⅔ cup sugar

2 eggs, well beaten

2 cups sifted flour

1 teaspoon baking powder

1 teaspoon soda

1 teaspoon salt

2 cups chopped apples

1 teaspoon lemon flavoring

⅔ cup chopped walnuts

Cream shortening and sugar until light and fluffy. Beat in eggs. Sift dry ingredients. Add alternately with apple to egg mixture. Add lemon flavoring and nuts. Batter will be stiff. Bake in greased and floured 9x5-inch loaf pan at 350 degrees for 50-60 minutes. Do not slice until cold.

Anne Rhoades
Sons Charles, 1998; Chris, 2005; Dan, 2007

In a 1985 Rockhurst High Review article, Drama Director Mr. Jerry Stark recalled some of his star pupils: Gerry McGonigle, 1976, a professional actor; Terry O'Malley, 1976, and Bob Ortega, 1976, both TV anchormen in Fairbanks, Alaska; Father Mike Rice, 1956, a priest; Mike Pace, 1967, in New York with a singing and acting group; Jeff East, 1976, was young Superman in the movie; Bill Zahner, 1973, a professional actor in Denver; Kevin Wall, 1971, a sportscaster in KC; Duane Sharp, 1982, a professional actor in KC; George Guastello, 1978, major roles at Worlds of Fun productions; David Muma, SJ, 1981, best supporting actor at state.

Cranberry Orange Bread

2 cups flour

1 cup oats (quick or old fashioned, uncooked)

¾ cup sugar

2 teaspoons baking powder

½ teaspoon baking soda

½ teaspoon salt, optional

¾ cup orange juice

2 eggs

⅓ cup vegetable oil

1 tablespoon orange zest

¾ cup chopped cranberries

½ cup chopped nuts, optional

Heat oven to 350 degrees. Grease and flour bottom only of 9x5-inch loaf pan. Combine flour, oats, sugar, baking powder, baking soda and salt, mixing well. Set aside. Beat orange juice, eggs, oil and orange zest until thoroughly combined. Add to dry ingredients, mixing just until moistened. Stir in cranberries and nuts. Pour into prepared pan. Bake 60-70 minutes or until wooden pick inserted in center comes out clean. Cool 10 minutes, remove from pan. Cool completely before slicing. Makes 12 servings.

Anne Rhoades
Sons Charles, 1998; Chris, 2005; Dan, 2007

Coconut Bread

1 cup coconut

1 egg

1½ cups milk

3 cups flour

1 cup sugar

1 tablespoon baking powder

½ teaspoon salt

1 teaspoon vanilla

Toast coconut on cookie sheet at 350 degrees for about 10 minutes. Watch closely as it burns quickly. Mix egg with milk and add remaining ingredients. Put into a greased loaf pan. Bake for 70 minutes.

Jean Bessenbacher
Husband James, 1949; Sons James, Jr., 1976; Steve, 1986
Grandson Edward, 2001

Applesauce Bread

½ cup shredded carrots, packed

1 cup applesauce (canned, sweetened)

½ cup oil

1 teaspoon vanilla

2 eggs

¾ cup sugar

2 cups flour

1 teaspoon baking powder

½ teaspoon soda

1 teaspoon cinnamon

½ teaspoon nutmeg

½ cup chopped nuts, optional

Topping:

5 tablespoons sugar

½ teaspoon cinnamon

Combine carrots, applesauce, oil and vanilla in bowl. Add eggs and sugar, mix. Mix dry ingredients and nuts. Stir in applesauce mixture, blend. Do not overmix. Pour into greased and floured loaf pan. Mix topping ingredients, sprinkle over batter. Makes a lot of topping -- I use all of it! Bake at 325 degrees for 1 hour.

Jan Carter
Son Sean, 2007

Lemon Tea Bread

2 cups flour

1½ teaspoons baking powder

¼ teaspoon salt

½ cup butter

1⅓ cups sugar, divided

2 eggs

⅓ cup milk

½ cup chopped walnuts or pecans

2 teaspoons lemon zest

¼ cup lemon juice

Lightly grease 9x5x3-inch loaf pan. Preheat oven to 350 degrees. Sift flour with baking powder and salt, set aside. Beat butter with 1 cup sugar until fluffy. Add eggs one at a time, beating after each egg. Beat in flour, alternating with milk, beginning and ending with flour mixture, just until mixed. Stir in nuts and lemon zest. Put in pan. Bake 55-60 minutes. Mix ⅓ cup sugar and lemon juice together and pour over bread as soon as it comes out of the oven. Let cool 10 minutes. Remove to rack.

Sande Novick
Sons Pete, 2003; Carl, 2005

I remember in Phys Ed class as a freshman and sophomore picking up rocks on the soccer field or Dasta stadium. Brother Eilert would have his tractor and a cart going around and we would be filling up buckets of rocks to improve field conditions. I guess all that bending over, reaching and carrying buckets was strength and flexibility conditioning!

- Jim Broski, 1979

Banana Tea Bread

2 eggs

½ cup butter, melted

1 cup ripe bananas (about 3)

1 teaspoon vanilla

1½ cups sugar

1½ cups self rising flour

1 cup chopped pecans, optional

Preheat oven to 350 degrees. Put eggs, butter, bananas, butter-milk and vanilla into blender. Mix thoroughly. Combine sugar and flour in a large bowl. Pour banana mixture over dry ingredients and mix well. Stir in nuts. Pour into greased loaf pan. Bake approximately one hour. It will get really brown on top. Check center with toothpick to make sure it is done. Cool. I keep it in the fridge wrapped in foil.

Sarah Jurcyk
Sons Jordan, 2006; Seth, 2008

This old southern recipe is unlike any banana bread I have had. It is almost cake-like, so I dubbed it "tea bread."

Fruit and Oat Scones

1½ cups flour

1 cup quick-cooking oats

2 teaspoons baking powder

¼ teaspoon salt

½ cup butter

½ cup milk

½ cup chopped fruit

½ cup white chocolate chips

Cinnamon sugar

Mix flour, oats, baking powder and salt. Cut in butter and add milk. Stir and add fruit and chips. Roll or pat out into a circle and cut with a pizza cutter into triangles. Sprinkle with cinnamon sugar. Bake at 400 degrees for 15-20 minutes on a pizza stone or baking sheet.

Sarah Jurcyk
Sons Jordan, 2006; Seth, 2008

Sturbridge Pumpkin Muffins

1 cup sugar	½ teaspoon baking soda
¼ cup vegetable oil	¼ teaspoon ground cloves
2 eggs	¼ teaspoon cinnamon
¾ cup canned pumpkin	¼ teaspoon nutmeg
1½ cups flour	¼ teaspoon salt
1 teaspoon baking powder	¾ cup raisins, optional

Preheat oven to 375 degrees. Mix sugar, oil, eggs and pumpkin. Sift together flour, baking powder, baking soda, spices and salt. Stir both mixtures together, fold in raisins. Fill muffin cups ⅔ full. Bake 16-20 minutes, until golden brown. Remove from oven and let cool a few moments in the pan. Makes 12.

Kate Mahoney
Son John, 2006

Apple Crisp Muffins

3½ cups flour	1 teaspoon vanilla
2 cups sugar	½ cup chopped pecans, optional
1 teaspoon salt	
1 teaspoon baking soda	
1 teaspoon cinnamon	**Streusel Topping:**
3 cups peeled, diced apples	1 cup flour
1¼ cups oil	1 cup brown sugar
2 eggs	½ cup butter, softened

Grease and flour 24 muffins tins or use paper liners. Mix flour, sugar, salt, baking soda and cinnamon. Add chopped apples and stir. Mix oil, eggs and vanilla, add to apple mixture. Add nuts. Fill muffin tins about half full. Mix streusel ingredients until crumbly, sprinkle over muffins. Bake at 350 degrees for 30 minutes. Makes 24.

Michelle Nemmers
Son John, 2008

I have also made this in a 9x13 pan and baked for 45-50 minutes.

Michigan Blueberry Muffins

½ cup butter	2 teaspoons baking powder
¾ cup sugar	½ teaspoon salt
4 egg whites	½ cup milk
2 cups flour	Pint of blueberries

Cream butter and sugar. Add egg whites and beat. Mix flour, baking soda and salt and add alternately with milk. Gently stir in blueberries. Spray muffin pan with cooking spray. Bake at 350 degrees for 25-30 minutes.

Donna Gutek
Son Brian, 2006

These are very light and delicious. For best flavor, use fresh berries.

"7 Week" Bran Muffins

15-ounce box Raisin Bran cereal	1 teaspoon salt
1 quart buttermilk	5 teaspoons baking soda
1 cup vegetable oil	1 tablespoon cinnamon
4 eggs	11½-ounce bag chocolate chips
3 cups sugar	2 cups chopped walnuts or pecan chips
5 cups flour	

Mix the first 5 ingredients in a large bowl. In another bowl, whisk together flour, salt, baking soda, cinnamon. Gradually add flour mixture to cereal mix, stirring after every cup is added. Add chocolate chips and nuts. Grease muffin tins, or use paper liners. The muffin mix can be kept in the fridge for 7 weeks, so you can make a few fresh muffins everyday. Bake at 400 degrees for 15-20 minutes.

Jo Marie Hogan
Husband Earl, 1953; Son Dan, 1986;
Grandson Jack Wendland, 2008

If you like having a bran muffin on hand at all times, this is the recipe for you. It stores in the fridge for 7 weeks. Dip in whenever you desire.

Checkmate Muffins

1 egg

1 cup milk

¼ cup melted butter

⅓-½ cup sugar (if fruit is very sweet, use the smaller amount)

1 teaspoon cinnamon

1 teaspoon vanilla

2 cups flour

3 teaspoons baking powder

2 cups fruit, ½-inch dice (frozen or fresh, frozen seems to keep the muffins more moist)

Mix all ingredients except fruit. Add fruit last. Bake muffins at 400 degrees for 20 minutes. Makes 12.

Valerie Davis
Dr. Michael Cusick
RHS Faculty members & Chess Club moderators

Sue Glatter-Judy would make these team favorites for us to take on the long drives to chess club tournaments.

Doughnut Muffins

⅓ cup unsalted butter

½ cup sugar

1 egg

1½ cups sifted flour

1½ teaspoons baking powder

½ teaspoon salt

¼ teaspoon nutmeg

½ cup milk

Coating:

6 tablespoons butter, melted

½ cup sugar

1½ teaspoons cinnamon

Mix all muffin ingredients. Grease or spray muffin tins. Drop about a tablespoonful of dough into each muffin cup. Bake at 350 degrees for 20-25 minutes. While muffins are hot, dip in melted butter, then roll in sugar and cinnamon combination. Makes 12 regular muffins or 24 mini muffins.

Rose Dorlac & Jim Bevan
Grandson Dennis Ogle, 2009

On the way to the chess-playing Hawklets 2005 State Championship and 2004 co-National Scholastic championship, 6-10 players would gather in the early morning outside the Rose Theater nearly every fall and winter weekend. They would drive with Dr. Michael Cusick or Mrs. Valerie Davis throughout Kansas and Missouri to compete in scholastic tournaments. Travel times and tournaments are opportunities to strategize, laugh, talk -- and eat. A favorite homemade treat on these journeys were Checkmate Muffins, hot from Mrs. Sue Glatter-Judy's (Nathan, 2005) oven.

Beignet (French Doughnut)

1¾ cups flour

½ cup sugar

½ teaspoon salt

1¼ cups club soda

2 eggs

⅛ teaspoon vanilla

9 tablespoons butter, melted

1 cup cocoa or ¾ cup flour and ¼ cup sugar

Powdered sugar

Mix flour, sugar and salt. Add club soda, eggs, vanilla and butter. Roll to ⅛-inch thickness on floured surface, using flour liberally on dough. Coat both sides with cocoa or the flour/sugar mixture. Cut into 2¼-inch squares. Fry in an inch or two of oil at 370 degrees, basting with oil continually on each side until puffy and light golden. Drain well. (Oil should be hot enough for dough to pop to surface in 8-10 seconds.) An electric skillet works best. Serve while hot. Sprinkle generously with powdered sugar and serve with maple syrup. Makes about 2 dozen. Add orange zest for variation.

Natalie Wolfe
Son Brad, 2007

Cream Cheese Squares

2 (8-ounce) cans refrigerated crescent dinner rolls, divided

2 (8-ounce) packages cream cheese, softened

1 teaspoon vanilla

1 egg, slightly beaten

¾ cup sugar, divided

2 tablespoons cinnamon

Preheat oven to 350 degrees. Grease a 9x13-inch pan and press 1 can crescent dough onto bottom to form crust. Press seams tightly to seal. Beat cream cheese, vanilla, egg and ½ cup sugar until well blended. Spread onto crust. Unroll remaining can of dough onto wax paper. Pat dough to form a 9x13 rectangle, pressing seams to seal. Invert over cream cheese mixture to form a top crust. Discard wax paper. Bake 30-35 minutes or until golden brown. Combine remaining sugar and cinnamon, sprinkle over top of cake. Cut into squares. Serves 24.

Carrie McCausland
Son Stuart, 2007

Sour Cream Coffee Cake

1 cup butter, slightly melted

1 cup sugar

2 eggs

1 teaspoon vanilla

1 teaspoon baking soda

½ teaspoon salt

2 cups flour

1 cup sour cream

¼ cup milk

Filling:

½ cup brown sugar

⅓ cup sugar

1 teaspoon cinnamon

1 cup chopped nuts

Glaze:

1½ cups powdered sugar

2½ teaspoons warm water

½ teaspoon vanilla

Cream butter and sugar together, add eggs and vanilla. Beat in dry ingredients, sour cream and milk. Beat 2 minutes. Spread half the batter in a greased and floured 9x13-inch pan. Sprinkle half the filling over the batter. Spread remaining batter over top, sprinkle rest of filling over top. Bake at 350 degrees about 35 minutes. When cake is cool, mix glaze ingredients until smooth, drizzle over cake.

Sarah Jurcyk
Sons Jordan, 2006; Seth, 2008

Frozen Fruit Cups

20-ounce can crushed pineapple, drained

16-ounce can apricots, drained, diced

2 (10-ounce) boxes frozen sliced strawberries in syrup, thawed

6 bananas, sliced

1 large can frozen orange juice concentrate

1 large juice can water

1 cup sugar

1 cup frozen blueberries

Mix all ingredients except blueberries. Pour into muffin tins lined with paper liners. Drop 4 or 5 blueberries on top of each cup. Freeze. Once frozen, cups can be removed from the tin and stored in freezer bags. Remove paper wrappers before serving.

Catherine Moussa
Son Alex VanMaren, 2007

Sherry Streusel Cake

Streusel:

⅔ cup melted butter

½ cup packed light brown sugar

¾ cup sugar

½ cup flour

1 teaspoon cinnamon

½-1 cup chopped pecans

Cake:

18.25-ounce package plain yellow cake mix

3.4-ounce package vanilla instant pudding mix

4 eggs

¾ cup oil

¾ cup sherry

1 teaspoon vanilla

2 teaspoons ground nutmeg

Mix streusel ingredients together, set aside. Preheat oven to 350 degrees. Lightly spray and flour a Bundt pan, set aside. Blend cake mix, pudding mix, eggs, oil, sherry, vanilla and nutmeg in a large mixing bowl on low speed for 1 minute. Scrape sides of bowl down, then increase speed to medium and beat 2 minutes, scraping sides of bowl again as needed. Batter should be well-combined and thickened.

Pour half of batter into prepared pan. Sprinkle with half the streusel mix, pour in remaining batter and top with remaining streusel. Gently swirl through with a knife. Bake 50-55 minutes, until golden brown and toothpick comes out clean. Run knife around edge of pan and invert onto a plate or rack, then onto another rack so cake is standing upright. Cool completely. Serves 16.

Kathy Huerter
Husband Dan, 1971; Son Drew, 2002

This cake is also good without the streusel, although I can't imagine not adding it. The cake is good as a coffee cake for brunch or as a dessert.

Cinnamon Roll-Ups

2 loaves sandwich bread

16 ounces cream cheese, softened

½ teaspoon lemon juice

1½ cups sugar, divided

2 egg yolks

2 tablespoons cinnamon

1 cup butter or margarine, melted

Cut crusts from bread and flatten, using a rolling pin. Beat together cream cheese, lemon juice, ¾ cup sugar and egg yolks. Spread over bread. Roll each piece like a jelly roll. Mix remaining ¾ cup sugar and cinnamon together. Dip rolled bread in melted butter and roll in sugar and cinnamon mixture. Slice each piece in half. Bake at 450 degrees for 10 minutes. Yields 20 to 40 roll-ups. Roll-ups are very easy to make ahead and freeze in a pan or zippered plastic bag.

Mary Ann Welsh
Sons Eddie, 2000; Steven, 2004

Baked Cinnamon French Toast

16-ounce loaf Pepperidge Farm Cinnamon Swirl Bread, cut into cubes

¾ cup dried cranberries or raisins, optional

6 eggs, beaten

3 cups half & half or milk

2 teaspoons vanilla

Cinnamon sugar or powdered sugar

Place bread cubes and cranberries in greased 3-quart shallow baking dish. Mix eggs, half & half and vanilla, pour over all. Cover and refrigerate 1 hour or overnight. Uncover and bake at 350 degrees for 45 minutes or until golden brown and set in center. Sprinkle with cinnamon sugar or powdered sugar. Serve with butter and syrup. Serves 8.

Anne O' Flaherty
Son Jack, 2008

Great for overnight guests!

In 1972, Mr. Ron Geldhof was fresh out of college and we were fresh out of grade school/junior high. As I recall on our first day of freshman Phys-Chem, Mr. Geldhof took the front of the class, sat on top of his desk, crossed his legs and began to address the class from his seated position atop the desk. He introduced himself as our new science teacher and went on to say that we could "just call him Ron". Before that first week was over he was no longer addressing us while seated on his desk, nor was he allowing us to address him as anything but Mr. Geldhof.

- Keith Connor, 1976

Crème Brûlée French Toast

½ cup butter

1 cup brown sugar

2 tablespoons corn syrup

6-8 slices country white bread, crusts removed

5 large eggs

1½ cups half & half

1 teaspoon vanilla

1 tablespoon Grand Marnier

¼ teaspoon salt

Melt butter, brown sugar and corn syrup. Pour into greased 9x13-inch baking dish. Line pan with bread to fit in one layer. Beat eggs, half & half, vanilla, Grand Marnier and salt. Pour over bread. Let sit in refrigerator for 8 hours, up to overnight. Bring to room temperature. Bake at 350 degrees for 35-40 minutes. It will puff up and deflate. Serve immediately.

Sarah Jurcyk
Sons Jordan, 2006; Seth, 2008

Apple Puff Pancakes

6 eggs

1½ cups milk

1 cup flour

3 tablespoons sugar

1 teaspoon vanilla

½ teaspoon salt

¼ teaspoon cinnamon

¼ cup butter

4 small apples, peeled, thinly sliced

2-3 tablespoons brown sugar

Preheat oven to 425 degrees. Combine eggs, milk, flour, sugar, vanilla, salt and cinnamon. Melt butter in a 9x13-inch pan in the oven. Add apples and return to oven until butter sizzles. Remove pan from oven and pour batter over apples. Sprinkle with brown sugar and bake 20 minutes or until golden brown and puffed. Serve hot with syrup. Serves 6-8.

Julie McManus
Sons Kevin, 1997; Tim, 2005

A favorite from when our sons were at Rockhurst!

Gingerbread Pancakes

2½ cups baking mix (Bisquick)

¾ cup apple butter

1 cup milk

2 tablespoons oil

¼ teaspoon cinnamon

¼ teaspoon ginger

¼ teaspoon nutmeg

2 eggs

Mix all together and pour ¼ cup on hot griddle. (If necessary, thin batter with extra milk.) Serve with warm syrup and freshly whipped cream. Makes 18-20.

Kate Brown
Husband Peter, 1976; Sons Chris, 2001; Kevin, 2003; Scott, 2010

Crispy Yeast Waffles

2⅔ cups flour

1 package dry yeast

2 tablespoons sugar

1 teaspoon salt

1¾ cups milk

¼ cup water

¼ cup butter

3 eggs

In a large bowl, combine flour, yeast, sugar and salt; mix well. In saucepan, or in microwave, heat milk, water and butter until warm. Butter does not need to melt. Add to flour mixture. Add egg. Blend at low speed until moistened, then beat 1 minute at medium speed.

Cover bowl with plastic wrap and foil. Refrigerate batter several hours or overnight. Stir down batter. Bake in waffle iron on medium heat. Serve hot with butter and toppings. Makes 6-8 waffles.

Kathy Huerter
Husband Dan, 1971; Son Drew, 2002

James Beckley took 1st place in the National Book Week oral book review contest.

- November 13, 1959 newspaper clipping

The 1974 Chess club, with over 40 active members, had two big victories over O'Hara and Washington High School. Club moderator was Larry Grace.

Baked Bananas

4 ripe bananas

¼ cup unsalted butter

2 tablespoons dry sherry

1 tablespoon fresh lime juice

⅓ cup loosely packed brown sugar

1 teaspoon ground cinnamon

Cut bananas into halves crosswise and lengthwise. Arrange in a single layer in a baking dish. Melt butter in a small saucepan and stir in sherry and lime juice. Pour over bananas; sprinkle with brown sugar and cinnamon. Bake at 375 degrees for 12-15 minutes or until golden brown and bubbly.

Linda Dro
Son Justin, 1997

For large groups, this recipe can easily be doubled or tripled.

Hot Glazed Pears

6 Bosc pears, cut in half, cored

¾ cup brown sugar

2 teaspoons butter, melted

1 teaspoon ground cinnamon

1 teaspoon cornstarch

2 teaspoons lemon juice

1 cup water

¼ cup slivered almonds, toasted, optional

Place pears cut side up in baking dish. Combine remaining ingredients except nuts, mix thoroughly. Pour evenly over pears. Bake at 350 degrees about 1 hour or until pears are soft and glazed. Baste a few times during baking to keep pears from drying out. Garnish with almonds, if desired. Serves 6.

Polly Mandl
Husband Richard, 1978; Son Ryan, 2006

Strawberry-Pineapple-Banana Kabobs

½ cup orange juice

Zest and juice of 1 lemon

¼ cup brown sugar

2 tablespoons honey

1 tablespoon cornstarch

¼ teaspoon ground allspice

1 quart strawberries, hulled

2 bananas, peeled and cut into 1-inch pieces (not too ripe)

½ pineapple, peeled and cut into 1-inch pieces (about 3 cups)

Glaze: Preheat broiler. In a small saucepan, stir together orange juice, lemon zest and juice, honey, cornstarch and allspice to dissolve cornstarch. Heat glaze mixture over medium heat, stirring occasionally until thickened, approximately two minutes. Remove from heat and cool.

Thread six metal skewers with a strawberry, banana, pineapple and then another strawberry, etc. Basically, alternate colors. Coat broiler pan rack with cooking spray. Place skewers on broiler pan rack. Generously brush all sides with cooled glaze. Broil 3-4 inches from heat for 2-3 minutes on each side or until fruit just starts to brown. Serve immediately.

Diane Rauschelbach
Husband Jerry, 1980; Son Parker, 2010

Fruit Dip

8 ounces sour cream

8 ounces thawed Cool Whip

1½ cups powdered sugar

1½ cups preserves, any flavor

Mix all ingredients and chill.

Rose Dorlac & Jim Bevan
Grandson Dennis Ogle, 2009

This is great with all fruits and can be made in any flavor you like!

Fresh Salmon Hash

1 medium russet or Idaho potato, peeled, sliced

3 tablespoons unsalted butter, divided

2 tablespoons safflower oil, divided

1 large clove garlic, minced

½ cup minced onion

⅓ cup chopped celery

2 tablespoons pimiento

2 tablespoons diced green bell pepper

6 tablespoons heavy cream

1 teaspoon salt

½ teaspoon white pepper

¼ cup minced fresh parsley

1½ cups cooked, flaked salmon (10 ounces)

Cook sliced potato in boiling water until just tender, 5-6 minutes. Drain, rinse under cold water, pat dry, dice. In heavy skillet over high heat, melt 1 tablespoon butter with 1 tablespoon oil. Add potato and cook until crisp and golden, 2-3 minutes, stirring frequently. Transfer potatoes to bowl, set aside. In same skillet, over medium-low heat, melt 1 tablespoon butter and 1 tablespoon oil. Add garlic, onion, celery, pimiento and green pepper. Cook until soft, about 6 minutes, stirring occasionally. Add to potatoes. Stir cream, salt and white pepper into potato mixture. Cool to room temperature. Add parsley and salmon. Cover and refrigerate up to 24 hours if made ahead. Sauté salmon hash in remaining butter until crisp and golden, about 4 minutes. Serves 6.

Suzanne Orscheln
Sons Joe, 2000; Dustin, 2002; Scott, 2005

When Rockhurst secured pool space at the Red Bridge YMCA in 2003, we finally had a place to call home and have morning practices. It soon became evident that getting up at 4:45 am, in the pool by 5:15 am, swimming until 7 am and getting to school by 7:45 am did not leave much time for eating and so the tradition of parents bringing breakfast to the Y began. At first it was simple fare: bagels, pop tarts, granola bars. We soon realized though that this did not fuel hungry boys who had just swum 3 or 4 thousand yards, so the fare expanded. Soon we were serving biscuits and gravy, egg casseroles, French toast, etc. No matter how much we made, there never seemed to be any leftovers. We like to think our early morning breakfasts helped fuel the race to win the team's first Missouri State Championship in 2005!

- Debra Webster
Sons William, 2005;
Kevin, 2007;
David, 2009

Sausage Gravy

½ pound ground pork sausage

1 tablespoon Crisco

3 tablespoons flour

3-4 cups milk or more

⅛ teaspoon sugar

Salt and pepper to taste

Brown sausage, add Crisco. After Crisco melts, add flour until sausage is coated. Gradually add milk, stir until gravy consistency. Add sugar, salt and pepper. Serve warm over biscuits.

Vicki Springs
Son Brett, 2000

Fire and Ice Eggs

5 strips bacon, cut into 1-inch pieces

3 cups hot cooked rice

1½ cups shredded Colby, cheddar, or Monterey Jack cheese, divided

½ cup sour cream

¼ cup picante sauce, plus additional for passing

¼ teaspoon salt

5 eggs

Cook bacon until crisp; drain well, set aside. Combine rice, 1 cup of the cheese, sour cream, picante sauce and salt; mix well. Spoon into 8-inch square baking dish. With back of spoon make 5 deep indentations in rice mixture. Drop an egg into each indentation. Arrange bacon around eggs and sprinkle with remaining ½ cup cheese. Bake at 350 degrees for 30-35 minutes or until eggs are cooked to desired doneness. Serve with additional picante sauce. Serves 5.

Ann Renne
Sons Ryan, 2001; Ross, 2003

Artichoke Oven Omelet

¾ cup picante mild sauce

6.5-ounce jar artichoke hearts, drained, chopped

4-6 ounces ham, chopped

6 eggs

8 ounces sour cream

Freshly ground black pepper

1 cup shredded Monterey Jack cheese

1 cup shredded cheddar cheese

¼ cup grated Parmesan cheese

Grease a 10-inch quiche or deep dish pie pan. Spread picante sauce evenly on the bottom. Distribute artichokes and ham over sauce. In a medium bowl, lightly beat eggs. Whisk in sour cream. Pour into pie pan. Grind pepper over top. Sprinkle evenly with three cheeses. Bake uncovered at 350 degrees for 40-45 minutes, until set. Cut into wedges and serve.

Bridget Winget
Sons Brian, 1999; Dave, 2001; John, 2004; Steven, 2007

Coach Davis, the football coach, broke up a fight between me and Gino Tutera, the big center on the football team, during a basketball game. Tutera had me in a headlock when Coach just looked at him and said "What are you doing, Tutera?" Obviously, for a football player to be headlocking a member of the speech and debate team (and definitely NOT a football player) was so ludicrous as to leave Coach Davis incredulous.

- King Stablein, 1962

McGill Masterpiece

1 pound mild pork sausage

1 pound spicy pork sausage

½ cup chopped onions

6 cups crisp rice cereal, divided

1½ cups rice, cooked

8 ounces shredded cheddar cheese

6 eggs

2 (10¾-ounce) cans cream of celery soup, reduced sodium

½ cup milk

1 tablespoon butter, melted

Grease a 3-quart rectangular baking dish. In a very large skillet, cook sausage and onion. Drain fat. In a large bowl, combine 5 cups of the cereal and cooked rice. Spread rice mixture evenly in bottom of baking dish. Spoon sausage mixture over rice layer. Sprinkle with cheddar.

Beat eggs, soup and milk with a wire whisk until combined. Carefully pour over layers in baking dish. Press down lightly with back of spoon. Toss remaining cereal with butter. Sprinkle over top. Bake at 325 degrees for 50-55 minutes or until golden brown and bubbly. Let stand 10 minutes before serving. Serves 12.

Betty Bailey
Son David, 1983
Grandsons Roland Sabates, 2000; Trey, 2003

Spicy Sunrise Eggs

¼ cup chopped green pepper

¼ cup chopped red pepper

4 eggs or Eggbeaters

Splash of non-fat milk

Colby Jack or American cheese

Toasted bagels

Frank's Hot Sauce

Mix peppers, eggs and milk. Cook and scramble the egg mixture. Melt in cheese. Serve on a toasted bagel. Top with Frank's Hot Sauce.

David Laughlin
Former RHS Principal

I don't cook much, but these will open your eyes. Use lots of Frank's Hot Sauce!

Here are a few quotes from some of my teachers. Ron Geldhof in freshman chemistry class: "This is made up of 7 ergs and spices." Father Mareno, when frustrated with students: "You sons of your parents" - which means nothing at all! Father Purcelli, in 4th year Latin, when picking a student to translate: "Round and round she goes and where she stops, nobody seems to give a damn, unless it's him." Beach Tuckness, introducing a 1 vs. 1 drill in freshman football: "Gentlemen, it's time for some tea and crumpets!" Al Davis, before an All School Mass: "Gentlemen, this gym has just become a chapel."

- Mike Gorman, 1979

Goat Cheese, Artichoke and Smoked Ham Strata

2 cups milk

¼ cup olive oil

8 cups 1-inch cubes sour-dough bread, crusts trimmed

1½ cups whipping cream

5 large eggs

1 tablespoon chopped garlic

1½ teaspoons salt

¾ teaspoon black pepper

½ teaspoon ground nutmeg

12 ounces soft fresh goat cheese, crumbled

1 tablespoon fresh sage, chopped

1 tablespoon fresh thyme, chopped

1½ teaspoons fines herbs or herbes de Provence

12 ounces smoked or regular ham, chopped into ½-inch cubes

3 (6-ounce) jars marinated artichoke hearts, drained, pieces halved lengthwise

1 cup grated Fontina cheese, packed

1 cup grated Parmesan cheese, packed

Whisk milk and oil together in large bowl. Stir in bread cubes. Let stand until liquid is absorbed, about 10 minutes. Whisk cream and next 5 ingredients in another large bowl to blend. Add goat cheese. Mix herbs in small bowl to blend. Grease 9x13-inch glass baking dish. Place bread mixture in prepared dish. Layer ham, artichoke hearts, herbs and cheeses over bread. Pour cream mixture over all. Cover and chill overnight.

Remove from refrigerator 30 minutes before baking. Bake uncovered at 350 degrees for about 1 hour or until golden brown.

Katherine Schorgl
Husband Jim, 1980; Son Christopher, 2007

My favorite subject/teacher was sophomore English with David Bishop, S.J., because he inspired me to read and write.

- David Chartrand, 1971

My favorite subject was sophomore English with Father William Kuehne because he taught me to love good writing.

- Jon Haden, 1975
Son Robbie, 2009

Bacon Quiche

2 pounds bacon, fried crisp, crumbled

2 cups shredded Swiss cheese

⅔-1 cup chopped green onion

2 unbaked pie crusts

4 cups half & half

8 extra large eggs

½ teaspoon white pepper

½ teaspoon ground red pepper (cayenne)

1 teaspoon salt

Preheat oven to 425 degrees. Coat 2 quiche pans with cooking spray. Put pie crusts in pans. Divide bacon and onion between 2 pans, sprinkle over crust. Top with half the cheese. Beat eggs and half & half. Add salt and both peppers. Pour over bacon and onions. Bake uncovered at 425 degrees for 15 minutes. Reduce temperature to 300 degrees, bake another 40-45 minutes, until knife inserted halfway between center and edge comes out clean. Let stand 10 minutes before cutting.

Josephine Nigro
Sons Michael, 2001; John-Paul, 2003

Variation: Substitute 1½ pounds cooked Italian bulk sausage for the bacon, 2 cups mozzarella for the Swiss cheese and 1 cup chopped onion for the green onion. Garnish with chopped tomatoes. Men love this!

Breakfast Burritos

¼ pound bulk chorizo sausage

2 tablespoons finely chopped onion

2 tablespoons finely chopped green bell pepper

2 eggs

2 tablespoons milk

Freshly ground pepper to taste

1 tablespoon butter

4 (6-inch) flour tortillas

1 tomato, peeled, seeded, chopped

½ cup shredded cheddar cheese

Burrito Sauce:

1 cup chopped onion

2 tablespoons vegetable oil

3½ cups finely chopped tomatoes

½ cup chopped green chilies

½ teaspoon sugar

½ teaspoon salt

¼ teaspoon garlic salt

Freshly ground black pepper to taste

2 tablespoons minced fresh parsley

2 tablespoons minced fresh cilantro

In medium skillet, cook sausage, onion and green pepper until done. Drain off grease, set aside. In small bowl, beat eggs, milk and pepper. Melt butter in 8-inch skillet over medium heat. Add egg mixture. Cook without stirring until eggs begin to set on bottom and around edges. Using a spatula, lift and fold partially cooked eggs so uncooked egg flows underneath. Continue until cooked through. Remove from heat.

Divide sausage mixture among 4 tortillas. Top each sausage mixture with ¼ of eggs, tomato and cheese. Fold in sides, fold bottom up and top down to enclose filling. Secure with wooden pick. Arrange on baking sheet. Bake at 350 degrees for 15 minutes or until heated through. Serve with warmed Burrito Sauce or salsa. Serves 2-4.

Burrito Sauce: Sauté onion in oil for 5 minutes. Add tomatoes, chilies, sugar, salt, garlic salt and pepper. Simmer for 15 minutes or until slightly thickened, stirring occasionally. Stir in parsley and cilantro. Makes 3 cups.

Vicki Springs
Son Brett, 2000

Italian Breakfast Pizza

1 pound bulk Italian sausage (or remove casings from links)

1 package refrigerated crescent rolls

1 cup frozen hash brown potatoes

1 cup mozzarella cheese

5 extra large eggs

¼ cup milk

1 teaspoon salt

¼ teaspoon pepper

½-1 cup chopped green onions, optional

1 cup sliced black olives, optional

2 tablespoons grated Parmesan cheese

Preheat oven to 375 degrees. Cook sausage in large skillet until browned, drain. Separate crescent roll dough into 8 triangles, place in ungreased 12-inch pizza pan with points toward center. Press over bottom and up sides to form crust, seal perforations.

Spoon sausage over crust, sprinkle with potatoes and top with mozzarella. Beat together eggs, milk, salt and pepper. Pour over pizza. Sprinkle with onions and olives. Top with Parmesan. Bake 25-30 minutes or until set. Cut into wedges and serve.

Josephine C. Nigro
Sons Michael, 2001; John-Paul, 2003

Great for a crowd or a teen sleepover!

Early in my son's freshman year, he was lamenting because he had forgotten an important assignment at school and it was too late to get back into the building.
I began to offer to write him a note to his teacher but before I could finish the sentence he interrupted with "Mom! A Rockhurst man finds a way to get it done."
I will never forget that day because he was no longer my little boy, but a Rockhurst Man, and he did find a way to get it done.

- Laura Brancato
Son Drew, 2002

SOUPS *AND* STEWS

1930s

National:

The 1929 stock market crash ushered in an economic depression that, coupled with the "Dust Bowl" drought of the 1930s, brought about an era of unparalleled economic hardship for the United States. But, at the same time, the U.S. made progress in ventures both lavishly large and sub-atomically small. Several marquee American landmarks- the Golden Gate Bridge, Empire State Building and Hoover Dam among them- were built during the decade, and scientists first split the atom in 1932. Wonder Bread began marketing pre-sliced bread nationwide in 1930. The company's product would became a staple of Hawklet sack lunches for years to come and gain acclaim as the greatest thing since, well, itself.

Local:

Even in the face of the Depression, the arts flourished in Kansas City in the 1930s. The Plaza Art Fair was born in 1932, and the Nelson-Atkins Museum of Art opened its doors a year later. Just blocks away from the Nelson-Atkins, the University of Kansas City, later incorporated into the state university system as the University of Missouri-Kansas City, held its first classes in 1933.

Apple Pork Stew

2 tablespoons olive oil, divided

1 pound pork tenderloin, cubed

3 tablespoons flour

Salt and pepper to taste

1 onion, chopped

1 teaspoon caraway seeds

2 cups chicken broth

2 cups water

1 tablespoon Dijon mustard

Half of a 16-ounce bag cabbage slaw mix

2 small potatoes, cubed

2 tart apples, unpeeled, cubed

2 tablespoons chopped fresh parsley

Heat one tablespoon olive oil in large pot. Toss pork with flour, salt and pepper. Brown in olive oil, transfer to plate, cover to keep warm. In remaining oil, cook onion and caraway seeds until onion is soft, about 3 minutes. Stir in chicken broth, water, mustard, slaw mix and potatoes. Bring to a boil, reduce heat and simmer, covered, for 15 minutes. Add chopped apples, cover, simmer 10 more minutes. Just before serving, add pork and chopped parsley and warm for an additional 2 minutes.

Martie Eftink
Son Jim, 2003

Do not overcook pork or it will become tough. I often use both a red and yellow apple for the color, but any kind may be used.

Irish Stew

2 tablespoons vegetable oil

3 pounds lean beef stew meat

¼ cup plus 2 tablespoons flour

3 onions, chopped

6 cups sliced fresh mushrooms

18 cloves garlic, minced

3 (6-ounce) cans tomato paste

6 cups beef broth

3 (12-ounce) cans or bottles Irish stout beer

12 cups sliced carrots

6 potatoes, peeled, diced

3 tablespoons cornstarch

3 tablespoons cold water

¾ cup chopped fresh parsley

Heat oil in large soup pot over medium-high heat. Coat beef cubes with flour, shaking off excess. Fry beef cubes until browned on all sides. Remove from pot.

Add onion, mushrooms and garlic to pot and cook, stirring constantly until onion is tender, about 3 minutes. Return beef to pot and stir in tomato paste, beef broth and beer. Add potatoes and carrots. Cover and simmer over low heat for about 1 hour.

Mix together cornstarch and cold water. Stir into stew and simmer until thickened. Sprinkle with parsley. Serves 18.

Bridget Thorne
Son Paul, 2007

This was served at the Irish table at the 2004 and 2005 Heritage Festivals at Rockhurst.

Sale-O-Chili

10 pounds hamburger

1 large onion, chopped

Salt and pepper

Garlic powder

1 cup Williams Chili Seasoning

1 #10 can tomato sauce

1 #10 can red beans

Brown meat with onions. Add salt, pepper and garlic powder, covering meat lightly with seasonings. Drain grease. Add chili seasoning and stir into meat. Add tomato sauce plus one #10 can of water. Cook over medium heat until meat is peeking out of the liquid. Rinse and drain beans, add to chili and heat. Chili may be frozen prior to adding beans. Serves 25.

John Lillis, 1984

The #10 cans can be found at wholesale clubs or use smaller cans for the equivalent of 13 cups, or 6 pounds and 15 ounces.

Steak Soup

3 large onions, diced

2 pounds sliced mushrooms

2 pounds bacon, diced

5 pounds cubed steak

3 (16-ounce) cans stewed tomatoes

3 (8-ounce) cans tomato sauce

1 quart water or red wine

2 (10-ounce) packages frozen mixed vegetables

2 envelopes dry Lipton onion soup mix

2 beef bouillon cubes

3 tablespoons sugar

2 tablespoons oregano

Black pepper

Sauté onions and mushrooms with bacon. Brown steak in same skillet. Add all ingredients together in large pot and simmer for about 2 hours. Serves 20.

Harold J. Reno, 1959
Sons Jay, 1985; Michael, 1994

Hal, who passed away in January 2005, developed this recipe for his trail ride and camping trips. He loved the outdoors and was an avid Rockhurst supporter.

Mike Lillis (Mr. Rockhurst) class of 1956, made chili for Sale-O-Rama for about 10 years. He'd make 400-500 pounds a year! My brother (Timothy, 1980) and I would go to Rockhurst with my dad and uncles the week before Sale-O. We would make all the chili and freeze it. It took about 8 hours or so to make all of it. All the Jesuits would come over, one by one, from the residence and sample the chili (actually they would have a couple of bowls) to make sure it met with the Jesuit seal of approval. Father Steiner (a.k.a. Father Sale-O) and Brother Eilert would always eat the most and would want 2 tubs any time we made the chili throughout the year. People at Sale-O would often say, "I love coming here to get a good deal and because they have the best chili!" Many people would buy it and take it home with them along with other treasures they found at Sale-O. The best thing was my dad would trade chili with the Cascones for their meatballs, both thinking they had the better part of the deal.

- John Lillis, 1984

Hearty Beef-Barley Soup

1 pound beef tenderloin, cut into ¾-inch cubes

¼ cup olive oil

1 cup finely chopped onion

2 cups chopped carrots

1 cup chopped celery

2 tablespoons minced garlic

6 cups beef stock or broth

½ cup tomato puree

¼ cup dry red wine or water

1 tablespoon fresh thyme or 1 teaspoon dried thyme

1½ teaspoons ground coriander

1 teaspoon freshly ground black pepper

½ teaspoon salt

1 cup quick-cooking barley

¼ cup chopped fresh flat leaf parsley

2 tablespoons fresh basil

Brown half of the beef cubes in hot oil over medium-high heat in a 4-quart Dutch oven. Remove meat and keep warm. Add remaining meat, onion, carrots, celery and garlic to the Dutch oven. Cook until meat is browned and onion is tender. Stir frequently. Return all meat to pan.

Stir in beef stock, tomato pureé, wine, dried thyme (if using fresh thyme, add later), coriander, pepper and salt. Bring to a boil and stir in barley. Reduce heat and simmer, covered, for 20-25 minutes or until meat and vegetables are tender. Stir in parsley, basil and fresh thyme (if using fresh.) Makes about 10 cups.

Betty Conway
Husband William, 1952; Son William, 1988

Tortellini Soup

1 pound Italian sausage	3 carrots, sliced
1 large onion, chopped	1 tablespoon sugar
2 cloves garlic, crushed	2 teaspoons Italian seasoning
3 (14-ounce) cans beef broth	2-3 zucchini, sliced
2 (14.5-ounce) cans Italian style diced tomatoes	9-ounce package fresh cheese tortellini
8-ounce can tomato sauce	1 cup shredded Parmesan cheese
1 cup dry red wine	

Cook sausage, onion and garlic until sausage is cooked through and vegetables are soft. Drain. Stir in broth, tomatoes, tomato sauce, wine, carrots, sugar and Italian seasoning and bring to a boil. Reduce heat and simmer 30 minutes. Skim fat. Stir in zucchini and tortellini and cook until done, about 15 minutes. Top servings with Parmesan.

Jane Sorrentino
Son Tom, 2008

Charlotte McGahan makes a similar soup but adds 1 chopped green pepper and 3 tablespoons chopped fresh parsley.

My brother Charles E. Elmer (1964) was so proud of his time at Rockhurst. Though he passed away in 2004, I know he would be proud to be included in this Heritage Cookbook. He was an honor student and was especially happy playing sports for RHS. He had the honor of being selected captain of his football, basketball and baseball teams. In 1964 he received the Edward F. Bukaty memorial award given to one senior for leadership both on and off the field. He was a member of the first Greater Kansas City All Star Team. He was also selected to be on the RHS All Time football team in 1970.

- Ms. Frances Harding

Mini Meatball Soup

2 tablespoons extra virgin olive oil

2 carrots, peeled, chopped

2 ribs celery, chopped

1 medium onion, chopped

2 bay leaves, fresh or dried

Salt and freshly ground pepper

1 pound ground beef, pork and veal combined

1 egg, beaten

3 cloves garlic, minced

½ cup Parmigiano-Reggiano cheese, grated

½ cup Italian breadcrumbs

½ teaspoon freshly grated nutmeg

8 cups chicken stock or broth

1½ cups dried pasta rings, or fettuccini broken into pieces

6-ounce bag fresh spinach, coarsely chopped.

In a deep pot over medium heat, heat olive oil. Add carrots, celery, onions and bay leaves. Season with salt and pepper. Cover and cook vegetables 5-6 minutes, stirring occasionally.

While vegetables cook, combine meat, egg, garlic, cheese, breadcrumbs and nutmeg in a bowl. Add salt and pepper as desired. Use a teaspoon to make small meatballs and place on wax paper.

Uncover soup pot and slowly add broth to the pot. Increase heat to high and bring soup to a boil. When soup boils, reduce heat a bit and carefully drop meatballs into soup. Add pasta to soup and stir. Cover and simmer 10 minutes. When pasta is tender, remove bay leaves. Stir in chopped spinach in batches. When spinach has wilted into soup, soup is ready. Serves 6-8.

Beth Selanders
Son Albert, 2008

Hearty Minestrone

1 pound Italian sausage links - hot, mild or sweet

2 tablespoons olive oil

1 large onion, chopped

1 large garlic clove, chopped

5 cups or more chicken stock

28-ounce can chopped tomatoes (or use fresh)

10-ounce package frozen chopped spinach

1½ cups sliced carrots

1½ cups fresh or frozen green beans or snow peas

1½ teaspoons dried basil

½ teaspoon dried marjoram

Pinch hot pepper flakes

19-ounce can white beans

¾ cup small shell pasta

1 cup grated Parmesan cheese

Prick sausage skins, cover with water in sauce pan and bring to a boil. Cover and simmer for 15 minutes. Drain, cut into slices. In large soup pot, heat oil and lightly brown sausages. Add onion and garlic, cook 2-3 minutes until softened.

Add chicken stock, chopped tomatoes with juice, spinach, carrots, green beans, basil, marjoram and pepper flakes. Bring to a boil. Reduce heat, cover and simmer for 10 minutes or until vegetables are almost tender.

Add white beans, including juice, and pasta. Simmer 5-7 minutes until pasta is al dente. Adjust seasonings with salt and pepper. Add more chicken stock if desired. Serve with freshly grated Parmesan.

Gerri Sopyla
RHS Counselor

This serves 6, but if you want to serve more, don't feel confined to doing exact math to increase portions.

To this day, when Thursday comes around I often think of Fr. Marko's freshman Latin class. You see, Thursdays were Culture Day and we were treated to slide shows of Rome, Pompeii and Paris.

- Jim Broski, 1979

Father Francis Fahey, S.J., taught at Rockhurst for 37 years, 1964-1980. He celebrated his Golden Jubilee with a reception at RHS in February 1981.

Wild Duck Gumbo

Raymond "Red" McKee,
class of 1925,
was a skinny red head
from St. Vincent
Academy.
He was an all-around
athlete: a flashy and
daring quarterback in
football, a nifty little
guard known for his
playmaking and
dribbling in basketball,
a clutch hitter in
baseball and a star in
tennis and golf.
He was inducted into the
Rockhurst High School
Athletic Hall of Fame.

Henry Massman IV,
class of 1980,
is the general contractor
for construction of
projects associated
with the RHS
"Foundations Forever"
campaign that include
a new theater-auditorium,
chapel and fine arts
classrooms.
Major benefactors
include
Dr. & Mrs. William Barry
(class of 1927) and
Mr. & Mrs. Robert
Pendergast,
(class of 1931.)

2 mallard ducks or 3 duck breasts, boned, skinned, cut into ½ inch pieces

Salt and freshly ground pepper to taste

Cayenne pepper to taste

½ cup vegetable oil

½ cup flour

2 medium onions, chopped

1 cup chopped celery

1 large green bell pepper, chopped

1 bunch green onions, chopped

2 cloves garlic, minced

2 quarts hot water

1 bay leaf

1 tablespoon Worcestershire

Pinch of dried thyme

Tabasco sauce to taste

2 (10-ounce) packages frozen sliced okra, thawed

⅓ cup tomato paste

1 pound smoked sausage, cut into ¼-inch pieces

¼ cup minced fresh parsley

6 cups cooked rice

Season duck well with salt, pepper and cayenne. In a large, heavy skillet, brown duck pieces in hot oil. Remove and keep warm.

Pour off all but ⅓ cup oil. Add flour and stir constantly over low heat until roux is dark brown in color. Add onions, celery, green pepper, green onions and garlic. Cook until onions are transparent. Pour in hot water. Add bay leaf, Worcestershire, thyme, Tabasco, salt, pepper, okra and tomato paste. Stir well.

Add duck and smoked sausage. Simmer uncovered over low heat for two hours or until duck is tender. Add water as needed. Shortly before serving, add parsley. Serve in bowls over rice.

Alison Ward
Sons Brian, 2004; David, 2004; Taylor, 2006

This recipe freezes well.

Mulligatawny Soup

4 tablespoons cooking oil

3 cups chopped carrots

3 cups chopped green peppers

3 onions, chopped

4 tart apples, peeled, chopped

15 cups hot water

8 large whole chicken breasts

15 chicken bouillon cubes

8 whole cloves

½ teaspoon mace

6-8 sprigs fresh parsley, chopped

2 tablespoons salt

6-8 drops Tabasco sauce

3 tablespoons paprika

3 (14½-ounce) cans peeled tomatoes

5 teaspoons Accent

4 teaspoons sugar

2 teaspoons curry powder

Heat oil in large soup pot. Add carrots, green peppers, onions and apples. Sauté over low heat for 15-20 minutes or until carrots are tender. Add hot water and chicken breasts with all other ingredients. Cover and simmer for at least one hour.

Remove chicken from pot and cut into small pieces. Return to pot and simmer for 30-45 minutes over very low heat.

Laura Koons
Sons Brett, 1999; Jeff, 2004

Karen makes a similar version of this soup but adds ½ cup raisins, ½ teaspoon lemon zest, ½ cup cooked white rice and ½ cup milk.

Karen McCracken
Husband Kevin, 1973
Sons Zachary, 2004; Daniel, 2006; Andrew, 2008

Chicken Noodle Soup

1 or 2 leftover cooked chicken breasts

3 quarts water

4 tablespoons chicken soup base or bouillon

1 onion, thickly sliced

1 medium carrot, peeled, diced

2-3 large stalks celery, including leaves, diced

¼ teaspoon dried tarragon

½ teaspoon dried thyme

2 teaspoons dried parsley flakes

Pepper to taste

24-ounce package Reames frozen egg noodles

(You can go to the trouble of using raw chicken if you want to waste the time. If you do, cook chicken in the water first, then add the rest of the ingredients after chicken is almost done.)

Put all ingredients except noodles in a large pot and bring to a boil, then lower heat and simmer for an hour, covered, until vegetables are soft. Add frozen noodles and cook for 45 minutes.

At this point I turn off the soup for an hour or so and remove the lid. Then, right before dinner I turn it on again, thereby tricking the soup into believing it is one day old! Soup, at least chicken noodle soup, never catches on. Then serve with…oh for cryin' out loud, it's SOUP! You know how to eat soup!

Joe Moore, 1955

Jim Walters was paralyzed from the neck down when he broke his neck on an outing with other youths at Sunny Shores Beach in Hickman Mills. For Christmas, fellow members of his senior class chipped in and bought a $130 machine which turns the pages of a book or magazine. Many students and teachers visit Jim, including Rev. Robert DeRouen, who has his English class write letters to Jim and answer mail for him.

- 1959 yearbook (Jim later married and was active at St. Elizabeth's parish in Kansas City. He passed away in 2006.)

Zucchini Soup

2 pounds ground beef or turkey	14.5-ounce can stewed tomatoes
6 cups water	1½ teaspoons dried basil
6 bouillon cubes	2 tablespoons butter
3 carrots, sliced	1 teaspoon salt
1 pound zucchini, sliced	1 teaspoon pepper
1 onion, chopped	15.5-ounce can prepared salsa

Sauté meat in skillet until browned. In large soup pot simmer water, bouillon, carrots, zucchini and onion until tender. Add tomatoes, basil, butter, salt, pepper and meat. Simmer 15 minutes then add salsa. Simmer an additional 30 minutes.

Jan Fakoury
Son Chris, 2006

Corn and Cheese Chowder

4 slices bacon	3 Yukon gold potatoes
1 tablespoon butter	⅛ teaspoon white pepper
1 red pepper, diced	½ cup cream
1 onion, chopped	2 cups corn, fresh or frozen and thawed
2 teaspoons dried cumin	2 cups shredded cheddar cheese
2 (14-ounce) cans chicken broth	Salt to taste

Fry bacon until crisp. Crumble and set aside; reserve 1 tablespoon bacon grease in pan. Add butter to pan, sauté red pepper and onion until softened, about 8-10 minutes. Sprinkle with cumin and cook 1 minute, stirring. Add chicken broth, potatoes and white pepper, simmer until potatoes are tender, about 10 minutes. Add cream and corn, bring to a boil. Turn off heat, stir in cheese until melted and season to taste with salt. Sprinkle with bacon to serve.

Sarah Jurcyk
Sons Jordan, 2006; Seth 2008

Martie Eftink uses ½ pound of breakfast sausage instead of bacon.

Boston Clam Chowder

1 pound bacon, diced

2 cups diced yellow onion

1½ cups diced celery

2 teaspoons finely chopped fresh thyme (or 1 teaspoon dried)

2 dry bay leaves

7 tablespoons flour

3 cups lobster stock

3 cups chicken stock

1¼ cups heavy cream or half & half

¾ cups milk

3 cups diced red potatoes, blanched in salted water

¼ teaspoon cayenne pepper

½ teaspoon cracked black pepper

Sea salt to taste

1½ cups chopped fresh clams (or 2 cups canned clams)

2 cups fresh yellow corn (or 2 cups canned corn)

4 teaspoons butter

Sauté bacon in a 5-quart saucepan over medium heat until crisp. Remove bacon and set aside. Add onions, celery, thyme and bay leaves to bacon grease, then sprinkle flour over mixture and stir. Cook for 2 minutes, stirring often.

Add a little of the stocks slowly so roux has a chance to absorb the liquid. Once liquid has been absorbed, add remaining stocks gradually, continuing to stir until smooth. Simmer for 5 minutes. Add cream and milk and cook for another 5 minutes. Add blanched potatoes, cayenne and cracked pepper. Taste for seasoning. Add sea salt if necessary.

Simmer on low heat for 20 minutes. Add clams and corn, continue to simmer on low for another 10 minutes. Ladle soup into bowls and garnish each with a sprinkle of bacon and ½ teaspoon of butter. Serve with warm sourdough bread.

Cyndi Lucas
Son Christopher, 2007

I use Better Than Bouillon Lobster Stock, available at Price Chopper.

ID2 Days (Ignatian Direction Days) -- this pastoral program began in 1976 and was developed to strengthen spiritual awareness. The junior and seniors and the freshmen and sophomores were paired together.

The Father's Club raffled off a TV in 1953.

Artichoke Shrimp Chowder

2 pounds medium shrimp

3 (14-ounce) cans quartered artichoke hearts

6½ cups chicken broth

8 green onions, chopped

1 tablespoon Creole seasoning

1½ teaspoons ground white pepper

1 teaspoon dried thyme

½ cup butter or margarine

⅔ cup flour

1 quart half & half

Grated Parmesan cheese

Peel and devein shrimp, set aside. Drain artichokes, reserving 1½ cups liquid. Place artichokes, reserved artichoke liquid, chicken broth and next 4 ingredients into a sauce pan and bring to a boil. Reduce heat, simmer 30 minutes. Melt butter in large soup pot over medium heat. Add flour and whisk constantly, 1 minute. Whisk broth mixture into flour mixture. Whisk in half & half, bring to a boil. Add shrimp, cook 3-5 minutes until pink. Ladle into bowls and sprinkle with Parmesan. Serves 8.

Beth Selanders
Son Albert, 2008

Smoked Shrimp Soup

½ gallon chicken broth

2½ pounds peeled, diced potatoes

3 small diced onions

2 cups diced celery

2 pounds Velveeta, diced

1 can Rotel tomatoes

2 (16-ounce) cans stewed tomatoes, puréed

½ gallon milk

Pepper to taste

½ tablespoon Wright's liquid smoke

2 pounds shelled shrimp

In large stock pot, heat chicken broth with potatoes, onions and celery. Simmer until vegetables are tender. Purée in blender, set aside. In stock pot, melt Velveeta and Rotel, stir in stewed tomatoes and milk, then add pepper and liquid smoke. Slowly add puréed vegetables, stirring well. Simmer on low 1½ hours. Add shrimp about 10 minutes before serving.

Shelley Looby
Sons Kevin, 2007; Colin, 2007

Lobster Bisque

6 tablespoons butter, divided

4 tablespoons green pepper, chopped

4 tablespoons onion, chopped

1 green onion, chopped

2 tablespoons parsley, chopped

1½ cups sliced fresh mushrooms

2 tablespoons flour

1 cup milk

1 teaspoon salt

⅛ teaspoon white pepper

Dash of Tabasco sauce

1½ cups half & half

1½ cups lobster meat

3 tablespoons dry sherry

Heat 4 tablespoons butter in skillet. Add green peppers, onion, green onion, parsley and mushrooms. Sauté vegetables until soft, about 5 minutes.

In saucepan, heat remaining 2 tablespoons butter. Stir in flour. Add milk and cook over medium to high heat, stirring constantly until thickened and smooth. Stir in salt and pepper, add Tabasco sauce to taste.

Add vegetables and half & half. Bring to a boil, stirring constantly, and then reduce heat. Add lobster. Simmer uncovered 5 minutes. Just before serving, stir in sherry.

Jane Sorrentino
Son Tom, 2008

Fire-Roasted Tomato Bisque

4 tablespoons unsalted butter, divided

1 small onion, finely chopped

1 medium carrot, finely chopped

1 celery rib, finely chopped

2 garlic cloves, finely chopped

3 tablespoons flour

4 cups chicken stock

14.5-ounce can diced fire-roasted tomatoes, drained

3 tablespoons tomato paste

2 teaspoons sugar

¼ cup heavy cream

Salt and freshly ground black pepper

½ cup feta cheese, optional

In a medium saucepan, melt 2 tablespoons butter. Add chopped onions, carrot, celery and garlic. Cover and cook over medium-high heat, stirring occasionally, until vegetables are just beginning to brown, about 5 minutes.

Sprinkle flour over vegetables and stir over low heat for 1 minute, or until flour is fully incorporated. Add chicken stock, tomatoes, tomato paste and sugar and bring to a boil. Cover and partially cook soup over moderate heat, stirring occasionally, until vegetables are tender, about 15 minutes.

Transfer soup to a blender and purée until smooth. Return purée to saucepan, add cream and cook until soup is just heated through. Season with salt and pepper and swirl in remaining 2 tablespoons butter. Ladle soup into bowls, garnish with feta cheese. Serves 4.

Barbara Dehaemers
Husband David, 1978; Sons Jason, 2005; Zach, 2006

This soup was served at two Teacher Appreciation dinners. The soup and salad bar has become a popular tradition served to teachers by Parents Club volunteers during Spring parent-teacher conferences.

The most fun I ever had at RHS was the senior trip to New York City. The bus ride there was a blast!

- Jon Haden, 1975
Son Robbie, 2009

As a freshman, I was always afraid of being chosen at the pep rallies!

- Clint Useldinger, 2008

North African Spice Soup

1 onion, chopped

5 cups vegetable broth

1 teaspoon ground cinnamon

1 teaspoon grated fresh ginger

Pinch of cayenne pepper

2 carrots, diced

2 celery ribs, diced

14-ounce can chopped tomatoes

1 pound potatoes, diced, lightly floured

14-ounce can chickpeas, drained

2 tablespoons fresh chopped cilantro

1 tablespoon lemon juice

Salt and freshly ground pepper to taste

5 strands saffron, optional

Combine all ingredients and simmer in a large pot 1 hour.

Ann Marie Scahill
Son Michael, 2009

Pumpkin Soup

2 tablespoons butter

8-ounce package sliced mushrooms

½ cup chopped onion

2 tablespoons flour

1 tablespoon curry powder

3 cups chicken broth

2 cups canned pumpkin

1 tablespoon honey

½ teaspoon salt

¼ teaspoon ground nutmeg

¼ teaspoon pepper

12-ounce can evaporated milk

Sour cream for garnish

Chives for garnish

Melt butter in a large soup pot. Add mushrooms and onion. Cook until tender, stirring often. Stir in flour and curry powder. Gradually add chicken broth and cook over medium heat. Stir constantly until mixture is thickened. Stir in pumpkin and next 4 ingredients. Reduce heat and simmer 10 minutes, stirring occasionally. Stir in milk and cook until heated thoroughly. Top with a dollop of sour cream and chopped fresh chives.

Jeanne Gorman Rau
Spouse Don, 1970; Son Zach, 2007

French Onion Soup

6 onions, sliced

2 tablespoons butter

1 tablespoon olive oil

1 teaspoon sugar

6 cups beef broth or consommé

Salt and pepper to taste

½ teaspoon Dijon mustard

6 slices French bread

1½ cups shredded Swiss, Gruyère or Parmesan cheese, or a combination

Cook onion in butter and olive oil for 20 minutes. Add sugar after first 10 minutes. Add beef broth. Cover and simmer 1 hour. Add salt, pepper and Dijon. Toast bread slices. Pour soup into oven-proof bowls. Top with bread and shredded cheese. Place under broiler until cheese melts. Serves 6.

Cyd Jokisch
Sons Craig Hakes, 1998; Pete Jokisch, 2002

Coyote Grill Tortilla Soup

1 onion, chopped

8-10 cloves garlic, minced

2 tablespoons bacon drippings or olive oil

3½ quarts chicken stock

8 ounces flour or corn tortillas

14.5-ounce can crushed tomatoes

1 small Anaheim pepper, diced

1 small red pepper, diced

6 tablespoons chili powder

1½ teaspoons thyme

4 tablespoons dried cumin

Shredded cheese, diced avocado and fried corn tortilla strips for garnish

Sauté onion and garlic in drippings or oil in a large soup pot over medium high heat, stirring frequently, 2-3 minutes. Add remaining ingredients except garnishes. Heat to boiling, reduce heat and simmer 1 hour or until mixture is reduced to 3 quarts. Tortillas will dissolve and create the desired texture. Strain soup through a food mill or use a food processor to purée. Garnish with cheese, avocado and tortilla strips. Serves 12.

Sarah Jurcyk
Son Jordan, 2006; Seth, 2008

The Homecoming theme was The Movies. Peter Perll's family allowed us to build our class float at their home. After hours of hammering, sawing, napkin stuffing and painting, we had erected the Frankenstein monster, 15 feet high. Back then, we still had Homecoming parades, which paraded from Rockhurst to the girls' schools. Well, our Franky was a bit wobbly, but with a few reinforcements, we headed up Ward Parkway to St. Teresa's. Picture the drive at STA, with all those mature and stately trees. Some with low and strong branches. You can guess the rest. Franky lost his head thanks to an oak. We picked him up and finished the drive to Sion, headless.

- Rick Bishop, 1979
Son Sean, 2008

Provençal White Bean and Mushroom Stew

1 cup chopped onion

2 tablespoons olive oil

1 pound fresh mushrooms, sliced

1 teaspoon garlic, minced

¾ teaspoon dried thyme

2 (14-ounce) cans vegetable broth

14.5-ounce can stewed tomatoes, with juice, cut into bite-sized pieces

¼ cup dry white wine

2 cans rinsed cannellini beans, divided

In soup pot, cook onion in oil on medium heat. Add mushrooms, garlic and thyme. Cook and stir 7 minutes or until onion is tender and mushrooms have softened. Add broth, tomatoes with liquid and wine. Bring to a boil. Cover and simmer 15 minutes. In a small bowl mash 1 cup beans until smooth, add to stew. Stir in remaining beans whole. Heat and serve. Serves 5.

Sarah Jurcyk
Sons Jordan, 2006; Seth, 2008

Wild Rice and Mushroom Soup

¼ cup wild rice

1½ cups water, divided

1 tablespoon butter

1 onion, chopped

1 clove garlic, minced

3 tablespoons flour

¼ teaspoon dry mustard

Dash Worcestershire sauce

2 (14-ounce) cans chicken broth

⅓ cup dry white wine

1 cup sliced fresh mushrooms

Rinse rice well. In a small pan, combine rice and ½ cup water, bring to a boil. Reduce heat, simmer 40 minutes. In large saucepan, melt butter and cook onion and garlic until tender. Blend in flour, mustard and Worcestershire. Add broth and 1 cup water. Cook over medium heat until thick and bubbly. Stir in rice, wine and mushrooms. Bring to a boil, reduce heat, cover and simmer 8 minutes.

Shelley Looby
Sons Colin, 2007; Kevin, 2007

1940s

National:

On December 7, 1941, a day labeled by President Franklin Delano Roosevelt as one "that would live in infamy," Japanese fighter pilots launched a surprise attack on Pearl Harbor. The following day, the U.S. entered World War II. War raged across the globe between the Axis powers and U.S.-led Allied forces until the Allies prevailed in 1945. The 1940s witnessed two major advances in aviation, as the sound barrier was broken in 1947 and the first non-stop flight around the globe was completed in 1949. The 40s marked the advent of the ballpoint pen, which revolutionized in-class essay writing for Rockhurst students, the Polaroid camera, the first computer and the microwave oven. American landmark Mt. Rushmore was completed in 1941, and George Orwell's 1984 was published in 1949, providing a staple of English class reading lists for future generations of Hawklets.

Local:

Two men with Kansas City ties made major headlines in the 1940s. "Dewey Defeated Truman" in the papers but not at the polls. Independence native Harry Truman was elected President of the United States in 1948 after filling that role for most of the previous term, when he succeeded the deceased Franklin Delano Roosevelt. In sports, former Kansas City Monarch Jackie Robinson broke baseball's color barrier in 1947, becoming the first African American to play Major League Baseball. While those two affected change nationally, Kansas City experienced changes as well. City Hall was wrestled from the control of the Pendergast political machine for the first time in nearly two decades, and WDAF-TV hit the airwaves in 1949.

Tomato and Jicama Salad

Salad:

1½ cups grape or cherry tomatoes, halved

1 cup jicama, peeled, cut into 1-inch cubes

2 tablespoons green onions, sliced

Dressing:

¼ cup canola oil

3 tablespoons wine vinegar

½ teaspoons salt

¼ teaspoons dried tarragon, crushed

⅛ teaspoon garlic powder

Dash of black pepper

Combine tomatoes, jicama and green onions. In a jar, combine dressing ingredients. Cover and shake. Pour over vegetables and toss. Cover and refrigerate for several hours, stirring occasionally. Serves 6.

Sue Dierks
Husband Bernard, 1955; Sons Chris, 1986; Michael, 1991

Good as a side dish with Mexican food.

President of Rockhurst from 1940-1946 was Rev. William H. McCabe, S.J. After the war years, Rev. Thomas M. Knapp, S.J. served from 1946-1951.

Mushroom Salad

Salad:

1 pound fresh mushrooms, brushed clean and sliced

½ pound Swiss cheese, grated

½ cup green onions, finely sliced

Dressing:

½ cup canola oil

⅓ cup seasoned rice vinegar

1 tablespoon Cavender's Greek Seasoning

Combine salad ingredients in a bowl. Mix dressing ingredients together. Toss with salad just before serving. Serves 6.

Lois Friedman

The early 1940s saw the continuation of the term of Principal Rev. Arthur J. Evans, S.J., 1935-1943. After him came Rev. August F. Guinta, S.J., 1943-1948 and Rev. Roman A. Bernert, S.J., 1948-1954.

Greek Potato Salad

2 pounds red potatoes, cut into 1-inch pieces (6 cups)

2 tablespoons red wine vinegar

¼ cup olive oil

1 tablespoon Dijon mustard

2 tablespoons chopped fresh oregano

½ teaspoon salt

¼ teaspoon black pepper

½ cup halved kalamata olives

1 cucumber, peeled, seeded, diced

½ cup chopped roasted red peppers

1 small green pepper, diced

½ very small red onion, diced

1 cup feta cheese

¼ cup chopped Italian parsley

Steam potatoes until just tender. Peeling is optional. Whisk together vinegar, oil, mustard, oregano, salt and pepper. Toss with potatoes while potatoes are still warm, cool. Stir in olives, cucumber, red and green peppers, onion, cheese and parsley.

Sally O'Neill
Sons Patrick, 2002; Peter, 2008

Summer Vegetable Salad Rolls

1 cup chopped green pepper

1 cup chopped cucumber

1 cup chopped tomatoes

4 tablespoons chopped red onion

4 tablespoons chopped fresh parsley

4 tablespoons chopped dill pickle

⅔ cup garlic-sour cream prepared dip

½ cup mayonnaise

½ teaspoon salt

1 teaspoon dried dill weed

8 ounces (or less) cream cheese, softened, optional

1 dozen hard rolls

Chop first 6 ingredients, drain excess juices. Combine with dip, mayonnaise, salt and dill weed, blend well. Add cream cheese to desired consistency, up to 8 ounces, and blend well. Slice and scoop out centers of hard rolls. Fill rolls with vegetable mixture and wrap individually. Chill well. Serves 12.

Sally Kampfe
Grandson Scott Miller, 2007

Warm Cabbage Salad

¼ cup canola oil

4 garlic cloves, minced

1 medium red cabbage

¼ cup red wine vinegar

Salt and pepper to taste

¾ cup toasted pecans

6 thick slices bacon, well cooked, chopped

8-ounce package crumbled goat cheese, room temperature

Heat oil and garlic in a sauté pan. Core cabbage, discarding several outer thick layers. Cut cabbage into ¼-inch slices. Add sliced cabbage to pan and sauté over medium heat until it begins to soften, tossing frequently. Add vinegar and stir to deglaze pan. Season with salt and pepper. Remove from heat and divide between individual plates. Sprinkle cabbage with pecans, bacon and goat cheese. Serve with good crusty bread. Serves 8.

Lois Friedman

Table-Side Caesar Salad For Two

1 tablespoon garlic

½ tablespoon anchovy

20 turns cracked pepper

1 tablespoon Dijon mustard

2 shots Tabasco

2 eggs

1 tablespoon Worcestershire

1 tablespoon balsamic vinegar

¼ cup olive oil

½ of a lemon, fresh squeezed

Romaine lettuce

2 spoonfuls Parmesan

2 spoonfuls croutons

Work first 4 ingredients into bottom of serving bowl with large spoon. Break one egg, coddle in soup cup of hot water and transfer yolk to serving bowl. Repeat with remaining egg. Add Worcestershire, balsamic vinegar, oil and lemon juice and whip with a large spoon. Toss in romaine, Parmesan and croutons, mix well. Serves 2.

Ed Holland, 1971
EBT Restaurant
Son Kevin, 1997

Ryan played soccer from when he was 4 or 5 until senior year in high school. That was the year Coach Lawson arrived, and Ryan decided he wanted to quit soccer, even though Coach Lawson had told the team he was planning on taking the team to state. (And did.) We told Ryan he needed to find another activity so he chose to be in the school play, "A Few Good Men." He was wonderful in the role of the 2nd attorney (not the Tom Cruise role.) And guess what? He is now an attorney! But first he returned to RHS as part of the Alumni Service Corps and became good friends with his old Coach, and even coached soccer.

- Laura Bailey
Son Ryan, 1995

Basil Tomato Salad with Hearts of Palm

Dressing:

2 tablespoons plus 1 cup extra virgin olive oil

½ cup red wine vinegar

2 tablespoons Dijon or Creole mustard

1 teaspoon salt

1 teaspoon freshly ground pepper

2 cloves garlic, minced

Salad:

5 heads red leaf lettuce, rinsed, torn

8 large tomatoes, cut into wedges

4 (14-ounce) cans hearts of palm, drained, cut into rounds

18 fresh basil leaves, chopped

8 ounces Roquefort cheese, crumbled

Dressing: Combine 2 tablespoons olive oil, vinegar, mustard, salt, pepper and garlic in a small bowl. Whisk in remaining 1 cup olive oil in a thin stream. Set aside.

Salad: Combine lettuce, tomatoes, hearts of palm and basil in a large salad bowl. Pour dressing over salad and toss. Sprinkle with Roquefort crumbles and serve. Serves 10-12.

Tina Montgomery
Son Connor, 2009

Best Dressing

½ cup tarragon vinegar

1 cup canola oil

½ cup sugar

1 teaspoon salt

1 egg white

2 tablespoons chopped green onions

Combine all ingredients in blender or food processor until smooth. Store in refrigerator up to 3 days. Toss with favorite salad greens.

Lois Veach

Sonoran Chop Salad

Dressing:

¾ cup canola oil

¼ cup balsamic vinegar

2 cloves of garlic, minced

1 teaspoon salt

4 teaspoons sugar

Fresh ground pepper to taste

Salad:

1-2 heads romaine, rinsed, chopped

1 large tomato, chopped

1 medium red onion, finely chopped

1-2 ripe avocados, peeled, chopped

4 ounces blue cheese, crumbled

8-10 slices bacon, fried, chopped

Combine dressing ingredients in a container and shake well. Place romaine on bottom of a large shallow serving bowl. Place chopped vegetables and bacon in individual rows atop romaine to make a colorful presentation. Add dressing just before serving and toss. Present to guests before tossing, it makes a great presentation. Serves 8 -10.

Tina Montgomery
Son Connor, 2009

Favorite Tossed Salad

Dressing:

½ cup mayonnaise

¼ cup sugar

¼ cup half & half

2 tablespoons poppy seeds

2 tablespoons white wine vinegar

Salad:

2 heads romaine, rinsed, torn

1 pint fresh strawberries, cleaned, hulled, sliced

2 ripe avocados, peeled, sliced

½ red onion, thinly sliced

Salt and pepper to taste

Whisk dressing ingredients together. Toss dressing with salad. Serves 10.

Lois Veach

Salad with Spicy Pecans

Spicy Pecans:

2 cups pecan halves

2 tablespoons butter

2 tablespoons brown sugar

1½ tablespoons sugar

½ teaspoon cayenne pepper

½ teaspoon ground black pepper

1 teaspoon salt

Salad:

2 heads romaine, rinsed, torn

2 (4-ounce) packages crumbled blue cheese

3-4 crisp Red Delicious apples, cored, chopped into large pieces

Dressing:

⅓ cup apple cider vinegar

3 garlic cloves

2 green onions, chopped

1 teaspoon ground pepper

1 tablespoon smooth Dijon mustard

1 tablespoon coarse Dijon mustard

⅔ cup pure maple syrup

1 cup canola oil

Spicy Pecans: Over medium to low heat, melt butter with pecans in a sauté pan. Add remaining Spicy Pecan ingredients and cook over medium heat until caramelized, stirring constantly. Watch carefully, they will burn easily. Pour onto wax paper and cool.

Combine all dressing ingredients in a blender and whirl at high speed until mixed. Chill in refrigerator. Combine salad ingredients and toss with dressing and spicy pecans. Serves 8 -10.

Annie Osborn
Son Scott Miller, 2007

Strawberry Salad with Chardonnay Dressing

Vinaigrette:

1 cup strawberries, hulled

½ cup Chardonnay wine

⅓ cup white wine vinegar

3 tablespoons sugar

1 tablespoon honey

1 teaspoon Dijon mustard

¼ teaspoon salt

⅛ teaspoon ground black pepper

1 cup vegetable oil

¼ cup chopped fresh mint leaves, optional

Salad:

Assorted greens

Fresh strawberries

Goat cheese, crumbled

Place all dressing ingredients except oil and mint in a blender and whirl until puréed. With blender running, add oil in slow, steady stream, pouring it through the hole in the blender cover, until vinaigrette thickens. Stir in mint. If not using right away, cover and refrigerate up to 3 days. Spoon vinaigrette over greens, with additional fresh strawberries and goat cheese.

Catherine Moussa
Son Alex VanMaren, 2007

Mountain Top Salad

Salad:

1 cup chopped walnuts

12-ounce container dry cottage cheese

5-ounce package crumbled blue cheese

1 bunch fresh spinach, cleaned, trimmed of stems

Dressing:

1 cup sour cream

¼ cup sugar

3 tablespoons apple cider vinegar

1½ teaspoons dry mustard

4 teaspoons or more prepared horseradish to taste

½ teaspoon salt

Toss walnuts, cottage cheese, and crumbled blue cheese into spinach. Blend all dressing ingredients. Pour dressing over salad. Serves 8 -10.

Annie Osborn
Son Scott Miller, 2007

Spinach Salad

Salad:

8 cups spinach

1 cup dried cranberries or dried cherries

4-ounce package crumbled feta cheese

1 medium red onion, thinly sliced

4-6 slices bacon, cooked, crumbled

½ cup slivered almonds, toasted

Dressing:

1 cup canola oil

¾ cup sugar

½ cup red wine vinegar

3-4 cloves garlic, minced

½ teaspoon salt

½ teaspoon paprika

¼ teaspoon ground pepper

¼ teaspoon cayenne pepper

Wash and dry spinach. Combine all salad ingredients in a large bowl. Mix all dressing ingredients in a container with tight-fitting lid. Cover and shake well to blend. Toss with salad.

Sally O'Neill
Sons, Patrick, 2002; Peter, 2008

I was sent home on the first day of school for 3 of the 4 years at RHS to get a haircut.
I played in a band, had long hair and round wire rimmed glasses.
I spent 4 years quietly rocking the boat, trying to be myself.
Years later, I realized what had happened to me.
The Jesuits did not explain the Ignatian paradigm.
They just did it to you, day in and day out.
You were made a "Man for Others" founded in the qualities of "Grad at Grad."
Students of my generation became independent thinkers, making decisions based on reflection tempered with what was right and just.

- John McEniry, 1968; RHS Faculty member

Mandarin Spinach Salad

Dressing:

¼ cup white vinegar

¼ cup canola oil

¼ cup sugar

1 tablespoon honey

Salad:

1 or 2 bunches fresh spinach, cleaned, trimmed of stems

11-ounce can mandarin oranges, chilled, drained

⅓ cup sliced almonds, toasted

In a jar, combine dressing ingredients. Shake well to mix, then chill. Just before serving, toss spinach, mandarin oranges and almonds together. Whisk dressing well before pouring over salad. Serves 8 -10.

Lisa Ledom
Sons Mark, 2007; Matthew, 2009

Add grilled chicken for a main dish variation. I brought this salad to several Class of 2007 Moms' Lunch Bunch gatherings and it was always devoured.

Crab Salad

2 (6.5-ounce) cans good quality jumbo lump crab-meat, or fresh cooked crab

1 tablespoon butter

12 ounces macaroni, cooked al dente, drained, cooled

3 hard-boiled eggs, chopped

⅓ cup chopped, fresh parsley

½ medium onion, chopped

3 medium potatoes, peeled, boiled, cooled, diced

2 celery stalks, chopped

1 teaspoon salt

½ teaspoon freshly ground pepper

Mayonnaise to taste

Drain crab. Melt butter in a small skillet over medium low heat and sauté crab in butter for several minutes, breaking up large chunks. Remove from heat and cool. Combine cooled crab meat with macaroni, eggs, parsley, onion, potatoes, celery, salt and pepper in a large bowl. Blend in enough mayonnaise to bind and add additional as desired. Correct for salt and pepper. Chill. Serves 8-10.

Karen Miyawaki
Son Brandon Busenbark, 2009

Between my junior and senior years I was involved in a severe auto accident that prevented me from playing football my senior year. My whole life revolved around football and I was selected as team captain senior year. The first home game I went out to midfield on my crutches for the coin toss. Knowing I would never play football again, I just lost it, crying uncontrollably. I was so embarrassed and hated the thought of going back to the bench because I could not stop crying. But my teammates consoled me and made me feel like a real part of the team. I guess that is what makes Rockhurst what it really is: all the guys are there for one another no matter what the circumstances. Even though I would not play another down for Rockhurst, my teammates made me feel appreciated and that made a huge impact on me. Rockhurst is the greatest school in Kansas City.

- Ed Holland, 1971
Son Kevin, 1997

Chinese Chicken Salad

3-4 chicken breast halves

½ cup cooking sherry

¼ cup olive oil

1 tablespoon lime juice

½ cup soy sauce

2 cloves garlic, minced

Salad:

1 head romaine

1 head iceberg lettuce

1 cup bean sprouts

1 red onion, sliced

1 can water chestnuts, drained, sliced

1 cup chow mein noodles

Dressing:

3½ tablespoons soy sauce

2 tablespoons vegetable oil

2 tablespoons rice vinegar

¾ tablespoon sugar

½ teaspoon pepper

½ teaspoon garlic powder

½ teaspoon sesame oil

Place chicken in a large ziplock bag. Combine sherry, olive oil, lime juice, soy sauce and garlic, mix well. Pour over chicken. Marinate chicken for 4-6 hours, then grill and thinly slice. Mix dressing ingredients, toss with salad, top with chicken and serve. Chicken can be warm or chilled.

Katie Hart

Thai Peanut Chicken Salad

½ bottle Thai peanut sauce

1 tablespoon mayonnaise

3 tablespoons lime juice

2 cooked chicken breast halves, diced

½ cup grated carrot

¼ cup sliced celery rib

1 medium red pepper, diced

¼ teaspoon salt

3 cups torn lettuce

Lime wedges

Stir peanut sauce, mayonnaise and lime juice together, set aside. Combine chicken, carrot, celery, red pepper and salt. Toss with half the peanut sauce dressing. Add lettuce, toss. Garnish plates with lime wedges, serve with remaining dressing.

Sarah Jurcyk
Sons Jordan, 2006; Seth, 2008

Chicken and Green Bean Salad

Salad:

2 tablespoons soy sauce

2 tablespoons olive oil

3-4 skinless, boneless chicken breast halves (about 1½ pounds)

Freshly ground black pepper

1 pound fresh green beans, trimmed, cut in half

1 cup (4 ounces) coarsely chopped, toasted walnuts

Curly greens or leaf lettuce

2 ounces goat cheese, crumbled

Fresh thyme

Dressing:

1 tablespoon balsamic vinegar or red wine vinegar

1 tablespoon Dijon mustard

⅓ cup olive oil

1 tablespoon minced green onions or shallots

2 teaspoons minced fresh thyme leaves

Mix soy sauce and oil in baking dish. Add chicken and toss well, top with black pepper. Bake at 375 degrees for 15-20 minutes or until chicken is cooked. Discard any cooking liquids. Chill. Cook beans in salted water until tender-crisp. Drain, rinse with cold water, drain again. Wrap in paper towels, put in plastic bag, chill.

Combine vinegar and mustard for dressing. Add oil very slowly while whisking rapidly. Stir in green onions and thyme. Set aside at room temperature if serving same day; if not, chill and let sit at room temperature 1-2 hours before serving.

To serve, combine chicken with dressing; gently fold in green beans and walnuts. Put curly greens or leaf lettuce on individual plates or platter, top with salad. Garnish with cheese and thyme. Serves 6.

Sally Kampfe
Grandson Scott Miller, 2007

If fresh green beans are not available, substitute 1 pound fresh pea pods, blanched and well drained or 2 (6-ounce) packages frozen snow pea pods, thawed, drained.

When asked to name an outstanding teacher, Mr. Chris Elmore is frequently mentioned. Mr. Elmore began his RHS career in 1997. He sets high standards for his honors and AP history and government classes and challenges students to elevate their work to meet those standards. He also is involved with various student activities, including Model UN competitions, and oversees the Total Ignatian Experience (T.I.E.) program.

The Stage Crew in 1970-71 included Bill Gleeson and Steve Farnen (carpenters), John Marencik, Joe Vogrin (painting), Mike Weaver (lighting), John DeGood (sound.) Fr. Wallace, S.J. was moderator.

Chicken and Wild Rice Salad

Salad:

2 whole chicken breasts

2 cups uncooked wild rice

5 cups chicken broth

⅓ cup fresh lemon juice

½ cup diced red pepper

2 cups sugar snap peas cut into pieces

1 avocado, chopped

1 cup pecan halves or pieces

Dressing:

2 cloves garlic, minced

1 teaspoon Dijon mustard

½ teaspoon salt

½ teaspoon sugar

¼ teaspoon pepper

¼ cup rice vinegar

⅓ cup olive oil

The night before, grill chicken and cut into 1-inch cubes. Also cook the rice according to directions, using chicken broth instead of water. While still warm, toss chicken and rice with lemon juice, refrigerate overnight.

Combine dressing ingredients in food processor. In large bowl mix dressing with all salad ingredients except avocado and pecans. Mix well. Add avocado and pecans immediately before serving.

Katie Hart

*Patrick Mason was a member of the first graduating class from RHS.
Pat wanted to play football, so he convinced teacher Charlie Alan to be the first football coach. In 1919, 2 years before he graduated Rockhurst College, Pat was hired as Rockhurst High School's football and basketball coach. For the next 2 years, he would practice with the college team, then grab his clipboard and whistle and lead the Hawklets in their workout. He was also an outstanding baseball player and played as catcher on several minor league and semi-pro teams. He never made it to the majors, but was a fierce competitor and set the standard and tone for Rockhurst sports. He left a legacy on which a successful high school athletic program was built. In 1991, Pat was inducted into the first class of the Rockhurst High School Athletic Hall of Fame.*

Minnesota Wild Rice Salad

5 cups chicken broth

2 cups wild rice

3 (6-ounce) jars marinated artichoke hearts, drained, chopped, reserve liquid

5 green onions, chopped

4-ounce jar stuffed green olives, sliced, drained

1 large green pepper, seeded, chopped

3 celery stalks, diced

½ cup chopped fresh parsley

2 cups mayonnaise

1 tablespoon curry powder

Salt and pepper to taste

Bring chicken broth and wild rice to a boil. Reduce heat to low, cover and simmer about 2 hours or until broth is absorbed. Cool to room temperature. Add artichokes, onions, olives, green pepper, celery and parsley. In a separate bowl, thin mayonnaise with half the artichoke marinade, add curry. Add to rice, stir. Season to taste. Chill for several hours or overnight. Serves 8-10.

Sarah Jurcyk
Son Jordan, 2006; Seth, 2008

Orzo Salad with Corn

Dressing:

2 tablespoons lemon juice

1½ tablespoons olive oil

1½ tablespoons red wine vinegar

½ teaspoon salt

¼ teaspoon pepper

3 garlic cloves, crushed

Salad:

1 cup uncooked orzo

2 cups fresh yellow corn kernels (about 4 ears)

2 cups chopped tomato

½ cup vertically sliced red onion

¼ cup finely chopped basil

Combine dressing ingredients in a jar, cover tightly and shake vigorously. Cook pasta according to package directions, omitting salt and fat. Drain, place in large bowl and pour half the dressing mixture over. Toss to coat, cool to room temperature. Add corn, tomato, onion, basil and remaining dressing to pasta mixture, toss to coat. Let stand 30 minutes. Serves 4.

Jennifer Dorman
Sons Taylor, 2008; Keaton, 2010

Pasta Salad with Spinach and Feta Cheese

Dressing:

¾ cup olive oil

¾ cup champagne vinegar

3 cloves garlic, minced

2 teaspoons Dijon mustard

½ cup Parmesan cheese, freshly grated

1 tablespoon fresh oregano, minced

Salt and freshly ground pepper to taste

Salad:

1 pound pasta shells or bows

1½ - 2 pounds fresh spinach, trimmed of stems, torn

3 ripe tomatoes, chopped

1 bunch green onions, finely chopped

1 cup crumbled feta cheese

2 cucumbers, peeled, thinly sliced

1 cup pine nuts, toasted

Combine dressing ingredients and blend well. Cook pasta in boiling water until just tender, al dente, drain. Toss cooked pasta with half the dressing, set aside. In large bowl, combine remaining salad ingredients with remaining dressing. Gently toss in cooled pasta, cover and refrigerate. Toss again before serving. Serves 10-12.

Harriet Kokjer
Nephew, Scott Miller 2007

Bow Tie Pasta Salad with Roasted Veggies

Dressing:

⅓ cup olive oil

¼ cup balsamic vinegar

Juice of ½ lemon

3 tablespoons Dijon mustard

1 teaspoon dried sweet basil

2 cloves garlic, minced

½ teaspoon salt

Salad:

16-ounce package bow-tie pasta

Olive oil cooking spray

1 large onion, coarsely chopped

1 sweet red or yellow pepper, seeded, chopped

8 ounces fresh mushrooms, brushed clean, halved

1 cup sliced carrots

1 medium zucchini, sliced

2 cups grape or cherry tomatoes

Whisk dressing ingredients together and store in an airtight container in refrigerator. While dressing flavors blend, prepare pasta according to package directions.

Preheat oven to 425 degrees. Spray a large baking sheet with olive oil cooking spray. Spread vegetables except tomatoes evenly on the baking sheet. Spray vegetables with olive oil cooking spray. Roast in oven about 15 minutes, turning once midway through cooking time. Toss veggies with pasta and tomatoes. Pour dressing evenly over top and toss gently. Serve at room temperature or cold. Serves 8-10.

Shea Walsworth

For Christmas 1960, RHS students Ken Knickerbocker, John Perry, Bill Gist, Frank Danzo and Dave Ransom designed, built, painted and installed a manger and nativity figures at school. Students John Abbick and Francis Riley handled the flood lighting for the scene. They were under the direction of Thomas Valiquette, physics and math instructor.

Yell leaders in 1998-99 included Joe Van Dyke, Kesler Pollard, Bo Keatley, Brad Thomas, Steven Phelps, Luke Hannan, Zach Ramirez, Willy Fagan, Matt Kopp, Joel Steed, Brian Degnan, JJ Cook, Andy O'Dower, Anthony D'Agnostino, Kevin Melgaard, Ryan Burns and Ryan Callahan.

Italian Pasta Salad

1 pound multicolored fusilli pasta (Colavita)

1 or 2 cans small black pitted olives

1 or 2 cans quartered artichoke hearts

1 pound Provolone cheese, cut into small strips

½ pound pepperoni slices, cut in half

1 onion, sliced, preferably red onion

Coarsely ground black pepper to taste

2-3 (16-ounce) bottles Wishbone Italian or Robusto Italian dressing

8-10 Roma tomatoes, sliced.

Cook pasta no more than 8-9 minutes, drain. Place pasta in large bowl, add olives, artichokes, cheese, pepperoni, onion and pepper. Add one bottle dressing, mix gently to coat. Add more dressing if needed, as pasta will absorb dressing. Cut tomato slices in half, if desired. Add to pasta. Cover and refrigerate. Add more dressing before serving if needed.

Josephine Nigro
Sons Michael, 2001; John-Paul, 2003

Summer Macaroni Salad

1 box Kraft macaroni and cheese

Miracle Whip Lite

Large can tuna packed in water, drained, or diced ham

½ cup chopped celery

½ cup chopped carrots

½ cup chopped onion

Red salad dressing (Catalina, French or Russian)

Paprika

Prepare macaroni and cheese as directed on box. Stir in Miracle Whip to desired consistency. Stir in tuna and vegetables, then red dressing to taste. Mix well. Sprinkle top liberally with paprika. Refrigerate. Better the next day. Serve with Triscuits or other crackers.

John McEniry, 1968
RHS Faculty member

A great quick and easy summer dish that is also inexpensive.

Orange, Spiced Walnut and Dried Cranberry Salad

Spiced walnuts:

6 tablespoons honey

1½ tablespoons water

¾ teaspoon ground allspice

½ teaspoon salt

¼ teaspoon (generous) ground ginger

1 cup walnut halves or pieces

2 teaspoons sugar

Salad:

¾ cup water

¾ cup cranberry juice or juice cocktail

½ cup dried cranberries

8 oranges, peel and white pith removed, sliced into ½-inch thick rounds, chilled

Fresh mint springs, optional

Preheat oven to 325 degrees. Line baking sheet with parchment paper. Mix first 5 ingredients in large bowl to blend. Add nuts, toss to coat well. Strain nuts, reserving liquid. Transfer nuts to baking sheet, sprinkle with sugar. Bake until golden brown, about 17 minutes. Cool completely. Store nuts in airtight container at room temperature.

Whisk ¾ cup water, cranberry juice and reserved liquid from nuts in medium saucepan to blend. Stir in dried cranberries, bring to boil. Reduce heat to medium-low and simmer until cranberries soften and liquid is reduced to thin syrup, about 20 minutes. (Can be made 3 days ahead. Cover and chill cranberry mixture.)

Arrange orange slices on platter. Spoon cranberry mixture over. Sprinkle with nuts. Garnish with mint. Serves 8.

Katherine Schorgl
Husband Jim, 1980; Son Christopher, 2007

My mother's green Cutlass convertible was in the Rockhurst Homecoming parade every year from 1971 through 1979. Ted Wiedeman borrowed it the first year, and between the Wiedeman boys and my brothers Bob, John and Pat McGannon, it was in use every year. It's probably a good thing that cars can't talk!

- Molly Sauder
Sons Bobby, 2004;
Ben, 2007

Rockhurst celebrates its 25 anniversary on the Greenlease State Line campus in 1987-1988 with a variety of ceremonies.

Fresh Fruit with Lemon-Mint Sauce

3 large oranges, peeled, sectioned

2 large red grapefruit, peeled, sectioned

2 cups seedless red grapes, halved

2 tablespoons chopped fresh mint

16-ounce container lowfat vanilla yogurt

2 tablespoons fresh lemon juice

1 teaspoon lemon zest

1 teaspoon honey

Fresh mint sprigs for garnish

Place oranges, grapefruit, grapes and mint in bowl, toss gently. Cover and chill. Just before serving, mix yogurt, lemon juice, zest and honey. Pour over fruit or serve on side. Garnish.

Mary Long
Sons Chris, 1998; Brad, 2003

Popular Assistant Admissions Director Amanda Pierce wed RHS theology instructor Corey Quinn in the summer of 2000.
The crowds of young men in her office each day did not diminish, however.

"Father Tom" (Cummings) knew every student by name. When he was in the school halls with a guest or potential donor, he always made the students stop and introduce themselves to the guest.

- Judie Scanlon, former secretary to Fr. Cummings Sons Steve, 1988; Kerry, 1994

Strawberry-Banana Gelatin Salad

6-ounce package strawberry gelatin

2 (10-ounce) packages frozen sweetened strawberries, partially thawed

20-ounce can crushed pineapple, undrained

1 cup mashed firm bananas, about 3 medium

½-¾ cup chopped walnuts

2 cups (16 ounces) sour cream

2 teaspoons sugar

½ teaspoon vanilla

Dissolve gelatin in 1 cup boiling water. Stir in strawberries, pineapple with juice, bananas and nuts. Pour half of mixture into 9x13-inch dish, refrigerate one hour. Set aside remaining gelatin. Combine sour cream, sugar and vanilla, mix well. Spread over chilled gelatin. Carefully spoon remaining gelatin over top. Chill overnight. Serves 12-15.

Maryhelen VanDyke
Husband Joe, 1940
Sons Mike, 1966; Jim, 1972; son-in-law Bryan Wilkerson, 1978
Grandsons Joe, 1999; Cory, 2003; Ryan, 2003; Jimmy, 2005

This dish was enjoyed at a Rockette (alumni mom) gathering in 2004.

Vegetables AND Grains

1950s

National:

The 1950s saw humans go higher and faster than they ever had before, as Edmund Hillary and Tenzing Norgay reached the summit of Mt. Everest in 1953 and Roger Bannister broke the four-minute mile in 1955. While U.S. troops went to war in Korea, Americans at home enjoyed a post-World War II boom, as the economy finally recovered to pre-Depression era levels. The 50s saw the advent of hula hoops, color TVs and Mickey D's, which soon became the world's largest fast-food joint and a hot lunch favorite for generations of Hawklets. McDonald's was first franchised in Des Plaines, Illinois in 1955, just a year before a young Elvis Presley got his big break on the Ed Sullivan Show.

Local:

Kansas City celebrated its centennial anniversary in 1950, marking the start of a decade during which the city experienced rapid and widespread expansion. The post-war boom led to the growth of suburban communities on the city's outskirts in all directions, many of which the Rockhurst student body draws from today. The growing city welcomed Major League Baseball in 1955, when Charlie Finley's Philadelphia Athletics came to town. And, as the 1950s came to a close, so, too, did Kansas City's street car era, as the city's electric trolley system was phased out in favor of more cars and interstate highways.

Red Cabbage

6-8 Granny Smith apples, peeled, cored, diced

1 large onion, chopped

¼ cup vegetable oil

¾ cup honey

1 cup raspberry vinegar

1 cup red wine

1 cup water

½ cup sugar

10-ounce jar or larger cranberry or cranberry-raspberry jam

2-3 heads red cabbage, shredded

2 cinnamon sticks

2-3 tablespoons whole cloves

3 tablespoons cornstarch, optional

Heat apples and onions in oil over medium heat. Add honey, vinegar, wine, water, sugar and jam. Add cabbage, stir. Bundle cinnamon sticks and cloves in cheesecloth, add to cabbage. Cover and simmer, stirring often, until most of liquid is evaporated. Cabbage is done when limp and apples have dissolved, about 1-2 hours. Remove cinnamon bundle.

If desired, mix cornstarch with water to make a paste and stir to thicken remaining liquid.

Kris Balderston
Son Blaine, 2007

This tangy sweet vegetable is heavenly and a surprise! Growing up in a German household, red cabbage was a staple. My grandmother passed this side dish down to our family. Just take the chance and you'll be hooked. We have this every Thanksgiving and every guest must try one tablespoon before being excused from the table. Generally, they are pleasantly surprised. Try and enjoy!

So-Good Mashed Potatoes

1 pound red potatoes

1 pound Yukon Gold (yellow) potatoes

1 fresh jalapeno pepper, sliced

12 ounces baby carrots

4 cloves garlic

10-ounce package frozen white corn, thawed

¼ cup butter

½ cup shredded cheddar cheese

Salt and pepper to taste

Place red potatoes, yellow potatoes, jalapeno pepper, carrots and garlic cloves in a large pot. Cover with water, bring to a boil over high heat. Cook 15-20 minutes or until potatoes are tender. Drain water from pot. Stir in corn and butter. Mash mixture with a potato masher until butter is melted and potatoes have reached desired consistency. Mix in cheese, salt and pepper. Serve hot. Serves 10.

Maraline Hayob
Son David, 2000

Layered Potatoes

2½ cups whipping cream

1 tablespoon butter

2 cloves garlic

5 large all purpose potatoes

1 onion, finely chopped

¼ cup freshly grated Parmesan cheese

Salt and pepper to taste

Simmer cream, butter and garlic in small saucepan for 15 minutes or until cream has reduced by half. Slice potatoes very thin and dry on paper towels. Butter a small casserole and arrange potatoes in even layers. On each layer sprinkle a little chopped onion, Parmesan, salt and pepper. Cover potatoes with reduced cream, adding additional cream if necessary to cover potatoes completely. Put lid on casserole and bake in preheated 350-degree oven for 1½ hours. Pour off any excess cream and save to enrich a soup or sauce.

Suzanne Orscheln
Sons Joe, 2000; Dustin, 2002; Scott, 2005

Sweet and Smoky Baked Beans

4 strips thick bacon, diced

Medium onion, chopped

½ green pepper, chopped

2 cloves garlic, minced

2 (15-ounce) cans Great Northern, large butter beans, black beans or combination, rinsed, drained

⅓ cup molasses

¼ cup barbecue sauce

¼ cup catsup

3 tablespoons brown sugar or to taste

1 tablespoon Worcestershire

1 tablespoon prepared mustard

1 tablespoon dry mustard

1 tablespoon cider vinegar

¼ tablespoon liquid smoke

Sliced chorizo or smoked sausage, optional

Salt and pepper

In heavy pot, cook bacon over medium heat about 5 minutes. Discard all but 2 tablespoons fat. Add onion, pepper and garlic and cook until vegetables are soft. Stir in beans and remaining ingredients except salt and pepper. Simmer uncovered until rich and thickly flavored, 10-15 minutes, stirring often. Or put in a deep baking dish and bake at 350 degrees for about 30 minutes. Add salt and pepper. Serves 4-6.

Pat Shealy
Sons John, 2007; Westly, 2010

Carrot Soufflé

16-ounce can carrots, drained, or 2 cups cooked carrots

1 cup sugar

3 eggs

3 tablespoons flour

1 teaspoon vanilla

1 teaspoon baking powder

½ cup butter, melted

Place carrots in blender or food processor and chop. Mix with remaining ingredients and place in a greased soufflé dish. Bake at 350 degrees for 1 hour.

Laura Murphy
Husband Matt, 1975; Sons Steven, 2002; Pat, 2005

Slow-Roasted Tomatoes

1 medium onion, chopped

3 garlic cloves, smashed

¾ cup extra-virgin olive oil, divided

9 fresh basil leaves

⅛ teaspoon dried hot red pepper flakes or to taste

12 plum tomatoes, halved lengthwise

1 teaspoon sugar

½ teaspoon kosher salt

Preheat oven to 250 degrees. Cook onion and garlic in 2 tablespoons oil in a 12-inch heavy skillet over moderate heat, stirring occasionally, until softened, 5-7 minutes. Remove from heat, stir in basil and red pepper flakes. In a bowl, toss tomatoes with sugar and salt. Arrange tomatoes, cut sides down, in roasting or 9x13-inch baking pan. Spoon onion mixture over tomatoes and add enough remaining olive oil to reach halfway up tomatoes. Braise in middle of oven, stirring gently halfway through cooking, until tomatoes are very tender but not falling apart, 2½-3 hours. Cool tomatoes, slip off skins, then use in recipes or freeze for future use.

Patty Crutchfield
Son Andy, 2003

Tomato oil keeps chilled in an airtight container up to 1 month. You can toss it with pasta, use it with chicken and pork or use it in dressings.

I was a tall, skinny guy, definitely not a jock. After attending my 40th reunion at Rockhurst, I began training and in 2005, my son and I completed a bicycle trip in Oregon, traveling 425 miles through the mountains over parts of the Lewis and Clark trail. I look back at my years at Rockhurst with nostalgia. Most of my teachers and some of my classmates are now gone. I wish the best to all who remain.

- George J. Frye, 1949

Mock Fried Cauliflower

1 cup milk

1 egg

1 or 2 heads cauliflower, cut up, steamed, rinsed to cool

½ cup breadcrumbs

½ cup Parmesan cheese

¼-½ cup butter

Mix milk and egg in small bowl. Pour over cauliflower, coating pieces well. Combine breadcrumbs and Parmesan, dredge cauliflower in mixture. Place pieces in greased baking dish. Drizzle with butter. Bake for 20 minutes at 325 degrees. Flavors blend even more if made the day ahead and reheated.

Sharon Davison
Sons Allen, 1999; Drew, 2003

Grilled Antipasto Vegetables

Vegetables:

4 red bell peppers, halved, seeded

4 red onions, each peeled and cut into 6 wedges

Cooking spray

2 teaspoons olive oil

6 (4-inch) portabella mushroom caps

2 pounds asparagus

⅓ cup Chile-Garlic vinaigrette

Chile-Garlic Vinaigrette:

1 tablespoon chopped serrano chile

¾ garlic cloves, crushed

3 tablespoons red wine vinegar

3 tablespoons water

2 tablespoons fresh lemon juice

1½ tablespoons extra-virgin olive oil

1½ tablespoons anchovy paste

Prepare grill. Coat bell peppers and onions with cooking spray. Place bell peppers and onions on grill rack, grill 15 minutes or until peppers are blackened, turning occasionally. Close peppers in a zip-top plastic bag, let stand 15 minutes.

Chop onions into 1-inch pieces, place in a large bowl. Peel and slice peppers into ½-inch strips, add to onions. Combine oil, mushrooms and asparagus, toss well to coat.

Place mushrooms and asparagus on grill rack. Grill 3 minutes on each side or until tender. Chop mushrooms into 1-inch pieces, add to onion mixture. Slice asparagus diagonally into 1½-inch pieces. Add to onion mixture. Drizzle ⅓ cup Chile-Garlic Vinaigrette over mixture to coat. Makes 11 cups. Store cooked vegetables in refrigerator for up to 3 days.

Chile Garlic Vinaigrette: Use this light vinaigrette to dress grilled vegetables or with pasta salads. Combine first 3 ingredients in food processor until paste-like mixture. Transfer to small bowl. Add garlic-paste mixture, vinegar and remaining ingredients, whisk. Makes ¾ cup. Store in refrigerator for up to 1 week.

Betsy Vossman
Son Eric, 2002

After Principal Tom Murphy passed away, leaving his wife and a very young daughter, the Mother's Club put together a memory book for his daughter. Everyone in the RHS community was encouraged to contribute a thought or memory for the book so that his daughter would be able to look through it as she grew older. The huge compilation was a loving tribute from those blessed to have known Mr. Murphy.

Creamy Mushroom Bake

1 pound mushrooms, stems removed

¼ cup butter, or to taste

2 tablespoons flour

½ cup half & half

½ cup beef or chicken stock

Dash of freshly ground pepper

¾ cup grated sharp cheddar cheese

½ cup grated Monterey Jack cheese

¼ cup cooking sherry

½ cup fresh fine or Italian breadcrumbs

½ cup freshly grated Parmesan cheese

Preheat oven to 350 degrees. Butter a shallow baking dish. Arrange mushrooms in dish, stem side down. Melt butter in a saucepan over low heat. Increase heat to medium-high, blend in flour and cook, stirring occasionally, for 3 minutes. Pour in half & half and bring to a boil. Mix in stock and pepper and return to a boil. Reduce heat to low.

Add cheddar and Monterey Jack cheeses, stir until blended. Add sherry, simmer until smooth. If thicker sauce is desired, add more cheddar cheese. Pour sauce over mushrooms, sprinkle with breadcrumbs.

Bake uncovered for 30 minutes. Sprinkle with Parmesan cheese and continue baking until cheese melts, about 5 minutes. Serves 4-6.

Suzanne Orscheln
Sons Joe, 2000; Dustin, 2002; Scott, 2005

Coaching from 1926-1936, Eddie Halpin put his indelible stamp on Rockhurst's sports legacy. He was the kind of coach who worked a player hard to make him do his best. His players gave their all because they didn't want to let Coach Halpin down. His teams were known for their tenacious spirit, tempered by the values of sportsmanship. Eddie was inducted as a charter member of the Rockhurst High School Athletic Hall of Fame.

Mushroom Ragout

16-ounce package shiitake and portabella dried mushrooms (or use fresh)

4 (1-ounce) packages Knorr peppercorn sauce

Bottle of red wine

2 onions, chopped

4-6 cloves garlic, minced

½ cup butter

¼ cup flour

Soak dried mushrooms in water overnight, drain and slice. Sauté onions and garlic in butter until soft. Add mushrooms, sauté a few minutes longer. Sprinkle flour over mushrooms, continue to cook for 10 minutes. Add wine while scraping pan. Prepare peppercorn sauce according to package directions, except do not heat. Add sauce to pan, cook until sauce thickens.

Lynne Knott
Son Keaton, 2007

Great with meats, especially beef tenderloin (p 199). This was served at the December 2004 faculty Christmas brunch by the Parents Club.

Layered Vegetable Casserole

16-ounce can French-style green beans, drained

12-ounce can white shoe-peg corn, drained

8-ounce can sliced or chopped water chestnuts

1 medium onion, chopped

1 can cream of celery soup

1 cup sour cream

2 cups shredded cheddar cheese

1 sleeve saltine crackers, crushed or 1 cup breadcrumbs

½ cup melted butter

½ teaspoon garlic powder

In 2-quart buttered casserole dish, layer vegetables in order listed. Combine soup and sour cream, spread over vegetables. Sprinkle with cheese. Combine crackers, butter and garlic powder, sprinkle over casserole. Bake at 350 degrees for 45 minutes or bubbly. Can prepare a day ahead without cracker topping. Add topping just before putting in oven. Serves 10-12.

Mary Jane Sirna
Sons Matthew, 2004; Aaron, 2008

I have a great deal of respect for Mr. Ron Geldhof. In 1972-73, I had Mr. Geldhof for Chemistry, his first job out of college. We thought he would be lucky to make it out of first semester. There were a few hi-jinks occurring, including the lighting of gas burners, various chemical concoctions and even a fight that broke out during one of his lectures. More than 30 years later he is one of the finest teachers and coaches at Rockhurst. Hats off to him!

- Mark Fitzpatrick, 1974
Sons Tim, 2002;
John, 2008

Swiss Green Beans

4 tablespoons butter

⅓ cup flour

1 teaspoon salt

1 teaspoon pepper

1 teaspoon sugar

½ teaspoon dried onion

1 cup sour cream

5 cans French-style green beans, drained

2 cups Swiss cheese, shredded

Melt butter and stir in flour, salt, pepper, sugar and onion. Mix in sour cream and cook, stirring, until sauce is hot and thickened. Fold in beans and cheese. Pour into baking dish. Bake at 400 degrees for 20 minutes. Serves 8-10.

Laura Murphy
Husband Matt, 1975; Sons Steve, 2002; Pat, 2005

Parmesan Green Beans

2 tablespoons vegetable oil

1 tablespoon wine vinegar

1 tablespoon chopped onion

¼ teaspoon salt

⅛ teaspoon pepper

1 clove garlic, crushed

2 pounds fresh green beans

2 tablespoons seasoned breadcrumbs

2 tablespoons grated Parmesan cheese

1 tablespoon butter

Preheat oven to 350 degrees. In a small bowl whisk oil, vinegar, onion, salt, pepper and garlic together to combine. Remove ends of green beans. Cook beans in boiling water until tender-crisp, about 7 minutes. Drain beans and coat with oil/vinegar mixture. Place coated beans in 9x11-inch glass baking dish. In a small saucepan, melt butter. Add breadcrumbs and Parmesan cheese and stir to create a crumbly coating. Drizzle mixture over beans. Bake 15-20 minutes. Serves 6-8.

Sue Dierks
Husband Bernard, 1955; Sons Chris, 1986; Mike, 1991

My husband Jerry (1980) came to Rockhurst his junior year from Washington, D.C. He played quarterback for Coach Severino. He still has many friends from there and we continue to support Rockhurst. Our son Parker is in the class of 2010.

- Diane Rauschelbach

1961: Tom Ruzicka of RHS was elected president of the city's southwest area youth council.

Sesame Green Beans

1 tablespoon olive oil

1 tablespoon sesame seeds

1 pound fresh green beans, cut into 2-inch pieces

¼ cup chicken broth

¼ teaspoon salt

Freshly ground black pepper to taste

Heat oil in a large skillet or wok over medium heat. Add sesame seeds. When seeds start to darken, stir in green beans. Cook, stirring, until beans turn bright green. Pour in chicken broth, salt and pepper. Cover and cook until beans are tender-crisp, about 10 minutes. Uncover and cook until liquid evaporates. Serves 4.

Mary Adair
Husband Bill, 1968; Son Chris, 2003

Broccoli Casserole

Broccoli head, cut up

1 teaspoon Worcestershire sauce

Juice of ½ lemon

1½ cups mayonnaise

1½ cups sour cream

Dash of onion juice

1 can sliced water chestnuts

½ cup buttered breadcrumbs

Steam broccoli until tender. Place in greased baking dish. Combine lemon juice, mayonnaise, sour cream, onion juice and water chestnuts in saucepan and heat slowly until slightly thickened. Pour over broccoli. Sprinkle buttered breadcrumbs over top. Bake at 350 degrees for 20 minutes or until sauce begins to bubble around the edges. Serves 6-8.

Betsy Vossman
Son Eric, 2002

When Fr. Thomas Pesci, S.J., became president, he interviewed all the faculty. I was one of the first called, and the first thing he said was "What would you say if you had to wear a tie every day?" Visualize 30 seconds of dead silence. Then I told him that a necktie was an outdated piece of clothing. I should have thought then to have an updated resume ready. But I also let him know that sometimes the boss makes a decision you don't agree with and you either do it or look for other employment. Well, we did start wearing ties and my collection grew from 3 to about 30.

- John McEniry, 1968; RHS Faculty member

Broccoli Au Gratin

2 cups milk

4 tablespoons flour

16 ounces cream cheese, softened

1 ounce blue cheese, room temperature

1 teaspoon salt

1 teaspoon pepper

2½ pounds broccoli

4 tablespoons breadcrumbs

¼-½ cup butter

Heat milk. Blend in flour, cream cheese, blue cheese, salt and pepper and stir over low heat until smooth. Cook broccoli until barely tender. Drain and place in 3-quart casserole. Pour cheese sauce over broccoli. May be prepared to this point a day before. Bake at 350 degrees for 50 minutes. Top with breadcrumbs, dot with butter and return to oven for 10 minutes. Serves 4-6.

Kathy Fallon
Sons Kevin, 1999; Brian, 2002

Baked Spinach Casserole

3 tablespoons grated onion

1 pound chopped mushrooms

3 tablespoons butter

3 tablespoons flour

2 teaspoons salt

¼ teaspoon white pepper

¼ teaspoon nutmeg

2 cups light cream

2 packages frozen spinach, thawed, drained

3 tablespoons grated Gruyère or Swiss cheese

Sauté onions and mushrooms in butter for 5 minutes. Blend in flour, salt, pepper and nutmeg. Gradually add cream, stirring to boiling point. Taste for seasonings and adjust if necessary. In buttered 8- or 9-inch square casserole, spread half the spinach; cover with half the mushroom sauce, then repeat. Sprinkle with grated cheese. Set casserole in larger pan of hot water. Bake at 325 degrees for 40 minutes. Serves 6.

Mary Adair
Husband Bill, 1968; Son Chris, 2003

My aunt Dorothy Flanagan drove us to school in the morning carpool. Many years later I learned she had a secret plan. She hated the silence of that morning drive with half-asleep teens, so she began getting up earlier every morning and reading the sports section front to back, just so she would have conversational items she thought would tempt my cousin Terry and me out of our silence. She continues to read the sports first to this day!

- B. Joseph Duffy, 1975

Asparagus with Parmesan Crust

1 pound thin asparagus spears

1 tablespoon extra virgin olive oil

1 ounce shaved Parmesan cheese

Freshly ground black pepper to taste

¼ cup balsamic vinegar or to taste

Preheat oven to 450 degrees. Place asparagus spears in single layer on a baking sheet. Drizzle with olive oil and toss to coat. Spread Parmesan cheese over asparagus and season with freshly ground black pepper. Bake 12-15 minutes in preheated oven, until cheese is melted and asparagus is tender but crisp. Serve immediately on warm plates, sprinkling with balsamic vinegar to taste. Serves 4.

Maraline Hayob
Son David, 2000

Stir-Fried Asparagus

3 tablespoons butter or margarine

1 teaspoon chicken bouillon granules

⅛ teaspoon celery salt

⅛ teaspoon pepper

1½ pounds fresh asparagus, trimmed, cut into 2-inch slices (about 4 cups)

1 teaspoon soy sauce

In a large skillet melt butter. Add bouillon, celery salt and pepper, mix well. Add asparagus and toss to coat. Cover and cook for 2 minutes over medium-high heat, stirring occasionally. Stir in soy sauce. Serve immediately. Serves 4.

Karen Van Dyke
Husband Mike, 1966; Sons Kevin, 1997; Cory, 2003; Ryan, 2003

Coach Tony Severino teaches Lifetime Sports to seniors. The class is always highly desirable. We'd go in early the first day of class sign-ups to get his coveted signature giving us the OK for the class. Students get to head off campus for their bowling, golf and tennis sessions. Coach Sev made sure each student knew exactly where the speed traps were on the way to these locations, but some students (not me, of course!) invariably got tickets anyway.

- Bryan Flanagan, 2002

Creamy Fried Confetti Corn

8 slices bacon

4 cups sweet corn kernels (8 ears) canned

1 medium white onion, chopped

⅓ cup chopped red pepper

⅓ cup chopped green pepper

8-ounce package cream cheese, cubed

½ cup half & half

1 teaspoon sugar

1 teaspoon salt

1 teaspoon pepper

Chop uncooked bacon in food processor or by hand. Fry chopped bacon in large skillet until crisp and brown. Remove bacon, drain on paper towels. Reserve 2 tablespoons drippings in skillet, set aside. Sauté corn, onion and peppers in skillet drippings over medium high heat, about 6 minutes or until tender. Remove from heat. Add cream cheese and half & half, stir until melted. Stir in sugar, salt and pepper. Top with bacon crumbles.

Amy Rodriguez
Son Richard, 2009

Sweet Potato Casserole

3 cups sweet potatoes (about 5), cooked, peeled, mashed

¼-½ cup sugar

½ teaspoon salt

2 eggs

½ cup butter, melted

½ cup cream

1 teaspoon vanilla

Topping:

⅓ cup butter

1 cup brown sugar, packed

⅓ cup flour

½ cup pecans

Beat together potatoes, sugar, salt, eggs butter, cream and vanilla. Pour into a shallow baking dish. Combine topping ingredients, sprinkle over potato mixture. Bake at 350 degrees for 35 minutes.

Karen Miyawaki
Son Brandon Busenbark, 2009

Oriental Zucchini Squash

2 large zucchini, sliced

2 large yellow squash, sliced

2 tablespoons soy sauce

1 tablespoon olive oil

1 teaspoon vinegar

1½ teaspoons sugar

2 teaspoons toasted sesame seeds

¼-½ teaspoon ground ginger

¼ teaspoon ground cumin

In a large saucepan, cook sliced zucchini and yellow squash in a small amount of water until tender-crisp. Drain well and place in a large bowl. In a small bowl, combine remaining ingredients. Mix well and pour over vegetables. Toss to coat. Serve warm or refrigerate and serve chilled.

Polly Mandl
Husband Richard, 1978; Son Ryan, 2006

Butternut Squash Gratin

2 tablespoons butter

1 medium yellow onion, chopped

2 cloves garlic, chopped

2 cups cream

2 teaspoons salt

½ teaspoon pepper

2½ pounds butternut squash, peeled, seeded, cut into ¼-inch slices

1½ cups pecans, chopped, toasted, divided

4 ounces goat cheese, crumbled

Parsley for garnish

Preheat oven to 350 degrees. Grease a 9x13-inch gratin pan. Melt butter in large skillet over medium-high heat. Add onions, cook for 5 minutes. Add garlic, cook for 1 minute. Add cream, salt and pepper, bring to boil. Add squash and ¾ cup pecans, return to boil. Reduce heat, simmer for 10 minutes. Transfer half the squash mixture to prepared pan, dot with half the goat cheese. Cover with remaining squash mixture, sprinkle remaining goat cheese over the top. Place gratin dish on a baking sheet. Bake until squash is very tender, cream is mostly absorbed and top is golden, about 45 minutes. Remove from oven and sprinkle with remaining pecans and parsley. Let rest 10 minutes before serving.

Sarah Jurcyk
Sons Jordan, 2006; Seth, 2008

Green Rice

3 cups cooked rice

1 cup chopped parsley

½ cup grated cheddar cheese

⅓ cup chopped onion

¼ cup chopped green pepper

1 clove garlic, minced

14½-ounce can evaporated milk

2 eggs, beaten

½ cup vegetable oil

1 tablespoon salt

1 teaspoon pepper

Juice of one lemon

Mix rice, parsley, cheese, onion, green pepper and garlic in greased 2-quart casserole. In a bowl, blend milk, eggs, oil, salt, pepper and lemon juice. Blend with rice. Bake at 350 degrees for 45 minutes. Serves 10.

Suzanne Orscheln
Sons Joe, 2000; Dustin, 2002; Scott, 2005

Wonderful Wild Rice

4 cups water

1 cup wild rice

4 cups beef stock

2 cups frozen peas, thawed

4 stalks celery, cut diagonally into thin pieces

8 green onions, sliced

½ cup slivered almonds, toasted

Dressing:

4 tablespoons red wine vinegar

2 tablespoons soy sauce

½ cup vegetable oil

4 teaspoons sesame oil

Bring water and rice to a boil, drain. Simmer rice in beef stock for about one hour, until rice is cooked. Drain. Add peas, celery, onion and almonds, mix well. Whisk dressing ingredients together in a separate bowl. Add to rice and mix well. Serve warm or cold. Serves 10-12.

Jan Flanagan
Husband Jim, 1971; Sons Bryan, 2002; Sean, 2004; Kevin, 2007

Recipe may be cut in half for a smaller crowd.

Baked Risotto with Asparagus, Spinach and Parmesan

1 tablespoon olive oil

1 cup finely chopped onion

1 cup uncooked Arborio rice

8 cups spinach leaves

2 cups chicken broth

¼ teaspoon salt

¼ teaspoon ground nutmeg

½ cup freshly grated Parmesan cheese, divided

1½ cups asparagus, sliced diagonally into 1-inch pieces

Preheat oven to 400 degrees. Heat oil in a Dutch oven over medium heat. Add onion, cook 4 minutes or until tender. Add rice, stir well. Stir in spinach, broth, salt and nutmeg. Bring to a simmer, cook 7 minutes. Stir in ¼ cup cheese. Cover and bake at 400 degrees for 15 minutes.

Stir in asparagus, sprinkle with remaining cheese. Cover and bake an additional 15 minutes or until liquid is almost absorbed. Serves 4.

Betsy Vossman
Son Eric, 2002

Recipe is easily doubled.

Bulgur with Leeks, Cranberries and Almonds

6 tablespoons butter

3 cups chopped leeks, white and pale green part only

5 cups chicken broth

3 cups bulgur

⅔ cup dried cranberries

⅔ cup sliced almonds, toasted

Salt and pepper to taste

Melt butter in large saucepan over medium high heat. Add leeks and sauté until very tender, about 12 minutes. Add chicken broth and bring to a boil. Stir in bulgur and boil 5 minutes. Add dried cranberries, remove from heat, cover and let stand for 5 minutes. Fluff with fork, mix in almonds. Season with salt and pepper.

Marianne Damon
Sons Paul, 2002; Quinn, 2008

Summer Couscous

3 medium red bell peppers

1½ cups (10 ounces) instant couscous

2¼ cups boiling water

½ teaspoon salt

¼ cup olive oil

¼ cup fresh lemon juice

1 teaspoon ground cumin

Freshly ground black pepper

Cayenne pepper

1 large cucumber, peeled, ½-inch dice

½ cup Moroccan or other small, black, oil-cured olives, pitted, coarsely chopped

2 green onions, white parts and about 3 inches green, minced

1 large clove garlic, minced

1 pound ripe beefsteak tomatoes, peeled, seeded, ½-inch dice

2 tablespoons finely chopped parsley

Preheat broiler. Put peppers on a sheet pan lined with foil and broil for about 15 minutes, turning once or twice to ensure they blister and blacken evenly. Remove to a bowl, cover with plastic wrap and let cool. Peel, seed and dice into ½-inch pieces. Set aside.

Put couscous in a large mixing bowl. Pour boiling water over couscous. Add ½ teaspoon salt and stir. Cover with plastic wrap and let stand for 10-15 minutes, or until swollen and tender. In a small bowl, combine olive oil, lemon juice and cumin. Season with additional salt, pepper and cayenne to taste.

Fluff couscous with a fork. Add cucumber, olives, green onions, garlic, tomatoes and roasted peppers. Pour dressing over couscous and toss to combine. Let stand at room temperature for at least 1 hour. Just before serving, stir in parsley.   Serves 4.

Maraline Hayob
Son David, 2000

Pasta
AND
Pizza

1960s

National:

What began as a "special forces" advisory exercise mushroomed into a controversial, divisive war in Vietnam, profoundly affecting many Rockhurst grads and their families. Back on U.S. soil, three of the most notable assassinations in national history occurred - John F. Kennedy in 1963, and Martin Luther King and Robert F. Kennedy in 1968. The space race heated up, with the Soviet Union putting a man in orbit in 1961 and the U.S. responding by putting Neil Armstrong on the moon in 1969. In the world of music, "Beatlemania" swept the globe and invaded the U.S.; the quartet from Liverpool paid a visit to Kansas City's Municipal Stadium in 1964. Woodstock, billed as the music festival of peace and love, took place in 1969, setting the standard for summer music festivals.

Local:

Our little "Cowtown" became better connected to the rest of the world in the 1960s, as Interstate 70 opened in Kansas City in 1962, and Kansas City International Airport followed in 1967. Both provided transportation for a steady influx of fans, as the Kansas City sports scene exploded in the 60s. Lamar Hunt and his Dallas Texans relocated to Kansas City and became the Chiefs in 1963. They wasted little time making a name for themselves, winning the AFL Championship and appearing in Super Bowl I in 1967. The Athletics skipped town for Oakland later that year. But within two years, Kansas City had baseball again, as the expansion Royals began play in 1969. Ward Parkway Shopping Center opened its doors in 1963, becoming the city's first enclosed shopping mall and, eventually, a hot spot for Rockhurst back-to-school shopping.

Seafood Lasagna

8 lasagna noodles

1 cup onions, chopped

2 tablespoons butter

8 ounces cream cheese, softened

1½ cups cream-style cottage cheese

1 egg, beaten

1 teaspoon dried basil, crushed

½ teaspoon salt

½ teaspoon pepper

2 cans cream of mushroom soup

⅓ cup milk

⅓ cup dry white wine

1-1½ pounds small shrimp, cooked, peeled

7-ounce can lump crabmeat, drained

¼ cup grated Parmesan cheese

½ cup grated sharp cheddar cheese

Cook noodles according to package directions, drain. Arrange 4 noodles on bottom of greased 9x13-inch baking dish. Cook onions in butter until tender, blend in cream cheese. Stir in cottage cheese, egg, basil, salt and pepper. Spread half on top of noodles.

Combine soup, milk and wine. Stir in shrimp and crab. Spread half over the cottage cheese layer. Repeat layers. Sprinkle top with Parmesan cheese.

Bake uncovered at 350 degrees for 40 minutes. Top with sharp cheddar cheese and bake for another 5 minutes. Let stand for 15 minutes before serving. Serves 8-10.

Diane Rauschelbach
Husband Jerry, 1980; Son Parker, 2010

The first alumnus to serve as President was Rev. Louis G. Mattione, S.J., class of 1932. He was President from 1962-1968. His successor was Rev. Carl G. Kloster, S.J., 1968-1975, who also served as Principal from 1954-1972.

Vegetable Cannelloni
with Sherry Sauce

8 Cannelloni Shells

Sherry Sauce:

2 tablespoons olive oil

2-3 cloves garlic, minced

1 shallot, minced

1 cup sherry

2 cups heavy cream

½ teaspoon cracked black pepper

Vegetable Mixture:

3 tablespoons olive oil

4 garlic cloves, minced

3 shallots, minced

1 small onion, chopped

1 cup chopped mushrooms

1 eggplant, chopped

1 cup chopped zucchini

1 yellow squash, chopped

1 roasted red bell pepper, chopped

Salt and pepper to taste

2 teaspoons dried basil

1 teaspoon rosemary

1 tablespoon dill weed

2 cups ricotta cheese

1 cup shredded Parmesan cheese

Cook cannelloni shells according to package directions, set aside. Begin sauce by heating olive oil over medium heat, sauté garlic and shallot. Add sherry and stir. Add heavy cream and pepper and heat, stirring as needed, so sauce does not boil over. Reduce heat.

For vegetable mixture, heat olive oil in large skillet, sauté garlic and shallots. Add onion, mushrooms and eggplant. After a few minutes, add zucchini, yellow squash and roasted red pepper. Stir. Add salt, pepper, basil, rosemary and dill weed. Add ricotta cheese and Parmesan. Stir and fold into mix. Vegetables should be cooked, but not mushy.

Fill cannelloni shells with vegetable mixture and place in 9x13-inch baking pan, side by side. Pour sherry sauce over filled shells to completely cover all shells. Bake at 350 degrees for about 30 minutes or bubbly. Serves 4-6.

Polly Mandl
Husband Richard,1978; Son Ryan, 2006.

Monterey Spaghetti

4 ounces spaghetti, broken into 2-inch pieces

1 egg

1 cup sour cream

¼ cup grated Parmesan cheese

¼ teaspoon garlic powder

2 cups shredded Monterey Jack cheese

10-ounce package frozen chopped spinach, thawed, drained

2.8-ounce can French-fried onions, divided

Cook pasta according to package. Meanwhile, in a medium bowl, beat egg. Add sour cream, Parmesan and garlic powder. Drain spaghetti, add to egg mixture with Monterey Jack cheese, spinach and half the onions. Pour into a greased 2-quart baking dish. Cover and bake at 350 degrees for 30 minutes or until heated through. Top with remaining onions and return to oven for 5 minutes or until onions are golden brown. Serves 6-8.

Sue Dierks
Husband Bernard, 1955; Sons Chris, 1986; Mike, 1991

Light Fettuccine Alfredo

1 tablespoon margarine

2 small cloves garlic, minced

1 tablespoon flour

1⅓ cups fat free half & half

3 tablespoons light cream cheese

1¼ cups freshly grated Parmesan cheese, divided

4 cups hot cooked fettuccine

2 teaspoons chopped fresh parsley

Freshly ground pepper

Melt margarine in a saucepan over medium heat. Add minced garlic and sauté 1 minute. Stir in flour. Gradually add half & half, stirring with a wire whisk until mixture is blended. Cook, stirring constantly, until mixture is thickened and bubbly. Stir in cream cheese, cook 2 minutes. Add 1 cup Parmesan, stirring constantly until Parmesan melts. Pour sauce over hot cooked fettuccine and toss well to coat. Top pasta with remaining ¼ cup Parmesan, chopped parsley and pepper. Serves 4.

Cathy Toth
Husband Robert, 1979; Son Kyle, 2009

Father Cummings had a dog named Rocksie. She was a big white hairy dog that Father often walked up and down the halls during school. The students loved that dog. Father took Rocksie to meetings with donors on a regular basis. One of Rocksie's biggest fans was Rose Teicher, a major benefactor for whom the Rose Theater is named.

- Judie Scanlon, RHS Special Events Coordinator Sons Steve, 1988; Kerry, 1994

There were 41 young men in the graduating Class of 1937, all dressed in coat and tie.

Baked Rigatoni with Bechamel Sauce

½ cup butter

½ cup plus 2 tablespoons flour

1 quart whole milk at room temperature

Pinch of fresh nutmeg

1 cup Fontina cheese, grated, divided

½ pound prosciutto, julienned

Salt

White pepper

1 pound rigatoni

3 tablespoons butter, diced

Melt butter in 2-quart saucepan over medium heat. Whisk in flour until smooth and cook about 1 minute. Gradually add milk, whisking until sauce is smooth and creamy. Simmer until sauce is thick enough to coat the back of a spoon, about 10 minutes. Remove from heat and add nutmeg, ½ cup Fontina, prosciutto, salt and pepper. Set aside.

Cook pasta for about 5 minutes, drain. Pasta will be cooked a second time, so don't overcook. Insides should still be hard. Combine pasta and sauce in pasta pot. Mix until pasta is well coated with sauce. Pour into a well-greased 9x13-inch baking dish. Sprinkle with remaining Fontina cheese and dot with butter. Bake at 425 degrees for 25 minutes or until bubbly and top is golden brown. Serves 8.

Pam Cowan
Son Alex, 2008

Cross Country Team Baked Ziti

1 pound ziti pasta

1 onion, chopped

1 pound lean ground beef

2 (26-ounce) jars spaghetti sauce

6 ounces Provolone cheese, sliced

1½ cups sour cream

6 ounces mozzarella cheese, shredded

2 tablespoons grated Parmesan cheese

Bring a large pot of slightly salted water to a boil. Add ziti, cook until al dente, about 8 minutes, drain. Meanwhile, in a large skillet, brown onion and ground beef over medium heat. Add spaghetti sauce and simmer 15 minutes.

Preheat oven to 350 degrees. Grease a 9x13-inch baking dish. Layer half the ziti, half the Provolone cheese, half the sour cream, half the spaghetti sauce mixture. Repeat layers. Top with grated Parmesan cheese. Bake for 30 minutes or until cheeses are melted. Serves 8.

Mary Ring
Son Gallagher, 2006

This ziti was served many Friday evenings at the Ring household as a pre-race carbo-loading dinner for members of the 2005 Cross Country team.

During the football season of 1960 against Ward, while playing defensive tackle, I picked up 3 fumbles and scored 3 touchdowns. It was featured in "Faces in the Crowd" in Sports Illustrated and in newspapers across the country. The week before, a blocked punt against Hayden of Topeka landed in my arms and I skipped in for a touchdown. Thus, I was tied for leading scorer in the city for a week. This was obviously the highlight of my career and used up my 15 minutes of fame! I think 3 touchdowns by a defensive lineman may still be a national high school record.

- Chuck Martin, 1961

Italian Meatballs and Sauce

Sauce:

1 onion, chopped

Olive oil

12-ounce can tomato paste

2 tomato paste cans of water, plus additional if necessary

1 teaspoon pepper

2 teaspoons salt

2 tablespoons sugar

Generous pinch of basil

1 bay leaf

Pinch of oregano

Pinch of parsley

Meatballs:

1 pound ground beef

Salt and pepper

½ cup bread crumbs

½ cup Parmesan cheese

1 egg

Small amount of milk (about 1-2 tablespoons)

3 large cloves garlic, finely chopped

Sauce: Brown onion in olive oil and add tomato paste and water. Add remaining ingredients. Simmer sauce for 2-3 hours while preparing meatballs. Add additional water if needed.

Meatballs: Mix ingredients for meatballs, using hands. Work it really well. This is the secret to a good meatball. I make my meatballs fairly small because I think the sauce can cook through them and give a better flavor. Brown meatballs in the oven at 350 degrees. Don't overcook. Add to sauce and simmer for several hours, stirring occasionally. Add more water if desired. Serve with spaghetti or your choice of pasta.

Cece Stabler
Husband Michael, 1970
Sons Nicholas, 1997; Matthew, 2000; Anthony, 2007

I sometimes add hard boiled eggs to the sauce, along with the meatballs. Multiply quantities for both sauce and meatballs as needed.

My mother-in-law Rose is a wonderful cook. Michael's parents were from Sicily and their name was Stabile. It was changed to Stabler when they came to the U.S. My husband wanted me to learn how to make their spaghetti and meatballs before we got married. Mama Rosa came over and we went through it step by step. To this day it is a family favorite.

An unforgettable memory for me is when my son Brent (2002) broke his arm during a game against Blue Springs his sophomore year. The break required surgery and 2 steel plates in his arm, which effectively ended his football career. It gave him the opportunity, though, to find another interest - technical theater. With the support and encouragement of Bill Murphy, the instructor, Brent became immersed in the program and had a great time.

- Chely Scarbrough

Rigatoni with Meat Sauce

1 pound bulk Italian sausage or turkey Italian sausage

1 medium onion, chopped

1 clove garlic, minced

28-ounce can tomatoes, undrained, broken up

15-ounce can tomato sauce

½ cup sliced black olives

1 teaspoon dried basil leaves

½ teaspoon fennel seeds

½ teaspoon salt

¼ cup grated Parmesan cheese

2-4 drops hot sauce, optional

1 pound rigatoni noodles

2 tablespoons dried parsley flakes

2 tablespoons olive oil

In a large skillet brown sausage, onion and garlic until sausage is no longer pink, drain. Add tomatoes, tomato sauce, olives, basil, fennel seed, salt, Parmesan and hot sauce. Bring to boil, reduce heat and simmer for 20 minutes. Prepare rigatoni according to package directions, drain. Toss rigatoni with parsley and olive oil. Arrange on a warm serving platter and top with meat sauce.

Karen Miller
Husband Sean, 1977; Son Ryan, 2008

I still remember the first time I experienced Rockhurst football. My nephew Matt Nolen (1988) was on the freshman team. I brought my son Nolen (1999) to the football game. As I sat in amazement watching the boys on the field grunting and hitting each other so hard I could hear the crack of their football pads, something caught my eye. On the practice field at the top of the hill was a group of huge individuals, all dressed in navy blue sweatsuits. Already in awe of the environment in which I was sitting, I asked my brother Chuck ever so sincerely, why the Marines were working out at Rockhurst. Needless to say, everyone around me had a good laugh. I am proud to say that my sons Nolen and Clark (2009) grew up to be two of those "Marines."

- Katy Nolen O'Dowd

Sausage and Spinach Fettuccine with Gorgonzola Sauce

1 pound hot Italian sausage, casings removed

10 ounces fettuccine

2 tablespoons butter

2 tablespoons flour

12-ounce can evaporated low-fat milk

¾ cup crumbled Gorgonzola cheese

¾ teaspoon salt

¼ teaspoon pepper

½ cup sundried tomatoes, chopped

5 - 6 ounce package fresh baby spinach

Brown sausage in skillet, drain, set aside. Cook pasta. While pasta is cooking, melt butter in medium saucepan over medium heat. Add flour and cook 1 minute, stirring constantly with whisk. Gradually add milk, stirring constantly. Reduce heat and simmer 3 minutes until sauce thickens. Remove from heat and add cheese, salt and pepper. Drain pasta, reserving ½ cup pasta water. Combine pasta, sauce, tomatoes and spinach. Toss gently to coat. If sauce is too thick, stir in some of reserved pasta water. Serves 8.

Pam Cowan
Son Alex, 2008

Rockhurst debt…
We owe Rockhurst for
27 years of blissful
marriage, three children,
and, well, so much more.
It was a hot summer
night of 1973, July 20.
Rockhurst had a mixer
for area high school kids.
When my good friend
Darlene Williams called
and asked me if I
wanted to go, I agreed.
Smart move! I met
incoming senior
Rob O'Byrne,
destined to be the man
of my dreams!
It was Jim Croce's
"Time in a Bottle"
that sealed the deal.

- Diane Campbell
O'Byrne

Shrimp in Red Pepper Sauce

7-ounce package vermicelli

12-ounce jar roasted red peppers, drained

8 ounces cream cheese, softened

½ cup chicken broth

3 garlic cloves, chopped

½ teaspoon ground red pepper (cayenne)

2 pounds cooked, peeled large shrimp

¼ cup fresh basil, chopped

Prepare pasta according to package directions. Process red peppers, cream cheese, broth, garlic and cayenne in food processor until smooth. Pour into skillet. Cook over medium heat 5 minutes, stirring often. Add shrimp, cook 2-3 minutes, until just heated through. Remove from heat, sprinkle with basil. Serve over hot pasta. Serves 6.

Lynne Knott
Son Keaton, 2007

Scallops with Angel Capers

3 large cloves garlic, minced

2 tablespoons olive oil

1½ pounds scallops

Juice of 1 lemon

25 capers

⅔ cup dry vermouth

1 pound capellini (angel hair) pasta, uncooked

½ cup breadcrumbs

½ cup Parmesan cheese

¼ teaspoon salt

¼ teaspoon pepper

Lemon slices, optional

Brown garlic in olive oil in skillet. Add scallops, cook until done. Mix lemon juice, capers and vermouth. Add to scallops, cook for 1 minute. Prepare pasta al dente (2-3 minutes.) In a small bowl, combine breadcrumbs, Parmesan, salt and pepper, set aside.

Drain scallops, reserving liquid. Toss ½ the reserved liquid with pasta in a large bowl, transfer to oven-proof platter. Ladle scallops over pasta, top with breadcrumb mixture and broil for 2 minutes or until lightly browned. Garnish with lemon slices. Use remaining reserved liquid to pour over pasta. Serves 6.

Pat Shealy
Sons John, 2007; Westly, 2010

I will probably never forget the smell of the local smokehouse down the street, nor how said smoke ruins lamb! Of course, I love burnt ends and beans and onion rings at Jack Stack. The pasta sampler at Lidia's at the Freight House is a favorite. I still miss all those family meals around the kitchen or dining room table with my Kansas City friends. They are special cherished moments.

- Rev. Thomas A. Pesci, S.J.,
RHS President
1993-2004

Farfalle alla Brigante

2 tablespoons basil olive oil

Medium yellow onion, diced

6 slices bacon, chopped

Juice and zest of 1 large lemon or 2 small lemons

¼ cup kalamata olives, sliced

¼ cup drained capers

Coarse sea salt

Cracked black pepper

Herbes de Provence

4 tablespoons unsalted butter

1 cup heavy cream

1 pound farfalle (bowtie) pasta

½ cup grated Parmigiano-Reggiano cheese

2 tablespoons roughly chopped Italian parsley

Prepare a pasta pot with salted water and place on high heat. Preheat basil olive oil in a large pan over medium-high heat. Add onions and bacon to pan and cook for 5 minutes. Add lemon juice to pan, cook for 2 more minutes. Add olives, capers and lemon zest, season with salt, pepper and herbs. Cook for 2 more minutes. Add butter and heavy cream, stir thoroughly and reduce heat to low.

Add pasta to boiling water and cook for 12 minutes or until al dente. After 6 minutes, add half the grated cheese and 3-4 grinds of pepper to cream sauce in pan, stir. When pasta is done, drain thoroughly. Fold sauce and pasta together and add parsley. Serve with a sprinkling of grated cheese.

Rob Messerli
Sons Robbie, 2007; Kyle, 2009

Herbes de Provence is a blend of dried herbs found in the spice section of the grocery. The aromatic mixture usually contains basil, fennel seed, lavender, marjoram, rosemary, sage, summer savory and thyme.

Creamy Artichoke and Mushroom Penne

3 tablespoons unsalted butter

¼ cup minced onion

1 clove garlic, crushed

8 ounces fresh sliced mushrooms

1 cup chopped canned or frozen artichokes

1 cup heavy whipping cream

2 tablespoons capers, rinsed, drained

Salt

Freshly ground pepper

12 ounces penne pasta, cooked

1 ounce Parmesan cheese, grated

2 tablespoons chopped fresh parsley

Melt butter in a large skillet over medium high heat, add onions and garlic. Saute until tender but not brown. Add mushrooms, saute 5 minutes. Stir in artichokes, heating thoroughly, about 2-3 minutes. Place artichoke mixture in a bowl and set aside.

Return skillet to heat and add cream. Boil until cream is reduced by half. Add artichoke mixture and capers, stir until combined. Season with salt and pepper. Toss warm sauce with pasta, gently stir in Parmesan and parsley. Serve immediately.

Tina Montgomery
Son Connor, 2009

One of our favorite teachers (1944-1948) was Joe Sheehan, S.J. He taught English 2A, among other things. One day someone had the bright idea of turning all our desks around to face the back of the room. That's the way we sat when he entered the room. He didn't jug us, but ordered us all to bring him a package of chewing gum as punishment!

- Jack Becker, 1948

Pesto

3 cups fresh basil leaves

⅔ cup olive oil

3 tablespoons pine nuts

3 cloves crushed, peeled garlic

1 teaspoon salt

⅔ cup grated Parmesan cheese

3 tablespoons grated Romano cheese

1 tablespoon hot water

2 tablespoons half & half, optional

Put first 5 ingredients in food processor and mix at high speed. Pour into a bowl and mix in cheeses by hand. Pesto may be frozen right after adding the cheeses for use at a later time. Or to serve immediately, add 1 tablespoon or so hot water and half & half to pesto. Toss with your choice of pasta.

Megan Viviano
Son Joseph, 2009

Chicken Pesto Pizza

1 pre-baked purchased pizza crust (like Boboli)

8 ounces spreadable cream cheese

8 ounces prepared pesto

2 chicken breasts, grilled or baked, sliced into thin strips

1 can or jar artichoke hearts, chopped

1½ cups shredded mozzarella cheese

Parmesan cheese, grated

Spread cream cheese on pizza crust. Spread pesto over cream cheese layer. Evenly sprinkle chicken and artichoke hearts on crust. Cover pizza with mozzarella cheese, then Parmesan. Bake at 300 degrees until cheese is melted. Slice and serve. Serves 3-4.

Lynne Hire
Son P.J., 2008

I remember when the freshman moms had to work clean-up duty after the Spectacular auction. All freshman moms had to go to the dock area and hose off the dishes before the caterer would take them back. We were there in the heat with the freshman boys, with garden hoses, rinsing off glassware, silver and dishes. Water was running all over us and we were all dripping in sweat equity. Those were the days…

- Rose Marie Fowler-Swarts Sons Stephen, 1998; Ryan, 2001

Pancetta and Potato Pizza

½ pound pancetta, thinly sliced, roughly torn into 1-2 inch pieces

1-2 tablespoons olive oil

6-8 fingerling potatoes or 2-3 Yukon Gold potatoes, peeled, cut into ⅛-inch slices

1 large zucchini, peeled, cut into ⅛-inch slices

1 prepared pizza crust (Boboli) or fresh 12-inch pizza dough, thin crust

Cornmeal

4 tablespoons heavy cream

4 ounces herbed cream cheese

Parmesan cheese

Preheat oven and pizza stone to 450 degrees. Place pancetta in a cold sauté pan with olive oil. Turn burner to medium-high and sauté about 10 minutes until starting to crisp. Stir occasionally to keep from sticking.

Meanwhile, slice potatoes and zucchini (a mandoline slicer works best). When pancetta is starting to crisp, remove with a slotted spoon and drain on a paper towel, leaving rendered fat and oil in pan. Add potatoes to pan and spread evenly. Cook until starting to soften, about 5 minutes. Add zucchini and spread evenly. Cook vegetables until softened through, about 5 minutes. Stir occasionally to keep from sticking. Add more olive oil if necessary. Pour vegetables into a strainer to drain off fat and oil.

Sprinkle pizza paddle with cornmeal and lay out dough. Ladle cream onto pizza dough and spread evenly. Spoon vegetable mixture onto pizza and spread evenly. Sprinkle pancetta bits over vegetables. Dot top of pizza with cream cheese. Sprinkle freshly grated Parmesan over the top. Slide pizza onto preheated pizza stone and bake 10-12 minutes, until crust is crispy on the bottom and cream cheese is starting to brown. Spread cream cheese with a knife after pizza comes out of oven if you wish.

Rob Messerli
Sons Robbie, 2007; Kyle, 2009

The 1952 Homecoming Queen was Miss Judy Carter of St. Teresa's Academy. Her attendants were Mary Alice Smith of Loretto Academy and Ann Wiedemann, Notre Dame de Sion.

After a summer 2001 trip to Italy, Doctor Jorge Taracido brought prayer cards back for all his classes. He integrated theology and history into our Honors Spanish IV course. I still have the prayer card in my wallet.

- Bryan Flanagan, 2002

Hot Wings Pizza

2 Boboli pizza crusts

4 boneless, skinless chicken breasts, cut into ½-inch cubes

1½ cups favorite hot wings sauce, divided

8 ounces blue cheese salad dressing (such as Ken's Chunky Blue Cheese)

3 ounces blue cheese crumbles

8 ounces shredded mozzarella

Bake crusts at 425 degrees for 3 minutes. In sauce pan, cook chicken in 1 cup hot wing sauce until chicken is cooked completely through, about 15-20 minutes. Cool.

Spread blue cheese dressing over entire crusts, sprinkle with blue cheese crumbles. Drain chicken and arrange over crusts. Drizzle remaining hot wing sauce over top. Sprinkle with mozzarella. Bake 20-25 minutes or until crusts are golden brown. Serves 12.

Pam Cowan
Son Alex, 2008

Deep Dish Pizza

1 pound frozen bread dough, thawed

4 cups mozzarella cheese, divided

1½ pounds very lean pork sausage (pre-cook and drain if not lean)

1½ teaspoons dried oregano

1½ teaspoons fennel seeds, crushed

3 (14-ounce) cans plum or Italian tomatoes, chopped, drained

½ cup fresh sliced mushrooms

Preheat oven to 500 degrees. Grease a 14x2-inch deep dish pizza pan. Roll dough on a flour dusted surface into a 16-inch circle. Press into bottom and 1½ inches up sides of pan. Sprinkle with 3 cups cheese. Crumble uncooked sausage over cheese. Top with oregano, fennel, tomatoes, mushrooms and remaining cheese. Place in 500 degree oven, immediately reduce heat to 400 degrees. Bake 40-50 minutes. Remove when crust is golden and sausage is cooked through. Serves 8.

Jan Flanagan
Husband Jim, 1971; Sons Bryan, 2002; Sean, 2004; Kevin, 2007

Fish AND Seafood

1970s

National:

The United States withdrew troops from Vietnam in 1973, during a decade in which several seemingly insignificant events turned out to be of major importance. In 1972, a break-in gone awry at the Watergate Hotel in Washington, D.C. snowballed into a scandal that involved many high-ranking government officials and led to the resignation of President Richard Nixon. In 1975, a Harvard dropout started a small software company in Albuquerque, New Mexico. Years later, that company, Microsoft, is one of the world's most powerful, and its products have become essential tools for term papers and computer applications classes for Hawklets. In the entertainment world, Star Wars was released and the miniseries Roots aired in 1977. Fans of Roots and other television programs enjoyed, for the first time, the ability to tape their shows of choice; the VCR hit the market in the 70s, as did the Sony Walkman.

Local:

New entertainment options abounded in Kansas City in the 1970s, as Crown Center, Worlds of Fun and the Truman Sports Complex all opened in 1972. The Chiefs, who earned redemption for their Super Bowl I loss with a 23-7 win over the Vikings in Super Bowl IV in 1970, kicked off at Arrowhead Stadium in '72, and the Royals opened at Royals (now Kauffman) Stadium in 1973. Also in 1973, the Kings basketball franchise came to town. Kansas City saw the continued growth of suburban areas in the 70s, as Corporate Woods Business Park opened in 1974, creating a business district to accompany the residential expansion into Johnson County. In 1976 "Walkin' Joe" Teasdale, an alum of both Rockhurst High School and College, was elected Governor of Missouri. The following year, a "500 year" storm caused Brush Creek and the Blue River to flood, resulting in damage to the Country Club Plaza and other parts of the metro area.

Asian Salmon with Summer Salsa

Salmon:

1½ pounds salmon fillets

2 tablespoons finely grated fresh ginger

2 tablespoons sesame oil

1 tablespoon chopped fresh cilantro

¼ teaspoon salt

¼ teaspoon black pepper

Salsa:

1 cucumber, seeded, chopped

¼ cup red bell pepper, seeded, chopped

1 jalapeno pepper, seeded, finely chopped

1 garlic clove, minced

3 tablespoons rice vinegar

2 tablespoons vegetable oil

¼ teaspoon sugar

¼ teaspoon salt

Place salmon fillets in ziplock bag. Combine ginger, sesame oil, cilantro, salt and pepper, pour over salmon. Place in refrigerator for 1 hour. Combine ingredients for salsa, store in refrigerator. Remove salmon from marinade. Grill over medium heat for 6 minutes on each side, or until fish flakes easily. Serve with salsa. Serves 4.

Catherine Moussa
Son Alex VanMaren, 2007

Brown Sugar Baked Salmon

2 pounds salmon fillets

½ cup packed brown sugar

4 tablespoons melted butter

3 tablespoons soy sauce

2 tablespoons lemon juice

2 tablespoons dry white wine

Line baking pan with foil. Place salmon on prepared pan. In a bowl, whisk remaining ingredients together and pour over salmon. Cover and refrigerate for 30 minutes or up to 6 hours. When ready to cook, preheat oven to 400 degrees. Uncover salmon and place on middle rack in oven. Bake 15 - 20 minutes, basting every 5 minutes or until salmon begins to flake. Do not turn. Serves 6.

Barb Haden
Husband Jon, 1975, Son Robbie, 2009

The first part of the decade saw the continuation of Rev. Carl G. Kloster's term as both President (1968-1975) and Principal (1954-1972.) He was succeeded as President (1975-1980) by alumnus Rev. Luke J. Byrne, III, S.J., class of 1952.

Rev. Carl G. Kloster, S.J., served as Principal 1954-1972. The next Principal was Rev. T. Patrick Lawless, S.J., 1972-1976, followed by Rev. Paul C. Pilgram, S.J., 1976-1980.

Various intramural tournaments were held throughout the year in the 1940s. Fall: handball, golf; Winter: boxing, bowling, basketball; Spring: tennis, more handball, golf, softball; All Year: ping pong, pool.

Salmon Fillets Southwest

4 (6 to 8-ounce) salmon fillets, boneless, skinless

1 cup prepared salsa, well drained

1 cup mayonnaise

1 tablespoon garlic, chopped

1 tablespoon fresh lime juice

1 tablespoon fresh lemon juice

4 tablespoons chopped fresh cilantro, divided

Combine salsa, mayonnaise, garlic, lime juice, lemon juice and 2 tablespoons chopped cilantro. Thoroughly coat both sides of the salmon fillets. Grill over medium-high heat, occasionally basting with sauce. Garnish with remaining chopped cilantro. Serves 4.

Katherine Huerter
Husband Daniel, 1971, Son Andrew, 2002

The basting sauce for this recipe is multipurpose, almost good enough to eat by the spoonful.

Mediterranean Salmon

2 pound salmon fillet

2 tablespoons olive oil, divided

½ cup chopped onion

½ cup chopped tomato

½ cup chopped parsley

½ cup chopped cucumber

½ cup chopped green pepper

Juice of 1 lemon

½ teaspoon salt

½ teaspoon ground black pepper

Preheat oven to 400 degrees. Cut salmon into 4 portions, 8 ounces each. With 1 tablespoon olive oil, grease baking pan large enough to hold salmon fillets in single layer. Place salmon in pan. Combine remaining ingredients, spoon over salmon. Bake 25-35 minutes or until done.

Mohamed Hamid
Son Shea, 2005

Mohamed is a longtime restaurateur whose Mohamed's Hummus products can be found in grocery stores.

Grilled Salmon with Creamy Horseradish Sauce

Salmon:

3 tablespoons olive oil

1 tablespoon prepared horseradish

2 tablespoons soy sauce

1 garlic clove, minced

½ teaspoon salt

¼ teaspoon black pepper

6 (1-inch thick) salmon fillets

Sauce:

¾ cup sour cream

¼ cup mayonnaise

2 tablespoons prepared horseradish

2 teaspoons soy sauce

2 tablespoons chopped fresh basil

1 tablespoon fresh lemon juice

1 tablespoon tarragon

Salt and pepper to taste

Whisk oil, horseradish, soy sauce, garlic, salt and pepper in bowl. Marinate salmon in mixture at least one hour. Mix all sauce ingredients together in small bowl, cover and chill.

Spray grill with non-stick spray. Or in oven, line a baking pan with foil. Grill salmon until opaque in center, about 4 minutes per side, or bake at 500 degrees for 30 minutes. Do not overcook. Serves 6.

Lynne Knott
Son Keaton, 2007

Jim "GeeGee" Gleeson, class of 1929, was a gifted athlete with a "can-do" personality. If you needed a touchdown or a clutch basket, Jim was your man. A member of the Rockhurst High School Athletic Hall of Fame, Jim played major league baseball with the Cleveland Indians, Chicago Cubs and Cincinnati Reds.

Tarragon Mustard Sauce

1 tablespoon Dijon mustard

1 teaspoon sugar

1 tablespoon white wine vinegar

1½ teaspoons finely chopped tarragon or ½ teaspoon dried tarragon

¼ cup olive oil

Combine all ingredients but oil, blend well, then slowly whisk in oil. Serve over salmon fillets.

Mary Reintjes
Husband Steve, 1975; Sons Steven, 2002, Peter, 2005

Salmon Burgers with Spinach

1 pound salmon fillet, skinned

4 ounces baby spinach, coarsely chopped (3 cups)

3 green onions, minced

1 tablespoon finely grated peeled fresh ginger

¼ teaspoon salt

¼ teaspoon black pepper

1 large egg white

1 tablespoon soy sauce

Vegetable oil

2 tablespoons pickled ginger, optional

Cut salmon into ¼-inch dice, then stir together with spinach, green onions, ginger, salt and pepper in a large bowl until well combined. Beat together egg white and soy sauce in a small bowl and stir into salmon mixture, then form into 4 patties. Patties can be formed 4 hours ahead and chilled on waxed paper-lined baking sheet, then covered with plastic wrap.

Heat a 12-inch non-stick skillet over moderate heat until hot and lightly brush with oil. Cook patties, carefully turning once, until golden brown and cooked through, 6-7 minutes total. Top with pickled ginger. Serves 4.

Laura Bluhm
Son Scott, 2007

Cashew-Garlic Butter

1 cup salted cashews

1 cup unsalted butter, room temperature

1½ teaspoons fresh lemon juice

1 tablespoon minced garlic

1 teaspoon salt

1 teaspoon hot pepper sauce

In food processor, coarsely chop cashews. Add remaining ingredients and pulse until well blended. Nuts should be finely chopped but not a paste. Serve with grilled or broiled fish.

Maraline Hayob
Son David, 2000

In 1950, the school was located on Troost. It was around 8:30 am and our class was at Mass. There were always two "proctors" who stood at the back of the chapel and on that memorable day it was Jim Taylor and me. Throughout the Mass smoke was appearing through the entrance of the chapel where Jim and I were making sure no one would try and sneak out during Mass.
Father Kellet was consecrating the host and had not taken notice of the smoke. Jim and I were getting increasingly nervous as the smoke was getting much thicker. We were frantically trying to signal Father, who still had his back to us. When he turned around with the Host up high for the prayer before distributing Communion, he saw what was happening and in stentorian tones (with host in hand) said "LET'S GET THE HELL OUT OF HERE!"

(Continued next page)

Salmon Rice Casserole

4 tablespoons butter

1 pound sharp cheddar cheese, grated

1 cup milk

1 onion, diced

4 cloves garlic, crushed

1 can Rotel

¼ cup chopped parsley

Salt and pepper to taste

4-8 drops hot pepper sauce

2 cans salmon, skinless, boneless

4 cups cooked rice

2 eggs, beaten

Preheat oven to 350 degrees. In a Dutch oven, melt butter over medium heat. Add cheese and milk, stirring until cheese has melted. Remove from heat and add onions, garlic, Rotel and parsley, blending well. Season with salt, pepper and hot pepper sauce. Fold in salmon and rice, mix well. Stir in eggs. Pour into a greased 9x13-inch casserole dish and bake uncovered until casserole is firmly set, about 45 minutes. Serves 6-8.

Kate Mahoney
Son John, 2006

Pan-Seared Lemon Sole

4 sole fillets

½ teaspoon kosher salt

¼ cup flour

4½ tablespoons unsalted butter, divided

1 lemon, cut into 12 thin circles

2 tablespoons capers, rinsed, drained

Season sole with salt, then coat in flour, shaking to remove excess. Melt one tablespoon butter in a large skillet over medium heat. Add lemon slices to skillet and cook until lemon is slightly browned, about 2 minutes. Push lemon to side of skillet and add sole. (Cook in batches if needed.) Cook until sole is the same color throughout and flakes easily, about 2 minutes per side. Add remaining butter and capers to skillet. Remove from heat, tilt skillet to swirl butter until melted. Place sole and lemon on serving plates, spoon capers and butter over top. Serves 4.

Sarah Jurcyk
Sons Jordan, 2006; Seth, 2008

(Continued from previous page)

Taylor and I tried our best to keep the panicked students from running over each other on the way out of the chapel. By this time there was total pandemonium and a few students jumped out the second story window. Shortly, we were all out of the building sitting on the grass when I suddenly remembered my lunch was in my locker in the basement and I ran back in to get it. One of the Jesuits observed this illogical action and said to me "Runyan, the only way you could be dumber is to be bigger." The reality is that when there is such a crisis and you're 14 or 15 years old, you tend to think about what's next and I immediately thought FOOD.

- Jack Runyan, 1951

Grilled Lemon-Mustard Fish Kabobs

½ cup lemon juice

1 tablespoon lemon zest

¼ cup Dijon mustard

¼ cup chopped fresh tarragon

¼ cup chopped fresh basil

¼ cup chopped fresh parsley

½ teaspoon salt

¼ teaspoon cracked black pepper

½ cup olive oil

Meaty firm fish, such as swordfish

Vegetables for grilling: cherry tomatoes, onions, mushrooms, peppers, etc.

Combine lemon juice, lemon zest, Dijon, mustard, tarragon, basil, parsley, salt and pepper in a small bowl. Slowly whisk in olive oil until well mixed. Cut fish and vegetables into large cubes. Place fish and vegetables in ziplock bag, pour marinade over. Marinate in refrigerator 2-4 hours. Thread fish and vegetables onto skewers, grill.

Wendy Zecy
Sons Kit, 2003; Connor, 2007; Cameron, 2009

Also good with chicken.

Marinated Grilled Swordfish

½ cup soy sauce

½ cup sherry

1 tablespoon lemon juice

¼ cup olive oil

1 clove garlic, crushed

6 swordfish fillets

Combine first 5 ingredients and blend well. Pour over fillets and marinate no longer than 3 hours. Preheat grill to high heat, or let coals burn until white. Brush grill with oil and cook fillets 5-8 minutes per side, or until cooked through. Serves 6.

Shelley Looby
Sons Colin, 2007; Kevin, 2007

Swordfish with Caper Sauce

2 tablespoons olive oil

½ cup chopped sweet onion

1 clove garlic, minced

1 (28-ounce) can plum tomatoes, coarsely chopped, liquid reserved

¼ cup dry white wine

½ cup chopped fresh basil

2 tablespoons capers, drained

¼ cup chopped kalamata olives

2 swordfish fillets

Cooking spray

Salt and pepper to taste

Heat oil over medium heat. Add onions, reduce heat, cook until soft, about 10 minutes. Add garlic, cook 1 minute. Add tomatoes and half the liquid. Simmer 15 minutes then add wine and cook 10 minutes or until liquid is reduced. Stir in basil, capers and olives.

Preheat grill until coals are white. Spray fish with cooking spray and season with salt and pepper. Grill five minutes per side or until cooked through. Spoon sauce over fillets. Serves 2-4.

Laura Bluhm
Son Scott, 2007

Potato-Rosemary Crusted Fish

12 ounces thick fish fillet, such as cod or halibut

1 small potato

Salt and pepper to taste

¼ teaspoon dried rosemary leaves, crushed

1 tablespoon extra-virgin olive oil

Rinse fish under cold water, pat dry. Cut in half. Sprinkle with salt and pepper. Peel potato and grate on large holes of grater. Squeeze excess water out of potato with paper towels. Season potato with salt, pepper and rosemary and press it around fish. Heat a nonstick frying pan over medium-high heat and add olive oil. Gently slide fish into pan.

Cook 3-5 minutes. Turn fish over and cook for another 3-5 minutes or until potatoes are golden and fish is done. Serves 2.

Sarah Jurcyk
Sons Jordan, 2006; Seth, 2008

In 2000, when we founded the Personal Finance & Investment Club, we knew our Accounting teacher and Coach Bernie Kreikemeier would be perfect as moderator. Coach helped us as we brought in guest speakers, conducted research and gave presentations on finance. Coach Kreik always challenged us in our club endeavors, just as he did in class. He would begin each class with a prayer, often one I came to very much appreciate - The Carpenter's House. I offered Coach a prayer I had always liked called The Player's Prayer. I later found out he had begun using this prayer with his teams before each game.

- Bryan Flanagan, 2002

Rare Tuna with Wasabi Aioli

1 tablespoon wasabi powder

½ teaspoon garlic powder

1 cup good quality mayonnaise

½ cup olive oil

1 tablespoon chopped fresh garlic

¼ teaspoon salt

¼ teaspoon fresh ground pepper

Good quality tuna steaks or fillets

Pickled ginger

Mix wasabi powder, garlic powder and mayonnaise. Put into a squirt bottle. Get grill hot, then mix olive oil, garlic, salt and pepper together and coat tuna with this mix. Immediately throw it on the grill. Time it for one minute, then turn and cook one minute more and you are done. Squirt wasabi aioli in an artistic fashion over tuna, top with pickled ginger.

Sean Cummings, "almost" class of 1981

Sean is chef-owner of several restaurants in Oklahoma City and Poco's Latino Cuisine in KC. He did not finish his high school career at RHS, (a decision made for him by the administration), but has fond memories of his Rockhurst days. In addition to this recipe, he shares several easy accompaniments to fish, which he calls "cheating": using some prepared ingredients to get a "made from scratch" taste.

Easy Tropical Fruit Salsa for Fish

16 ounces good, fresh pico de gallo (in most grocery stores)

1 good mango, diced

1 good kiwi, diced

2 tablespoons rice wine vinegar

1 teaspoon chopped mint

1 teaspoon chopped cilantro

Mix together and enjoy!

Sean Cummings, "almost" class of 1981

Red Pepper Coulis for Fish

1 jar roasted red peppers

1 cup chicken broth

½ teaspoon fresh ground pepper

¼ cup cream

Put all in a blender and whirl until smooth. Then put in a pan and bring to a boil. Serve under the fish, placing fish in an artistic manner on top of the sauce.

Sean Cummings, "almost" class of 1981

Fish with Quick High-End Green Chili Sauce

8-ounce can green chili sauce (also called green mole)

1 clove garlic

½ cup chicken broth

Fish fillets

Milk

Tortilla chips, ground in food processor

Heat green chili sauce, garlic and chicken broth together. Roll fish in milk, then in ground tortilla chips. Sauté until internal temperature is 120 degrees. Go buy the cheap $5 thermometer. Serve over green chili sauce.

Sean Cummings, "almost" class of 1981

Membership in the "R" Club was the zenith of any athlete's career during the early years of the high school.

June 4, 1928 - Rockhurst Circle honors the high school graduates of 1928 with a dance at the Garrett.

Asian Sole

1½ tablespoons toasted sesame oil

½ ounce dried shiitake mushrooms

8 (4-ounce) sole fillets

⅓ cup rice vinegar

3 tablespoons tamarind sauce

⅓ cup thinly sliced green onions (white part only)

1 tablespoon finely diced fresh ginger

½ cup chopped fresh cilantro

1 teaspoon sugar

2 tablespoons cornstarch

1 tablespoon cold water

Preheat oven to 350 degrees placing rack in the bottom third. Wipe a glass pie dish or other baking dish with some of the sesame oil. Discard shiitake stems and break caps into pieces. Grind in a blender until reduced to a fine powder. (About ⅓ cup.) Sift mushroom powder onto a large sheet of aluminum foil.

Carefully pull sole fillets apart. Coat fillets lightly in mushroom powder. Starting at thick end, roll each fillet into a paupiette (roll) and place in prepared baking dish spiral side up. Add vinegar, tamarind and remaining sesame oil to baking dish. Sprinkle fillets with green onions, ginger and remaining shiitake powder.

Bake fish for 18 minutes, remove from oven, and turn off oven. Transfer fish to an oven-proof serving dish and return to oven with oven door open to keep fish warm. Pour liquid from baking dish into a small saucepan (should be about ¾ cup). Add cilantro and bring to a boil. Add sugar, cook 2 minutes. Mix cornstarch and water, add to sauce and stir until thickened, about 30 seconds. Remove fish from oven. Spoon sauce over paupiettes and serve. Serves 6-8.

Shanthi Eckert
Husband Bill, 1982; Son Ryan, 2008

Red Snapper Veracruz

4 (6-ounce) red snapper or tilapia fillets

Cooking spray

½ teaspoon ground cumin

¼ teaspoon salt

¼ teaspoon ground red pepper

¼ cup chopped fresh cilantro

¼ cup chopped pitted green olives

¼ cup bottled salsa

16-ounce can black beans, drained

14.5-ounce can diced tomatoes, drained

4 lime wedges, optional

Preheat grill of broiler. Coat both sides of fish with cooking spray. Sprinkle fish with cumin, salt and pepper. Place fish on grill or broiler pan coated with cooking spray; cook for 5 minutes on each side or until fish flakes easily when tested with a fork.

Combine cilantro, green olives, salsa, black beans and tomatoes to make a salsa. Serve fish with salsa and lime wedges. Serves 4.

Laura Bluhm
Son Scott, 2007

Baked Roughy with Artichokes

2 pounds orange roughy fillets, cut in 4 pieces

1 tablespoon butter

½ medium onion, diced

2 stalks celery, diced

½ cup tomatoes, diced

14-ounce can artichoke hearts, drained, quartered

½ cup white wine or juice of 1 lemon

1 bay leaf

¼ cup freshly grated Parmesan cheese

Preheat oven to 350 degrees. Place fish in a baking dish. Melt butter in a medium pan. Add onion, celery, tomatoes and artichoke hearts and sauté for 1 minute. Add wine and bay leaf, cook for 3 minutes. Pour sauce over fish. Cover with foil, bake 15 minutes. Uncover, bake 5 minutes. Discard bay leaf and sprinkle with cheese. Serves 4.

Michelle Nemmers
Son John, 2008

Doug Bruce (class of 1967) and I are the only faculty who have been here for every president since the Greenlease campus opened. I am quite proud of that.
I still play rock and roll with my old bandmates. I am sure I have the distinction of being the only faculty member who has been told to get a haircut 4 times now by 3 different administrations. The boat rocking goes on. But the Jesuits made me the way I am.

- John McEniry, 1968; RHS Faculty member

Halibut with Feta Crumb Crust

6 tablespoons olive oil, divided

3 cups thinly sliced onions

2 tablespoons slivered garlic

1 cup thinly sliced fennel bulb

4 anchovies, rinsed, minced fine, optional

2 tablespoons chopped parsley

3 pounds plum tomatoes, chopped or 3 cups diced canned tomatoes, drained

Salt and pepper

2½ pounds halibut, cut into 1-inch pieces

¼ cup fresh basil

3 tablespoons capers, drained

¼ cup dry red wine

⅓ cup Parmesan cheese

½ cup crumbled feta cheese

3 tablespoons chopped pine nuts

½ cup panko or other dry breadcrumbs

1 tablespoon minced fresh thyme

Preheat oven to 350 degrees. In 3 tablespoons oil, saute onions, garlic and fennel until softened. Add anchovies and parsley and cook 2 minutes. Remove from heat

Lightly oil a 3-quart baking dish with 2 tablespoons olive oil. Spread half the onion mixture in bottom of dish. Scatter half the tomatoes on top and season with salt and several grindings of pepper. Arrange fish evenly on top of tomatoes and scatter basil and capers on top. Season well with more salt and pepper. Drizzle with red wine. Layer with remaining onion mixture, followed by tomatoes. Sprinkle top with Parmesan.

Combine feta, pine nuts, bread crumbs, thyme and remaining 1 tablespoon oil. Scatter over top of halibut. Casserole can be covered and refrigerated for up to 6 hours. Bake 30-35 minutes (40-45 minutes if refrigerated) or until fish is done and topping is a light golden brown. Serves 6-8.

Pat Shealy
Sons John, 2007; Westly, 2010

Sherried Crabmeat Pastries

¼ cup shallots, chopped

¼ cup finely chopped red pepper

⅓ cup butter, melted

¼ cup flour

¾ cup milk

1 pound lump crabmeat

¼ cup mayonnaise

2 tablespoons sherry

1 teaspoon Old Bay seasoning

½ teaspoon black pepper

5 dashes hot sauce

2 refrigerated pie crusts

Cook shallots and red peppers in butter over medium-high heat until tender. Whisk in flour. Cook one minute, whisking constantly. Gradually whisk in milk, and cook, whisking constantly until thick and bubbly. Stir in crab, mayonnaise, sherry, Old Bay, pepper and hot sauce.

Unfold pie crusts. Cut each in half. Divide crab mixture between pie crusts, placing on one side of the crust. Brush pastry edges with water, fold over into triangle and pinch to seal. Put on a baking sheet lined with parchment. Bake at 425 degrees about 20 minutes or until golden. Serves 4.

Jan Flanagan
Husband Jim, 1971; Sons Bryan, 2002; Sean, 2004; Kevin, 2007

Spicy Dipping Sauce

¾ cup mayonnaise

¼ cup spicy cocktail sauce

2 teaspoons fresh lemon juice

¼ teaspoon cayenne

¼-½ teaspoon Old Bay seasoning

Mix ingredients, cover and chill. Serve with shrimp, catfish nuggets, etc.

Tom Bergman
Grandsons Bryan Flanagan, 2002; Sean, 2004; Kevin, 2007

I like to jazz up plain cocktail sauce!

Principal Tom Murphy: His red hair and accompanying red face were a constant, his laugh hearty, his voice always filled with energy, passion and drive. Even during the worst of his illness as the ravages of cystic fibrosis took a toll on his body, he continued on. Every morning at 6:30, I would deliver school material to his home and keep him informed of happenings at the Rock. After one of those visits, I knew he would not return to his beloved school again. He did not. Tom died on December 28, 1999 at age 42.

- Larry Ruby, RHS Principal

Shrimp Stuffed with Crabmeat

8 tablespoons butter or olive oil, divided

1 pound crabmeat

Pinch of dried basil

Pinch of oregano

Pinch of thyme

¼ cup minced celery

½ cup minced onion

¼ cup chopped fresh parsley

1 tablespoon minced garlic

¼ cup mayonnaise

1 egg, beaten

1½ teaspoons hot sauce

3 tablespoons fresh lemon juice

1 tablespoon Worcestershire sauce

1½ cups crushed butter crackers (like Ritz), divided

Salt and pepper

20 fresh jumbo shrimp (about 2 pounds)

Paprika

Grease a large baking dish with 1 tablespoon butter or olive oil and set aside. Season crabmeat with basil, oregano and thyme. Cover and refrigerate.

Melt 4 tablespoons butter in medium skillet. Sauté celery and onion, stirring until transparent. Add parsley and garlic, stir and let cool. Add sautéed vegetables to crabmeat and toss with mayonnaise, beaten egg, hot sauce, lemon juice and Worcestershire sauce. Stir gently. Add 1 cup cracker crumbs, salt and pepper. Stir gently.

Peel shrimp, leaving on tail and first connecting segment. Devein and butterfly shrimp. Place 2 tablespoons crab mixture into each shrimp and press down. Sprinkle tops with remaining ½ cup cracker crumbs. Drizzle with 3 tablespoons melted butter, sprinkle with paprika. Bake at 325 degrees for 25 minutes. Serves 4-5.

Ann Marie Scahill
Son Michael, 2009

Shrimp Jambalaya

1 tablespoon vegetable oil

1 medium green pepper, cut into thin strips

½ cup chopped onion

½ cup chopped celery

1½ pounds boneless, skinless chicken breasts, cut into strips

2 tablespoons Creole seasoning, divided

14½-ounce can diced tomatoes, undrained

1 cup water

8-ounce can tomato sauce

½ pound medium shrimp, peeled, deveined

2 cups brown rice, uncooked

In a large skillet add oil, pepper, onions and celery and cook until tender but still crisp. Toss chicken with 1 tablespoon Creole seasoning. Add to skillet. Cook 2-3 minutes until chicken is cooked through. Add tomatoes, water, tomato sauce, shrimp and remaining 1 tablespoon seasoning. Mix well. Bring to a boil. Stir in rice, cover. Simmer for 5 minutes. Remove from heat and let stand, covered, 5 minutes. Fluff with fork. Serves 6-8.

Sondra Estes
Sons Joe, 2007; Vernon, 2009

Shrimp Etouffée

6 tablespoons butter

3 tablespoons flour

1 cup chopped onion

6 green onions, including tops, chopped

½ cup chopped bell pepper

½ cup chopped celery

2 cups water

3 pounds shrimp, peeled

¼ cup chopped parsley

Salt and pepper to taste

1 small bay leaf

Hot pepper sauce to taste

Cooked rice

In a skillet, melt butter, stir in flour. Stir constantly until this roux is a rich brown. Add vegetables, cook until tender. Stir in water, shrimp, parsley and seasonings. Simmer uncovered 20 minutes or until shrimp are done. Remove bay leaf. Serve over hot rice.

Jeannette Reintjes
Husband Bob, 1974;
Sons Robert, 2002; John, 2004; Paul, 2007; Michael, 2009

Shrimp Enchiladas Con Queso

Father William Steiner definitely fit his nickname of Mr. Sale-O-Rama. He knew in his head just how Sale-O had to be set up. He was great at giving a little TLC to donated items. A little glue, maybe a few nails, and many items were good as new. For many years he said Mass for us Sale-O moms on our Wednesday work day. Mass was celebrated in the Jesuit chapel, but in later years, Father said Mass in the basement of the Jesuit residence, in the midst of all the treasures of Sale-O!

- Mary Elizabeth Heiman Sons William, 1970; Terence, 1974; Gregory, 1978; Kevin, 1985; John, 1985

4 tablespoons olive oil, divided

½ cup chopped red bell pepper

½ cup minced onion

1 jalapeno pepper, cored, seeded, diced

1 fresh green chili pepper, cored, seeded, diced

½ teaspoon minced garlic

½ teaspoon dried oregano

½ teaspoon salt

Freshly ground black pepper to taste

Pinch cayenne

6 tablespoons flour

6 tablespoons water

2 cups milk

1½ cups Monterey Jack cheese, divided

½ cup sour cream

1½-2 pounds medium shrimp, peeled, deveined

¾ cup green onions, chopped, divided

2 medium tomatoes, peeled, seeded, chopped, divided

8 (8-inch) flour tortillas

Guacamole

Chipotle Tomatillo Salsa or purchased salsa

Chipotle Tomatilla Salsa:

2 tablespoons olive oil, divided

1 pound tomatillos, husked, quartered

1 small red onion, diced

2-3 dried or canned chipotle peppers, seeded, finely minced

½ cup loosely packed chopped fresh cilantro

1 tablespoon red wine vinegar or balsamic vinegar

Shrimp Enchiladas: Preheat oven to 350 degrees. Grease a 9x13-inch baking dish. In a heavy saucepan, heat 2 tablespoons olive oil over medium heat. Add bell pepper, onion, jalapeno, green chili, garlic and oregano. Cook until tender, about 5 minutes, stirring occasionally. Stir in salt, pepper, and cayenne.

In small bowl, combine flour and water, whisk to blend and add to bell pepper mixture. Add milk and stir until well blended. Reduce heat and simmer until slightly thickened, stirring constantly about 3 minutes. Add 1 cup Monterey Jack and stir until melted. Remove from heat and stir in sour cream.

In large skillet, heat remaining 2 tablespoons olive oil over high heat. Add shrimp and ½ cup green onions. Stir until shrimp just turn pink, about 2 minutes. Stir in half the bell pepper mixture and half the tomatoes. Remove from heat. Spoon approximately ½ cup shrimp mixture onto 1 tortilla and roll tightly. Place seam

Continued on next page

side down in prepared baking dish and repeat with remaining tortillas. May be prepared to this point up to 2 hours in advance. Cover and chill.

Top enchiladas with remaining bell pepper mixture. Cover with foil and bake 30-40 minutes, until thoroughly heated. Top with remaining Monterey Jack, green onions and remaining tomatoes. Garnish with guacamole and salsa. Serves 6-8.

Chipotle Tomatillo Salsa: In skillet, heat 1 tablespoon olive oil over medium-high heat. Add tomatillos and cook 5 minutes. Remove, chop and set aside. Add remaining 1 tablespoon olive oil to skillet. Add red onion and reduce heat to medium. Cook until browned, about 8 minutes. Return reserved tomatillos to skillet and stir in chipotle chilies. Remove from heat and stir in cilantro and vinegar. May be prepared up to 2 days in advance. Cover and chill. Serve warm or at room temperature.

Patti Gound
Sons Ryan, 2003; Matthew, 2007

Shrimp Diane

10 tablespoons unsalted butter, divided	**¼ teaspoon basil**
¼ cup minced green onion	**⅛ teaspoon oregano**
½ teaspoon salt	**2 pounds shrimp, peeled, deveined**
¼ teaspoon cayenne	**½ pound mushrooms, thinly sliced, optional**
½ teaspoon white pepper	
¼ teaspoon black pepper	**¼ cup vegetable broth or dry white wine or fish stock**
½ teaspoon minced garlic	**3 tablespoons chopped fresh parsley**
¼ teaspoon thyme	

Heat 8 tablespoons butter in large skillet over high heat. When butter is almost melted, add green onions, salt, cayenne, white and black peppers, garlic, thyme, basil and oregano. Stir well. Reduce heat, add shrimp and sauté until pink, about 1-2 minutes, shaking pan instead of stirring. Add mushrooms, broth and remaining butter, shaking pan until butter sauce is smooth. Garnish with parsley. Serve over pasta. Serves 4.

Tim O'Brien
Sons Kyle, 2005; Evan, 2008

Shrimp and Feta

2 tablespoons vegetable oil

4 cloves garlic, minced

2 (14-ounce) cans stewed tomatoes

½ cup chopped kalamata olives, optional

1 teaspoon dried oregano

2 tablespoons chopped parsley

Salt and pepper to taste

1 pound raw shrimp, peeled, deveined

2 ounces crumbled feta cheese

In a large skillet, heat oil over medium-high heat, add garlic and cook until just beginning to brown. Add tomatoes, olives, oregano, parsley, salt and pepper. Reduce heat to low and simmer until thickened, about 20 minutes. When sauce has thickened, add shrimp and feta. Cook until shrimp are pink, about 5 minutes. Ladle over cooked rice or pasta. Serves 4.

Jan Flanagan
Husband Jim, 1971; Sons Bryan, 2002; Sean, 2004; Kevin, 2007

Scallops in Wine

2 pounds scallops

2 cups dry white wine

¼ cup butter, plus additional for topping

4 shallots, thinly sliced

24 mushrooms, thinly sliced

2 tablespoons chopped parsley

2 tablespoons flour

2-4 tablespoons heavy cream

Breadcrumbs

Paprika

Simmer scallops about 5 minutes in wine. Drain, reserve liquid. Melt ¼ cup butter and sauté shallots, mushrooms and parsley. Stir in flour and add reserved liquid and cream. Add scallops to the hot mixture. Place in a shallow casserole dish and cover with a mixture of dry breadcrumbs, dots of butter and paprika. Broil until golden brown. Serves 6-8.

Lynne Knott
Son Keaton, 2007

Poultry AND Meats

POULTRY *AND* MEATS

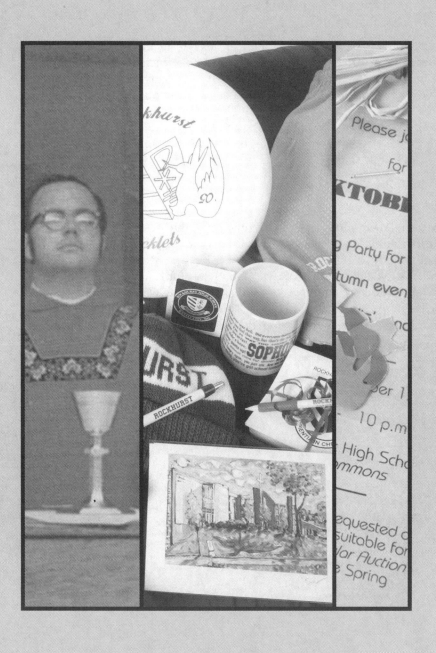

1980s

National:

Such acronyms as CNN and PC entered the American lexicon in the 1980s. Ted Turner's Cable News Network began broadcasting in 1980, and IBM introduced the personal computer the following year. The fledgling news network had plenty of compelling stories to cover in its early years: the underdog US national hockey team pulled off the "Miracle on Ice" against the Soviet Union at the 1980 Lake Placid Olympic Games, the Mir Space Station entered orbit, the Berlin Wall came tumbling down, and the Exxon Valdez spilled millions of gallons of oil into Prince William Sound during the decade. "Rad" 80s trends included Cabbage Patch Kids and Rubik's Cubes.

Local:

The Kansas City Royals learned in the 1980s that, sometimes, the second time is the charm. After falling to the Philadelphia Phillies in the 1980 World Series, Kansas City beat cross-state foe St. Louis in the controversy-laden "I-70 Series" to become baseball's World Series champions in 1985. Not all sports news was good news for Kansas City in the 80s, as the basketball Kings left for Sacramento in 1986. Sadly, the decade was marred by two fatal disasters; in 1981 the Hyatt skywalk collapsed killing 114, and in 1988 six firefighters battling a pre-dawn blaze on the city's east side died when highway construction ammonium nitrate was ignited. In the world of business, Westwood-based United Telecommunications Inc. and Connecticut-based GTE Corp. merged into what would become Sprint, establishing headquarters in Westwood.

Grilled Mulberry Street Chicken Thighs

8 chicken thighs (skin on if grilling, removed if baking)

6 cloves garlic, finely chopped

½ bunch flat leaf parsley, finely chopped

leaves from 1 stem fresh oregano, finely chopped

1 cup olive oil

1 cup freshly squeezed lemon juice (about 6 lemons)

1 teaspoon sea salt

1 teaspoon freshly ground pepper or to taste

2 large celery stalks with leaves for basting, if grilling outside

Combine all ingredients in a large freezer ziplock bag and marinate overnight in refrigerator, turning occasionally. Before cooking, bring to room temperature to let olive oil liquify.

If grilling, remove chicken, reserving marinade, and place on grill that is not too hot. Grill for about 30 minutes, using celery stalk and leaves to brush on marinade frequently. If cooking in oven, pour all ingredients into a baking dish together and cook uncovered for 30 minutes at 350 degrees, then pour off most of the marinade and bake or broil, marinating chicken a few times until browned. Serves 4.

Joy Blake-Krug
Son Colin, 2003

This is a great dish to serve in the summer as it can easily be served at room temperature.

Pantry Drummies

16 chicken drummies or wings

1 cup ketchup

¼ cup Dijon mustard

¼ cup hot sauce

¼ cup soy sauce

1 tablespoon light brown sugar

In a large, shallow baking dish, combine ketchup with mustard, hot sauce, soy sauce and brown sugar. Add chicken and turn to coat. Cover and refrigerate overnight.

Prepare grill. Remove chicken from sauce; reserve remaining sauce. Grill drummies over medium-hot fire, turning and basting with reserved sauce until nicely charred and cooked through, about 30 minutes. Stop basting during last 5 minutes of grilling and discard any remaining sauce. Serve drummies hot or at room temperature. Serves 4.

Alison Ward
Sons Brian, 2004; David, 2004; Taylor, 2006

Serve with celery stalks and blue cheese or ranch dressing. Easily doubled. Great for a tailgate.

Granny's Mustard

3 tablespoons dry mustard

3 tablespoons sugar

3 tablespoons cider vinegar

2 eggs

¼ cup butter

Mix mustard, sugar and vinegar in double boiler until hot. Stir in eggs and cook until thick, stirring constantly over lowest heat. Add butter, stir until melted and mixed in well. Keeps for 2-3 weeks in refrigerator. Great with ham or spring rolls.

Sarah Jurcyk
Sons Jordan, 2006; Seth, 2008

I remember David Cone throwing 95 mile an hour fastballs against the cafeteria wall.

- Jim Russell, 1981

Senior (1997) Chris Heier won the Silver Key award at the Western Missouri Regional Art Awards for a piece of pottery he created. Chris was in Mrs. Connie Greany's advanced hand pottery class.

Grilled Chicken with Lemon Vinaigrette

4 boneless skinless chicken breasts

½ cup balsamic vinegar

½ cup olive oil

Honey to taste

½ cup or more olive oil

Kosher salt and freshly ground pepper to taste

Vinaigrette:

Zest, juice and pulp (without seeds) of 2 lemons

1 tablespoon fresh rosemary, chopped

Garnish:

4 ounces feta cheese, crumbled

Kalamata olives

Fresh rosemary sprigs

Marinate chicken breasts in olive oil and balsamic vinegar for at least 1-2 hours before grilling. Meanwhile, combine all vinaigrette ingredients except olive oil in a mixing bowl. Add olive oil to the other ingredients slowly while constantly whisking to form an emulsion. Taste vinaigrette for balance, adding more lemon, olive oil and/or honey as needed. Season with salt and pepper.

Grill chicken breasts over charcoal until chicken is tender and fully cooked, turning once. Place chicken on serving platter or individual plates and drizzle with lemon vinaigrette. Garnish with feta, olives and fresh rosemary sprigs. Serve immediately or at room temperature. Serves 4.

Laura O'Rourke
The Culinary Center of Kansas City
Husband Kevin, 1972; Sons Delaney, 2008; Devin, 2010

Father Frommelt was the advisor to the Camera Club. Contest winners were Joseph Flaherty, first place for "Monkey Island"; John Sullivan, 2nd place for "The Scout."

- 1947 yearbook

Chicken Curry

1 teaspoon salt

½ teaspoon pepper

¼ teaspoon garlic powder

¼ teaspoon seasoned salt

2 tablespoons curry powder

4 whole chicken breasts, cut into 1-inch strips

4 tablespoons butter

2 tablespoons olive oil

4 tablespoons green onions, chopped

2 cups or more chicken broth

6 tablespoons slivered almonds, chopped

2 small apples, peeled, chopped

1 onion, chopped

2 celery stalks, chopped

2 teaspoons cornstarch

½ cup heavy cream

½ teaspoon cayenne pepper

Ground nutmeg

Combine first 5 ingredients, coat chicken strips. Melt butter and olive oil in a skillet. Sauté chicken and green onions until lightly browned.

Cut chicken into bite-sized pieces and return to skillet. Add chicken broth, almonds, apples, onion and celery to skillet and bring to a boil. Reduce heat and simmer 25 minutes. Combine cornstarch, cream, cayenne and nutmeg. Stir into chicken and bring to a boil again. For a more intense curry flavor, add an additional 1 teaspoon curry to chicken mixture.

Serve over white rice with an assortment of traditional accompaniments: chopped green onions, chopped bacon, flaked coconut, peanuts, raisins, currants, chutney and chopped green pepper. Serves 8.

Annie Osborn
Son Scott Miller, 2007

I serve this on Christmas Eve.

Mediterranean Chicken with Feta Cheese

8 ounces orzo pasta

2 pounds boneless, skinless chicken breast halves, fresh or frozen

2 tablespoons olive oil

1 large onion, chopped (about 2 cups)

1 tablespoon minced garlic

1 teaspoon dried oregano

1 teaspoon dried basil

1 cup white wine

2 (14-ounce) cans chopped tomatoes with garlic and oregano

8 ounces feta cheese

1 cup chopped fresh parsley

Bring 2½ quarts unsalted water to a boil in a 4½-quart or larger Dutch oven or soup pot. Add orzo to boiling water and cook 8 minutes or until orzo is tender. Drain and set aside.

Heat oil over medium heat in an extra deep 12-inch non-stick skillet. Add onion. Cut chicken (fresh or partly defrosted) into bite-sized pieces, adding pieces to the skillet as you cut. After about a ½ cup chicken is in the pan, increase heat to medium-high and continue to cut and add remaining chicken to pan. Cook chicken, stirring from time to time, until it is no longer pink outside, about 3 minutes. While chicken cooks, add garlic, oregano and basil. Stir frequently.

When chicken is cooked through, stir in wine and cook 1 minute. Add tomatoes with juice and feta cheese. Add parsley. Stir and cook 1 more minute and then serve over orzo. Serves 4.

Mary Reintjes
Husband Steve, 1975; Sons Steven, 2002; Peter, 2005

The 1959 freshman football team coached by Beach Tuckness was undefeated, untied, and unscored upon!

Construction of a new stadium will include an artificial turf field, permanent homefield stands and an eight-lane Mondo Track. Other parts of the Phase II renovations will include a new parking lot and closing of the circle drive.

- 2002 yearbook

Chicken Cacciatore

Salt and pepper

3-4 boneless chicken breasts

¼ cup olive oil

2 cloves garlic, crushed

2 yellow peppers, sliced

1 medium onion, sliced

8 ounces mushrooms, sliced

Garlic salt to taste

Basil

Parsley

28-ounce can crushed tomatoes

1 can tomato paste

¼ cup Merlot wine

12-16 ounces fettuccini, cooked

Grated Parmesan cheese

Salt and pepper chicken. Brown chicken in olive oil with crushed garlic in a large fry pan. When browned, reduce heat. Add peppers, onion, mushrooms, garlic salt, basil and parsley. Add crushed tomatoes, tomato paste and wine. Stir mixture and cook covered until vegetables are soft, 20-25 minutes. Serve over a bed of fettuccini with grated cheese. Serves 3-4.

Fred Campisano
RHS Faculty member

Bruschetta Chicken Bake

14.5-ounce can diced tomatoes, undrained

2 cloves garlic, minced

6-ounce package Stove Top Stuffing Mix for Chicken

½ cup water

1½ pounds boneless, skinless chicken breasts, cut into bite-sized pieces

1 cup dried basil leaves

1 cup shredded mozzarella cheese

Preheat oven to 400 degrees. Place tomatoes with liquid in a medium bowl. Add garlic, stuffing mix and water; stir just until stuffing mix is moistened. Set aside. Place chicken in a 9x13-inch baking dish, sprinkle with basil and cheese. Top with stuffing mixture. Bake 30 minutes or until chicken is cooked through. Serves 6.

Jean Barnhart
Sons Nicholas, 1983; Lucas, 1987; Alexander, 2000
RHS Cafeteria manager

Rosemary Chicken with Pinot Noir Risotto

Bottle of Pinot Noir wine

2 (14½-ounce) cans chicken broth

¼ cup butter or margarine, divided

2 large shallots, chopped

1 carrot, chopped

2 leeks, cut into 2-inch strips

1 celery stalk, chopped

4 garlic cloves, minced

1½ cups uncooked Arborio rice

1½ teaspoons salt, divided

1½ teaspoons pepper, divided

1 tablespoon chopped parsley

1 tablespoon chopped fresh rosemary

6 skinned and boned chicken breast halves

Fresh rosemary sprigs to garnish

Heat wine and broth in a large saucepan over medium-high heat, keep hot. Melt 2 tablespoons butter in a large heavy skillet over medium-high heat, add shallots, carrots, leeks, celery and garlic and sauté until tender. Add rice and sauté, stirring constantly, 1 minute. Reduce heat to medium, add ½ cup hot wine mixture. Cook, stirring constantly, until liquid is absorbed. Repeat procedure with remaining wine mixture, ½ cup at a time. Cooking time is about 30 minutes. Stir in ½ teaspoon salt, ½ teaspoon pepper and parsley, keep warm.

Sprinkle remaining 1 teaspoon salt, remaining 1 teaspoon pepper and chopped fresh rosemary evenly over chicken. Melt remaining 2 tablespoons butter in a 12-inch skillet over medium heat. Add chicken and cook 3 minutes on each side or until done. Cut chicken lengthwise into slices, cutting to within ½ inch of opposite end. Spoon risotto onto serving plate. Top with chicken, spreading slices to fan. Garnish, if desired. Serves 6.

Wendy Zecy
Sons Kit, 2003; Connor, 2007; Cameron, 2009

The Vincent P. Dasta memorial athletic field was a gift from friends of the Kansas City builder and civic leader who died in March 1963 at the age of 49. The 10-acre tract cost $130,000.

In National Forensic League competition, Tom O'Malley took 2nd honors in Oratorical Declamation and 5th in Original Oratory. Tom Shine was 4th in Humorous. Ted Brockman took 6th in Serious Declamation.

- 1950 Chancellor Yearbook

Turkey Tenderloins Florentine

1 lemon

¼ pound sweet Italian sausage

4 tablespoons olive oil, divided

1 onion, chopped

1 celery rib, chopped

1 cup Italian breadcrumbs

½ (10-ounce) package frozen spinach, thawed, squeezed dry

1 egg

2 large boneless, skinless turkey breasts

4 tablespoons flour, divided

¼ teaspoon paprika

¼ teaspoon salt

1 cup water

2 tablespoons dry white wine

¼ cup cream or half & half

Cut 4 thin slices from lemon and reserve for garnish. Squeeze 1 teaspoon lemon juice, set aside. Cook sausage over medium heat in 2 tablespoons olive oil, add onion and celery. Remove skillet from heat and stir in breadcrumbs, spinach and egg until well blended. Cut turkey into four equal pieces and using a meat mallet, pound each piece into ¼-inch thickness. Place ¼ the sausage mixture in middle of each turkey piece, roll up and secure with a toothpick.

Mix 2 tablespoons flour, paprika and salt, then dredge turkey pieces in mixture. In a skillet over medium heat in remaining 2 tablespoons olive oil, brown turkey on all sides. Add water, wine and reserved lemon juice. Reduce heat to low, simmer for 30 minutes. When turkey is done, remove to warm platter. Mix cream with remaining 2 tablespoons flour until blended. Stir cream mixture into bubbling liquid in skillet, stirring until smooth. Spoon over turkey and garnish with lemon slices. Serves 4.

Martie Eftink
Son Jim, 2003

I will never forget the sight of my classmates, in our RHS navy coats and ties, as we formed an honor guard at the funeral service of our classmate Tyler Hansen, who passed away our freshman year during PE class.
We were all nervous and scared and unsure of what to do when one of our own had fallen.
I think it made us come together as a class early on.

-Bryan Flanagan, 2002

Chicken with Tarragon Sauce

4 boneless skinless chicken breast halves

Salt and pepper

2 tablespoons flour, plus additional for dusting

3 tablespoons butter

1 cup chicken broth

½ cup light cream

1-2 teaspoons dried tarragon

Pound chicken breasts between sheets of plastic wrap to about ½-inch thickness. Pat chicken dry. Sprinkle with salt and pepper, then dust with flour to coat. Melt butter in skillet and add chicken breasts. Brown chicken in butter 15-20 minutes. Remove to warm serving platter.

Stir 2 tablespoons flour into skillet drippings. Cook for 2 minutes. Add chicken broth and light cream. Cook over moderate heat for 10 minutes, stir in tarragon. Pour over warm chicken breasts. Serve with rice and asparagus spears. Serves 4.

Mary Reintjes
Husband Steve, 1975; Sons Steven, 2002; Peter, 2005

Chicken Breasts and Goat Cheese

4 boneless chicken breasts with skin

8 ounces herbed goat cheese

12-29 fresh basil leaves

Salt and pepper to taste

Olive oil

1 tablespoon butter

2 shallots, chopped

¾ cup heavy cream

¼ cup chicken stock

Cut a 1x2-inch pocket in center of breasts directly under skin of chicken. Wrap ½-ounce piece of goat cheese in two basil leaves and place leaves directly under skin on top side of breast. Season with salt and pepper. Sauté chicken in light film of olive oil and a pat of butter for 10 minutes. Simmer shallots with cream and stock until sauce is reduced by ⅔. Put remaining basil leaves into sauce for 1-2 minutes. Slice chicken and arrange over sauce. Serves 4.

Joy Blake-Krug
Son Colin, 2003

The 1975 Quarry pictures a benefit basketball game with Rockhurst faculty members playing members of the Kansas City Chiefs.

Varsity soccer won state the 2nd year in a row with a final record of 27-1-1. Team members included Managers Mike Strain and Bobby Mata, Scott Siegel, Brent Coppage, Jarrett Devereaux, Ryan Raybould, Matt Bowen, Jason Woods, Lance Snodgrass, Brendan Matthews, Luke Maese, Joe Burns, Chris Hentzen, Jeff Tanner, Jim Davey, Josh Williams, Jamie Brecheisen, Matt Jewett, Will Banning, Matt Darby, Brian Siegel, Head Coach Chris Lawson and coaches Kevin Charcut and Kevin McArdle.

- 2000 yearbook

Crockpot Lemon Chicken

3 pound broiler-fryer

Salt and pepper

½ teaspoon dried rosemary, divided

1 teaspoon dry oregano, divided

3 garlic cloves, minced, divided

2 tablespoons butter

¼ cup sherry or chicken broth

¼ cup lemon juice

Wash chicken and pat dry. Season generously with salt and pepper. Sprinkle half the rosemary, oregano and garlic inside cavity of chicken. Melt butter in frying pan. Brown chicken on all sides. Transfer to a slow cooker or crockpot, sprinkle with remaining rosemary, oregano and garlic.

Add sherry to frying pan and stir to loosen browned bits. Pour into crockpot. Cook on low for 7 hours, then add lemon juice and cook an additional hour. Remove chicken from pot, cut into pieces. Serve juices over chicken. Serves 4.

James Flanagan, 1937
Sons James, 1971; Terry 1975
Grandsons Bryan, 2002; Sean, 2004; Kevin, 2007
Grandson Nick Vaughn, RHS Faculty member

Easy and delicious!

Sweet and Sour Chicken

6-8 chicken breast halves

18-ounce jar apricot preserves

8-ounce bottle Russian dressing

1 envelope dry onion soup mix

Place chicken in shallow baking dish. Combine remaining ingredients, pour over chicken. Bake covered at 350 degrees for 1 hour 15 minutes.

Kathleen Murphy-Marx
Son Ian, 2004

Macadamia Nut Chicken

½ cup breadcrumbs

½ cup chopped macadamia nuts

¼ teaspoon salt

4 boneless, skinless chicken breasts

1 egg

¼ cup butter, divided

1 tablespoon olive or salad oil

½ cup chicken broth

½ cup orange juice

Radicchio or Boston lettuce leaves

Orange sections

Combine breadcrumbs, macadamia nuts and salt on a sheet of waxed paper. Beat egg with a fork in a pie plate. Dip each breast into egg, then in breadcrumb mixture.

In a large skillet, heat 2 tablespoons butter with oil, add chicken breasts. Cook until golden on all sides, approximately 5 minutes. Reduce heat to low, cover and cook an additional 5-7 minutes until chicken is fork tender. (If chicken breasts are thick, they may need to be baked an additional 15-25 minutes at 350 degrees.) Remove chicken and keep warm.

Pour chicken broth and orange juice into skillet. Heat to boiling. Cook until sauce is reduced by ⅓. Blend in remaining butter 1 tablespoon at a time until sauce thickens. Pour over chicken. Serve with radicchio leaves and orange sections. Serves 4.

Laura Foley

The 1987 football state semi-finals were on Jeff City's home field. I remember watching the football sail through the uprights as time expired, ensuring another RHS march to the championship (which we then won.) Students, parents and faculty poured from the visitor's bleachers and trampled the chain link fence separating the field from the stands. Being in the middle of the victory swarm at mid-field is a favorite memory. And then we cheered ecstatically at the championship pep rally when our school president said that paying Jeff City for the damaged fence was the best check he ever wrote.

- Rob Rastorfer, 1989 [editor's note to students: don't even think about it today!]

Baked Chicken and Artichokes

6-8 boneless, skinless chicken breasts

1 tablespoon salt

½ teaspoon paprika

¼ teaspoon pepper

¼ cup plus 2 tablespoons butter or margarine, divided

9-ounce package frozen artichoke hearts, thawed

¼ pound fresh mushrooms, sliced

2 tablespoons flour

⅔ cup chicken broth

3 tablespoons dry sherry

Sprinkle chicken with salt, paprika and pepper. Melt ¼ cup butter in large skillet, brown chicken over low heat. Transfer to a greased shallow 2-quart casserole. Reserve drippings in skillet. Arrange artichoke hearts between chicken breasts, set aside.

Add remaining butter to reserved drippings, melt over low heat. Add mushrooms, sauté 4-5 minutes. Stir flour into mushrooms, gradually add chicken broth and sherry, mixing well. Cook over medium heat, stirring constantly until thickened, about 5 minutes. Pour sauce over chicken and artichokes. Cover and bake at 375 degrees for 40 minutes. Serves 6-8.

Joan Jones
Son Spencer, 2006

Chicken Adobo

1 cup white vinegar

1 head garlic

1 bay leaf

4 tablespoons soy sauce

Whole chicken, cut into pieces

2 tablespoons salt

1½ cups water or Sprite

Combine vinegar, garlic, bay leaf and soy sauce in large pot. Add chicken and salt, soak 20-10 minutes. Add water or Sprite, simmer uncovered until tender.

Elvie Leone
Son Jonathan, 2009

Chicken Chalupas

12 ounces Monterey Jack cheese, grated

12 ounces sharp cheddar cheese, grated

1 bunch green onions, tops only, chopped

2 (10-ounce) cans cream of chicken soup

4-ounce can chopped green chilies

16-ounce carton sour cream

1 cup sliced black olives

8 boneless chicken breast halves, cooked, cut into 1-inch pieces

12 (6-inch) flour tortillas

Combine cheeses, reserve half for topping and half for filling. Divide green onion tops into two equal portions. Combine ½ the cheeses, ½ the onion tops, soup, chilies, sour cream and olives. Set aside 1½ cups of this mixture for topping. Add chicken to the remainder for filling. Mix well.

Put 3 heaping tablespoons of filling on each tortilla and roll. Place tortillas seam side down in a lightly buttered 9x13-inch baking dish. Arrange tortillas in a single layer, using two baking dishes if necessary. Spread reserved topping mixture over tortillas. Cover with reserved cheeses and onion tops. Cover and refrigerate for 6 hours or overnight.

Preheat oven to 350 degrees. Bake uncovered for 45 minutes. Let stand a few minutes before serving. Serves 8-10.

Diane Bradshaw
Son Andrew, 2003

Physics was most fun under Fr. Frommelt. He was happy to encourage my interest. I was like a kid in a candy store exploring all the fun things stored on the shelves in the lab. I took a special interest in the spark generators. One afternoon we were visited by the principal Fr. Guinta, and when he leaned on the metal edge of the lab bench, I let him have it with the spark generator. Luckily he had a sense of humor and I did not get expelled!

- George J. Frye, 1949

Baked Chicken Chimichangas

1 onion, diced

16 ounces picante sauce

7 cups cooked chicken (about 6-8 breasts)

2½ teaspoons cumin

1½ teaspoons oregano

Salt and pepper

12 ounces shredded cheddar cheese (or other cheese)

20 flour tortillas

Olive oil

Toppings: guacamole, chopped tomatoes, diced green onions, diced black olives, shredded lettuce

Sauté onion and combine with 1½-2 cups picante sauce and next 4 ingredients. Cook over medium-low heat stirring often until liquid has evaporated, about 25 minutes. Cool slightly. Add cheese. Place about ⅓ cup mixture down center of each tortilla. Fold ends in and fold lids over each other to make a package.

Place on a cookie sheet that has been brushed or sprayed with olive oil or cooking spray. Spray tops of tortillas with olive oil. Preheat oven to 425 degrees. Bake 8 minutes. Turn chimichangas over and spray or brush with olive oil. Bake 5 minutes more. Serve with salsa and toppings. Makes 12-18.

Karen Reintjes McLeese
Father Robert, 1945

Chicken Picante

1½ cups picante sauce

3 tablespoons packed brown sugar

1 tablespoon Dijon mustard

4 boneless chicken breast halves

3 cups hot cooked rice

Mix picante sauce, brown sugar and mustard. Place chicken in shallow baking dish, pour sauce over. Bake 20 minutes at 400 degrees or until done. Serve with rice. Serves 4.

Sue Dierks
Husband Bernard, 1955; Sons Chris, 1986; Michael, 1991

Chicken Pockets

3-ounce package cream cheese, softened

3 tablespoons butter, softened, divided

2 cups diced, cooked chicken breast

1 tablespoon chopped pimientos

1 tablespoon chopped chives

½ teaspoon dried tarragon

¼ teaspoon salt

⅛ teaspoon pepper

2 tablespoons milk

8-ounce can refrigerated crescent rolls

¾ cup crushed seasoned croutons

Preheat oven to 350 degrees. In mixing bowl, combine cream cheese and 2 tablespoons butter. Add chicken, pimiento, chives, tarragon, salt, pepper and milk. Blend well. Set aside.

Separate crescent roll dough into 4 rectangles. Press seams together well. Fill each rectangle with ¼ the chicken mixture. Pull up corners and pinch all seams closed. Melt remaining 1 tablespoon of butter and brush on dough. Dip lightly in crushed croutons. Place on an ungreased baking sheet and bake 20-25 minutes or until golden brown. Serves 4.

Diane Bradshaw
Son Andrew, 2003

Great for a luncheon, baptism, or large family gathering.

Being involved as a parent at Rockhurst has been a great experience and blessing to our whole family. From hosting refreshments for music or sports ceremonies, potluck dinners, serving hungry boys in the cafeteria, cheering them on in sports, music, plays and academics. It's been amazing to see our sons nurtured as young "Men for Others." Thank you!

- Dan & Terri Bly
Sons Ryan, 2002;
Andrew, 2005

Chicken Pot Pie

1 can cream of chicken soup

½ cup milk, plus additional for brushing on crust

½ teaspoon garlic salt

½ teaspoon black pepper

2 cups chopped cooked chicken

8-ounce bag frozen mixed vegetables (corn, carrots, peas, green beans)

2 cups diced potatoes, cooked

4 ounces chopped mushrooms, sautéed in 1 tablespoon butter, optional

2 refrigerated pie crusts

Preheat oven to 350 degrees. In large mixing bowl, blend together soup, milk and seasonings. Add in chicken, frozen vegetables, potatoes and mushrooms. Mix gently until combined. Place one crust in an ungreased 9-inch deep dish pie pan. Pour mixture into crust, top with remaining crust. Flute crust edges, cut vents into top of crust. Brush with milk. Bake 55 minutes or until crust is golden brown. Let stand 15 minutes. Serves 6.

For Individual Pot Pies: Preheat oven to 350 degrees. Cut 2 pie crusts into quarters, to yield 8 equal pieces. Coat insides of 4 small aluminum foil pans (4½ inches in diameter, 1¼ inches deep) or 4 ramekins with cooking spray. Line bottom of each with a quarter of the crust, molding it with fingers to fit. Spoon about ⅔ cup mixture into each ramekin. Top each with a pie crust quarter. Pinch edges together and cut vents in the top. Place on baking sheet and bake 25-35 minutes or until golden brown. Serves 4.

For another crust option, try Phyllo-Parmesan Crust:
6 tablespoons melted butter
16-20 sheets phyllo, thawed
¼ cup finely grated Parmesan cheese

Preheat oven to 425 degrees. Pour pot pie mixture into a 9x9-inch casserole pan. Place 1 phyllo sheet on work surface (cover remainder with a damp cloth). Brush phyllo with butter, covering entire surface. Using both hands, gently scrunch buttered phyllo into a loose ball about 2½-3 inches in diameter. Set balls on top of chicken mixture. Repeat with remaining phyllo sheets until filling is covered. Sprinkle with Parmesan. Bake 15 minutes, reduce heat to 350 degrees, and bake for 20 minutes. Tent with foil to prevent over-browning. Serves 4.

Alison Ward
Sons Brian, 2004; David, 2004; Taylor, 2006

Jim Flanagan scored both goals as Rockhurst High clinched the championship of the Inter-State Soccer federation with a 2-1 victory over Hogan. Hogan is in 2nd place in the 7 team league, followed in order by Ward, Pem-Day, DeLaSalle, Miege, Savior of the World.

- newspaper clipping Feb 11, 1971

Chicken with Figs

2 chickens (2½-3 pounds each), cut into 8 pieces each

6 large cloves garlic, finely minced

2 tablespoons dried thyme

1 tablespoon ground cumin

1 teaspoon ground ginger

1 teaspoon salt

½ cup red wine vinegar

½ cup olive oil

4 teaspoons green peppercorns (packed in water), drained

1 cup black olives

1½ cups dried apricots

1 cup dried small figs or large fig pieces

¼ cup packed brown sugar

½ cup Madeira

1 cup large pecan pieces

Grated zest of 2 lemons

One day before, combine chicken, garlic, thyme, cumin, ginger, salt, red wine vinegar, oil, peppercorns, olives, apricots and figs in a large bowl. Cover and marinate in refrigerator overnight. Remove bowl from refrigerator 1 hour before cooking.

Preheat oven to 350 degrees. Arrange chicken in single layer in large shallow baking pan. Spoon marinade mixture evenly over chicken. Sprinkle with brown sugar and pour Madeira between pieces. Cover pan with aluminum foil, bake for 20 minutes. Remove foil and bake, basting frequently with pan juices, until juices run clear when a thigh is pierced with a sharp skewer, 40-50 minutes.

Using fork and slotted spoon, transfer chicken, olives and dried fruit to a large serving platter. Drizzle with a few spoonfuls pan juices and sprinkle with pecans. Sprinkle lemon zest over all. Pass remaining pan juices in a sauceboat. Serves 6.

Joy Blake-Krug
Son Colin, 2003

The 1985 Sale-O raised more than $111,000. The sale gained national attention after being mentioned by Willard Scott on the NBS Today Show. Father Hunthausen appeared on the local Mike Murphy radio show to promote the event and thanked the mothers and alumni mothers for over 10,000 volunteer hours which made the 1985 Sale-O successful. Chair was Cathy Cussen with co-chairs Mary Winne, Marilyn O'Brien, Yolanda Knox and Pat Bolin.

- 1985 newsletter

Mixed Grill with Asian Flavors

Mr. Petersen, my math
teacher for 3 of the 4
years, gave me my first
demerit without either of
us saying a word.
He caught me knocking
books out of the hands
of my fellow student
coming down the stairs.
He looked at me.
I handed him my card.
He marked it without
comment.

- King Stablein, 1962

Soy Marinade:

⅓ cup soy sauce

3 tablespoons seasoned rice vinegar

2 tablespoons packed brown sugar

2 tablespoons minced, peeled fresh ginger

1 tablespoon vegetable oil

2 garlic cloves, crushed

2 green onions, thinly sliced

¼ teaspoon crushed red pepper

½ teaspoon Asian sesame oil

Meats:

2 beef flank steaks (1¼ pounds each)

2 whole pork tenderloins (1 pound each)

10 medium skinless, boneless chicken breast halves (6 ounces each)

40 large shrimp, shelled, deveined

Herb Rub:

2 limes

2 cups loosely packed fresh cilantro leaves, chopped

2 cups loosely packed fresh mint leaves, chopped

2 tablespoons brown sugar

2 tablespoons minced, peeled fresh ginger

3 garlic cloves, crushed

2 green onions, thinly sliced

2 teaspoons salt

1 teaspoon crushed red pepper

Creamy Peanut Dipping Sauce:

¾ cup creamy peanut butter

¼ cup boiling water

¾ cup well-stirred unsweetened light coconut milk (not cream of coconut)

½ cup packed fresh cilantro leaves, chopped

¼ cup boiling water

2 tablespoons packed brown sugar

2 tablespoons soy sauce

5 teaspoons seasoned rice vinegar

½ teaspoon crushed red pepper

Soy Marinade: In jumbo ziplock bag, combine all ingredients. Add 1 flank steak, 1 pork tenderloin and 5 chicken breasts, turning to coat. Seal bag, pressing out excess air. Place bag on plate; refrigerate at least 30 minutes or up to 1 hour. Add 20 shrimp to marinade during last 10 minutes of marinating time.

Continued on next page

Herb Rub: From limes, grate 1 tablespoon zest, then squeeze 2 tablespoons juice. In jumbo ziplock bag, combine lime zest, juice and remaining rub ingredients. Add 1 flank steak, 1 pork tenderloin and 5 chicken breast halves, turning to coat. Seal bag, pressing out excess air. Place bag on plate; refrigerate at least 30 minutes or up to 1 hour. Add remaining 20 shrimp to bag during last 10 minutes of marinating time.

Creamy Peanut Dipping Sauce: In medium bowl, with wire whisk, mix peanut butter and boiling water until blended. Stir in coconut milk and remaining ingredients until combined. Refrigerate sauce until ready to serve. Let stand at room temperature 30 minutes before serving to allow flavors to develop. Makes about 2¼ cups.

Heat grill. Remove meat from Soy Marinade; discard marinade. Remove meat from Herb Rub, spoon any herb mixture remaining in bag on meat. Place shrimp on skewers. Place flank steaks and tenderloins on grill over medium heat.

Cook flank steak 15-20 minutes for medium rare or until desired doneness, turning once. Cook tenderloins about 20 minutes or until browned on the outside and still slightly pink in the center, turning occasionally. (Temperature on meat thermometer in tenderloins should reach 155 degrees, internal temperature of meat will rise to 160 degrees upon standing.)

Place chicken breast halves on grill and cook 10-12 minutes, turning once, until juices run clear when thickest part is pierced with tip of knife. Place shrimp on grill and cook 4-6 minutes, until shrimp turn opaque throughout, turning once.

Transfer cooked meats to cutting board. Thinly slice flank steak and tenderloins. Cut each chicken breast in half lengthwise, transfer to large platter. Arrange shrimp on same platter. Serve with Creamy Peanut Dipping Sauce.

Anne O'Flaherty
Husband Vince, 1980; Son Jack, 2008

This recipe might look intimidating, but it is not difficult. It just takes some prep time, which can be done the day before, and it is worth every minute!

The Mothers Club Board of Directors approved a new project, publishing a new cookbook. Jean Sanderson will chair the project and asks that everyone consider submitting 3 of your favorite recipes. We hope to have the cookbook ready for sale before May 1.

- November 1973 Mothers Club minutes, Charleen Brain, president

Cornish Game Hens in Cognac Sauce

2 Cornish game hens, split in half

Salt and pepper

¼ cup butter

1 tablespoon oil

½ pound sliced mushrooms

½ teaspoon rosemary

1 package long grain & wild rice, prepared according to package directions

2 tablespoons cognac

½ cup heavy cream

Season hens with salt and pepper. Melt butter and oil in a skillet over medium-high heat. Brown hens well on all sides. Add mushrooms and rosemary. Reduce heat to low, cover and cook until tender, 20 minutes.

Spread cooked rice on a platter. Warm cognac in a small saucepan over low heat. Sprinkle cognac over hens and ignite, shaking pan gently until flame is out. Place on rice. Add cream to pan and cook gently for 5 minutes. Pour sauce over hens and rice. Serves 4.

Wendy Zecy
Sons Kit, 2003; Connor, 2007; Cameron, 2009

Foolproof Beef Tenderloin

Whole beef tenderloin   **Montreal Steak Seasoning**

Olive oil

Coat tenderloin in olive oil and sprinkle generously with steak seasoning. Wrap tightly in plastic wrap and refrigerate overnight.

The next day, let beef come to room temperature, at least 45 minutes. Preheat oven to 400 degrees (450 for crisp crust on meat). Place beef in roasting pan. Cook 10 minutes at 400 (or 450) degrees, then reduce heat to 375 degrees for 20 minutes for medium-rare. Remove from oven, let sit for 30 minutes before slicing. Excellent with Mushroom Ragout (in Vegetable section, page 131.)

Lynne Knott
Son Keaton, 2007

This was a favorite at the December 2004 Faculty Christmas luncheon sponsored by the Parents Club and chaired by Debra Webster.

At the first Sale-O-Rama we were pricing small kitchen appliances when we opened a waffle iron and found a burnt waffle still in it!

- Maryhelen VanDyke
Sons Mike, 1966;
Jim, 1972

T-Bone with Blue Cheese Butter

2 tablespoons unsalted butter

2 tablespoons blue cheese, room temperature

1 tablespoon snipped fresh chives

4 T-bone steaks (10-12-ounces each), 1-inch thick

Salt and pepper

In a small bowl, mix together butter, blue cheese and chives until well blended. Refrigerate for up to 24 hours. Bring to room temperature before serving. Grill steaks directly over heat source 4-6 minutes per side for medium-rare. Top each steak with a dollop of blue cheese butter, then let rest for 3 minutes. Serve steaks hot.

Catherine Moussa
Son Alex VanMaren, 2007

I remember when we had an awesome outdoor pep rally and bonfire for Homecoming.

- Jim Broski, 1979

When the fire alarm rang
in the middle of our
3rd floor religion class
that chilly morning
March 9, 1950, my first
thought was how
disrespectful to have a fire
drill when the other half of
school was at Mass.
We began to trudge
down the stairway that
normally was reserved for
Jesuit faculty only,
but which was our
planned fire exit.
I stayed behind, since it
was my week to make
sure all the windows
were closed when
we left the room.
I then began to leave
rather nonchalantly,
but immediately
smelled and tasted
the acrid smoke.
I began to panic,
and then saw
Father Phil Kellet still
in the bright red chasuble
he wore to say Mass.
He was carrying a
ciborium with the
Blessed Sacrament,
covering it in the folds
of his chasuble.
Without hesitating,
I turned and followed
him. He was a big, stocky
man, but I also reasoned
that surely I'd be safer
from earthly fires
close to a priest.

(Continued next page)

Simply Elegant Steak

1½ pounds beef round steak	½ cup dry sherry
1½ tablespoons vegetable oil	4-ounce can sliced mushrooms, drained, reserve liquid
2 large onions, cut in half (separate slices into rings)	
10¾-ounce can cream of mushroom soup	1½ teaspoons garlic salt
	3 cups cooked rice

Cut steak into thin strips. (Easier to slice if partially frozen.) Brown meat in oil over high heat. Add onions and sauté until tender crisp. Blend soup, sherry, liquid from mushrooms and garlic salt. Pour over steak. Add mushrooms. Reduce heat, cover and simmer for 1 hour until steak is tender. Serve over rice.

Donna Tulipana
Son Joe, 2008

Marinated Flank Steak

Juice of 1 lemon	1 large clove garlic, sliced
½ cup soy sauce	Pepper to taste
¼ cup or more dry red wine	Chopped green onion
2 tablespoons Worcestershire sauce	1-1½ pounds flank steak, trimmed

Mix all ingredients, pour over meat. Marinate in refrigerator, turning occasionally, 2-12 hours. Grill meat over hot coals 5 minutes per side for rare meat. Slice meat on the diagonal across the grain and serve. Serves 3-4.

Pat Wells
Son Chris, 2008

Carbonnade of Beef Flamande

2 tablespoons butter

2 tablespoons oil

3 pounds chuck or rump roast, cut into slices ½-inch thick

1½ pounds yellow onions, thinly sliced

Salt and freshly ground pepper to taste

2 cloves garlic, crushed

12 ounces beer

1 cup beef stock or beef consommé

1 tablespoon brown sugar

Bouquet garni: bay leaf, thyme, parsley

2 tablespoons cornstarch

2 tablespoons vinegar

Chopped parsley for garnish

Heat butter and oil to sizzling. Brown beef slices, removing from pan as each slice finishes browning. Reduce heat and brown onions in same fat. Season with salt and pepper, stir in garlic.

Layer beef and onions in casserole dish. Pour in beer and beef stock, stir in brown sugar. Poke bouquet garni down into casserole. Cover and cook at 350 degrees 2½ hours or until meat is fork-tender. Discard bouquet garni. Mix cornstarch and vinegar, stir into gravy to thicken. Garnish with parsley. Serves 6-8.

James Flanagan, 1937
Sons Jim, 1971; Terry, 1975
Grandsons Bryan 2002, Sean, 2004, Kevin, 2007
Grandson Nick Vaughn, RHS Faculty member

(Continued from previous page)

*I followed him until
he descended down steps
and I could not see
in front of me.
Again panic set in.
I froze. A set of windows
was on a nearby landing
and I saw students
outside on the lawn.
I opened a window to
jump, but then saw
the thick, heavy vines
covering Sedgwick Hall.
I grabbed a vine and
lowered myself the 20 feet
or so to the ground.
Some other students also
climbed down the vine.
One sophomore,
Don Donnelly, did jump
and was severely injured.
No other students were
hurt that day as I recall.
Some students and a
teacher were briefly
trapped on the 3rd floor,
above the chemistry lab,
but the firemen arrived
early on and took care of
everything. We students
were without coats,
so after awhile, we starting
drifting away. I walked
home, wondering how
many days we'd get off
because of the fire.
The yearbook pictures of
the fire were captioned:
Fulfillment of a
Student's Dream!*

- Tom Cooke, 1951

Mexican Pot Roast

1 tablespoon oil

½ cup chopped onion

4-ounce can chopped green chilies

2 jalapeno chilies, seeded, finely chopped

1 clove garlic, minced

2½ pounds boneless chuck roast, cut into 8 pieces

½ cup beef broth

1½ teaspoons chili powder

½ teaspoon cumin

⅛ teaspoon cayenne

½ teaspoon salt

Flour tortillas

Accompaniments: shredded lettuce, salsa, sour cream, guacamole, black olives, shredded cheese

Heat oil in Dutch oven over medium heat. Sauté onions, chilies, jalapenos and garlic about 2 minutes, stirring frequently. Add beef, broth and spices. Reduce heat to low, cover. Simmer 2-2½ hours until beef is tender. Shred beef with forks and mix well with pan juices. Serve in flour tortillas with accompaniments. Serves 8.

Pam Cowan
Son Alex, 2008

Sherried Beef Tips

2 cans cream of mushroom soup

½ cup sherry

1 envelope dry onion soup mix

¾ cup water

3 pounds beef stew or sirloin tip roast

Mix all but meat together in crockpot. Add meat and stir until coated. Cook 4 hours on high or 8 hours on low. Serve with rice or pasta.

Rita & Steve Snodell, 1977

Hank Stram's
Oriental Pepper Steak

1½ pounds round steak

2 tablespoons cooking oil

Salt and pepper to taste

Garlic powder to taste

1 tablespoon sugar

2 tablespoons vinegar

5 tablespoons soy sauce

1 cup plus 3 tablespoons water, divided

2 green peppers, cut in strips

2 tablespoons cornstarch

2 tomatoes, cut in chunks

Cut steak in very thin strips. Brown in hot oil. Add seasonings, sugar, vinegar, soy sauce and 1 cup water. Cover and cook 1-1½ hours over low heat. Add green pepper strips and cook an additional 10 minutes. Blend cornstarch and 3 tablespoons cold water and stir into prepared mixture. Add tomatoes and cook 5 minutes. Serve over steamed white rice.

Jan Carter
Son Sean, 2007

Italian Beef Chicago-Style

4-5 pounds boneless rump or chuck roast

2 teaspoons garlic powder

1½ teaspoons oregano

1½ teaspoons fennel seed

1⅛ teaspoons black pepper

1½ teaspoons anise seed

½ teaspoon paprika

2½ teaspoons salt

12-ounce can tomato sauce

2 cups water

Place roast in deep roaster pan or pot. Mix remaining ingredients together and add to pot. Cover and bake at 350 degrees for 1 hour. Reduce heat to 300 and bake for 3 hours. Baste meat with pan juices every 30 minutes until done. Remove meat and cool. Slice as thinly as possible or shred chuck roast. Return meat to sauce and rewarm. Serve on crunchy French rolls. May be cooked in a crockpot overnight on low. Serves 12-14.

Alice Mumford
Son John, 2004

The Model UN group won 4 awards in the trip to the Georgetown competition in Washington, DC. Co-moderators were Mr. Chris Elmore and Dr. Jerry Goben. Wining awards were Zach Thomas, Joel Blevins, Brian Shroeder, Jerry Sirna, Brian Dress, Jamie Huppe and Nick Carr.

- 2000 yearbook

Shredded French Dip

3 pounds boneless beef chuck roast, trimmed

10½-ounce can French onion soup, undiluted

10½-ounce can beef consommé, undiluted

10½-ounce can beef broth, undiluted

1 teaspoon beef bouillon granules

8-10 French or Italian rolls, split

Cut roast in half and place in a crockpot or slow cooker. Combine soup, consommé, broth and bouillon, pour over roast. Cover and cook on low 6-8 hours or until meat is tender. Remove meat and shred with forks. Serve on rolls. Skim fat from cooking juices and serve as dipping sauce. Serves 8-10.

Catherine Moussa
Son Alex VanMaren, 2007

Slow Cooker Sherried Beef Tips

2 cans cream of mushroom soup

½ cup cooking sherry

1 package onion soup mix

¾ cup water

3 pounds beef stew or sirloin tip roast, cut into small pieces

Mix all ingredients other than beef together in crock pot. Add beef and stir until coated with soup mixture. Cook about 4 hours on high or 8 hours on low. Serve over rice or pasta.

Rita & Steve Snodell, 1978

Beef broth or additional water can be substituted for the cooking sherry.

Beef Brisket

1 trimmed brisket

1 can of beer

1 bottle of catsup

1 sliced onion

Barbecue sauce

Place brisket in large baking pan with cover. Pour beer and catsup over brisket. Layer sliced onion on top. Bake at 325 degrees for 5-6 hours. Cool, slice and put in baking dish. Heat with favorite barbeque sauce and serve. Serves 25-30.

Mary Jo Barton
Sons Brett, 2005; Scott, 2007

Absolutely no fail, best brisket. Everyone always wants to know where it came from. So easy and so good that I have given the recipe to butchers at grocery stores and they have printed it and handed out to customers. This is my mom's recipe (Gen Poskin). She put 5 boys through Rockhurst. It is a family favorite and has been served hundreds of times over the past 30-40 years. My mom was a dedicated and loyal RHS mom. Greg, 1971; Joe, 1975; David, 1978; Donald, 1981 and Richard, 1981 are her sons. Chris Poskin, 2001; Joel Hodes, 2004; Jamie, 2002, and Brady, 2003, Poskin; Brett, 2005, and Scott, 2007, Barton; Jeff, 2005; Derek, 2007 and Zach, 2009, Poskin are her grandsons who have attended or are attending RHS, with more to come.

Orange Brisket

5 pound beef brisket

1 cup orange juice

1 cup beef bouillon

3 cloves garlic, crushed

½ cup red wine

1 tablespoon soy or Worcestershire sauce

Salt and pepper

Cut as much fat as possible from brisket. Combine orange juice, bouillon, garlic, wine and soy or Worcestershire, pour over brisket. Sprinkle with salt and pepper. Cover and bake at 275 degrees about 5 hours, or until tender, about 1 hour per pound. Uncover if more browning is necessary.

Harriet Kokjer
Nephew Scott Miller, 2007

Mrs Pat Shieffer chaired the 1989 Sale-O. The sale occupied the Jesuit residence basement, weight room, wrestling room, little theater, gym, gym lobby and downstairs school hallways, every inch covered with donations of both new and used merchandise.

- 1989 newspaper clipping

Scott Andre, assisted by Mike Weaver, managed the Quarry photography duties.

- 1971 yearbook

Texas-Style Baby Back Ribs

2 tablespoons canola oil

2 full racks baby back ribs (4½ pounds)

6 quarts chicken broth

3 cups barbecue sauce

Salt and pepper to taste

Preheat oven to 375 degrees. Heat oil over medium high heat. Add ribs, flesh side down, and cook 3-4 minutes, until browned. Transfer ribs to large roasting pan and cover with chicken broth. Cover pan tightly with foil. Roast 3-3½ hours, until fork-tender. Remove from oven and cool in liquid. Refrigerate overnight if desired.

Prepare a medium-hot grill. Brush ribs with barbecue sauce, sprinkle with salt and pepper. Place flesh side down on grill and cook, turning once, for 6-8 minutes, basting ribs with sauce until sauce forms a crispy crust. Serve immediately.

Nancy Fitzpatrick
Husband Mark, 1974; Sons Tim, 2002; John, 2008

Father Tom Pesci and my mother Janet Stephenson became good friends. They met when he sat next to her at a Chiefs game and she kept hitting him on the shoulder with a rolled up program when she got excited. When she found out she was sitting with my boss, she called me and said "You are going to get fired!"

- Judie Scanlon, RHS Special Events Coordinator Sons Steve, 1988; Kerry, 1994

Corned Beef Brisket

5 pound or larger boneless corned beef, preferably point cut

Red wine or red wine vinegar

Rub:

3 tablespoons ground peppercorns

2 tablespoons coriander seeds

1 tablespoon onion powder

3 teaspoons salt

3 teaspoons garlic powder

2 teaspoons dried thyme

2 teaspoons paprika

1 teaspoon sugar

Drain meat, rinse with water, pat dry. Mix Rub ingredients together, rub into meat. (If desired, marinate overnight, but I have good luck without the overnight wait.) Preheat smoker or grill to 225 degrees. Prepare shallow pan with ¼-inch deep mixture of ½ water and ½ red wine. Place meat in pan. Cook until center temperature is 170 degrees, approximately 1½-2 hours per pound. Let stand 15 minutes before slicing across the grain.

Terry Flanagan, 1975

Crockpot Baby Back Ribs

4 pounds pork baby back ribs

2 tablespoons sweet or hot paprika

1 tablespoon kosher salt

¼ cup dark brown sugar, firmly packed

2 tablespoons chili powder

1 tablespoon minced garlic

1 tablespoon ground cumin

1½ teaspoons dry mustard

¼ teaspoon cayenne

18-ounce bottle barbeque sauce

Cut each rack of ribs to fit into crockpot. Combine paprika, salt, brown sugar, chili powder, garlic, cumin, mustard and cayenne in a small bowl. Mix well, then rub over ribs. Cover ribs and refrigerate for 4 hours or overnight. Cook ribs in crockpot on low for 8 hours. When almost done, preheat oven to 300 degrees. Transfer ribs to rimmed sheet pan or pyrex dish, reserve juices from crockpot.

In large saucepan, combine juices from crockpot with barbeque sauce. Bring to boil over high heat and simmer for 10 minutes to thicken slightly. Reserve ½ cup of simmered sauce to serve on the side. Spread the rest over the ribs. Bake for 15 minutes so ribs are crisp. Serve immediately. Serves 4.

Joe Doyle, 1974
Sons Patrick, 2008; John, 2010

Crockpot Pork or Beef

2 pounds country pork ribs or beef

1 large onion, cut in rings

12 ounces barbecue sauce

Place meat on heavy duty foil, top with onion rings, tuck more underneath meat. Wrap tightly to avoid leaks. Cook in crockpot on low 7-8 hours. Remove meat and onions from foil, add barbecue sauce. Cook another 2 hours. Break up meat and serve on buns.

Ann Marie Scahill
Son Michael, 2009

As a member of the Poster Club I recall helping make a gymnasium-long poster highlighting the basketball season.

- Bradley Thedinger, 1971
Sons Seaton, 1998; Blair, 2000

The 1981 Homecoming theme was Halloween. Floats echoed the theme: Seniors "Wrap up the Kewpies"; Juniors "Spirit Behind the Hawklets"; Sophomores "Legend of Dasta Hollow"; Freshmen "Fall of the House of Kewpies".

-1981-82 yearbook

Texas-Style Pesto with Pork Tenderloin

2 pork tenderloins	¼ cup toasted pecans
Salt and pepper	2 cloves garlic
2 cups fresh cilantro leaves, plus additional for garnish	¼ cup fresh lime juice
1 tablespoon finely chopped jalapeno	½ cup grated Parmesan cheese
	½ cup canola oil

Preheat oven to 350 degrees. Season pork with salt and pepper and sear in hot skillet to seal in juices. Finish cooking in oven at 350 degrees for 30-40 minutes. Don't overcook pork. Take pork out and tent with foil. Let rest for 10-15 minutes.

Meanwhile, prepare pesto by combining cilantro, jalapeno, pecans, garlic, lime juice, Parmesan, salt and pepper in a food processor. Add canola oil in a steady stream with processor running. Blend well. Set aside until ready to use.

To serve, place a spoonful of rice (I use a Spanish rice) on plate, top with slices of pork, and drizzle pesto on top of pork.

Marianne Damon
Sons Paul, 2002; Quinn, 2008

Balsamic Pork Tenderloin

¼ cup balsamic vinegar	2 pounds pork tenderloins
3 tablespoons honey	1 teaspoon salt
2 garlic cloves, minced	1 teaspoon pepper
½ teaspoon dried crushed red peppers	

Combine balsamic vinegar, honey, garlic and crushed peppers. Place pork tenderloins in a large ziplock plastic bag. Pour marinade over tenderloins and seal bag. Refrigerate 8 hours or overnight. Drain tenderloins, sprinkle with salt and pepper. Grill with lid on. Let stand about 10 minutes before slicing.

Jim Flanagan, 1971
Sons Bryan, 2002; Sean, 2004; Kevin, 2007

Citrus Pork Tenderloin

¼ cup soy sauce

2 cloves garlic

2 inches fresh ginger, chopped

Small can orange-pineapple juice concentrate

1 teaspoon cinnamon

1 tablespoon balsamic vinegar

2 pork tenderloins

¼ cup honey

Sesame seeds, lightly toasted

Mix together soy sauce, garlic, ginger, juice concentrate, cinnamon and vinegar. Pour over pork tenderloins. Marinate overnight. Drain, reserving marinade, and pat dry. Roll in honey and toasted sesame seeds. Barbecue in double pans for 20 minutes, basting with reserved marinade. Finish on grill for 5 minutes, turning often.

Pat Wells
Son Chris, 2008

Raspberry Sauce for Pork Tenderloins

18-ounce jar raspberry preserves

2 ounces red wine vinegar

1 ounce soy sauce

½ tablespoon horseradish

½ tablespoon catsup

1 tablespoon minced garlic

Mix all ingredients and bring to a boil in saucepan. Boil 2 minutes, stirring constantly. Turn to low and simmer 5-10 minutes. Serve with pork tenderloins.

Sally O'Neill
Sons Patrick, 2002; Peter, 2008

Oriental Pork Tenderloin

1 cup soy sauce

⅓ cup sesame oil

3 large cloves garlic, minced

1 tablespoon ground ginger

3 large pork tenderloins or 1 whole trimmed beef tenderloin

Mix first 4 ingredients, pour over tenderloin. Marinate overnight. Grill, basting frequently with sauce.

Annie Osborn
Son Scott, 2007

Pork, Cashew and Vegetable Stir-Fry

¼ cup reduced-sodium soy sauce

2 teaspoons cornstarch

1 pound pork tenderloin, cut into thin strips

2 teaspoons dark sesame oil

1 tablespoon minced, peeled fresh ginger

2 cloves garlic, minced

¼ cup fat-free, less-sodium chicken broth

16-ounce package frozen stir-fry vegetables

2 cups hot cooked rice

¼ cup chopped unsalted cashews, toasted

Combine soy sauce and cornstarch in a medium bowl and add pork, stirring to coat. Cover and let stand 5 minutes. Coat skillet with cooking spray. Heat oil over medium-high heat. Add ginger and garlic; sauté 1 minute. Add pork mixture; stir-fry about 2 minutes, or until pork is done. Add chicken broth and cook an additional 1 minute. At this point the pork mixture can be placed in a plastic freezer bag and frozen for up to 3 months. Remove from freezer the morning before you would like to serve the dish. Place pork mixture into a skillet sprayed with cooking spray. Add frozen vegetables. Simmer about 3 minutes. Serve over rice, sprinkle with cashews.

Catherine Moussa
Son Alex VanMaren, 2007

The Rockhurst Enrichment Program (REP) was begun in the summer of 1988 as an intense but fun program of instruction in literature, grammar, math and basic computer skills for incoming 8th grade students. It is also hoped that the program will help diversify the RHS student body. The inaugural class had 10 students, the 2nd class in 1989 had 22. Instructors were Mr. Gene Morris, S.J., Mr. Frank Lyngar, Mr. Mark Bubalo. Student assistants were Tim Mozee, 1990, Juan Melendez, 1990 and Scott Weinzerl, 1991.

Pork Tenderloin Burrito Fiesta

¼ cup freshly squeezed lime juice

½ cup freshly squeezed orange juice

½ teaspoon ground cumin

¼ teaspoon salt

¼ teaspoon freshly ground black pepper

1½ pound whole pork tenderloin

12 (10-inch) flour tortillas or corn tortillas

Additional condiments: fresh cilantro, chopped green onions, sour cream, grated cheddar or jack cheese

Tomato Salsa Fresca:

1 pound ripe tomatoes, diced

¼ cup red onion or green onions, finely chopped

½ cup lightly packed cilantro, finely chopped

1 garlic clove, minced

1 jalapeno or serrano chili, seeds discarded, minced

1 tablespoon olive oil

2 tablespoons freshly squeezed lime juice

Salt and pepper to taste

In a baking dish or shallow bowl, mix all juices and seasonings. Place tenderloin in marinade so that meat is covered in the marinade. Cover and marinate for 2 hours in refrigerator. Combine all salsa ingredients in a bowl, let sit for 1 hour at room temperature to allow flavors to blend.

Grill tenderloin on a grill or under a preheated broiler for about 8 minutes on each side, or until cooked throughout (160 degrees). Avoid overcooking. Cut tenderloin into thin slices. Place inside warm tortillas with Tomato Salsa Fresca and additional condiments. Serves 6.

Rita & Steve Snodell, 1978

Pecan Crusted Double-Cut Pork Chops

4 (10-ounce) pork chops, thick-cut, bone-in

Salt and freshly ground black pepper

2 tablespoons olive oil, divided

1 cup pecans, chopped

Ancho Chili Pepper Barbeque Sauce:

5 cups catsup

½ tablespoon chopped garlic

½ cup cider vinegar

½ cup brown sugar

½ tablespoon liquid smoke

½ cup beer

½ cup honey

1½ cups water

¼ cup Worcestershire sauce

1 teaspoon onion powder

1 teaspoon dry mustard

½ teaspoon black pepper

1 dried ancho chile pepper, crushed

½ teaspoon ham or chicken stock

Preheat oven to 350 degrees. Season pork chops on both sides with salt and pepper. Pour 1 tablespoon olive oil on a plate and spread pecans on another plate. Lay each pork chop in olive oil, coating both sides, then coat both sides with chopped pecans.

Heat remaining olive oil in a large skillet over medium heat. Add pork chops and cook until pecans are light brown on that side. Turn chops over in pan and place in oven until an internal temperature of 165 degrees is reached, about 10 minutes. Drizzle chops with Ancho Chili Pepper Barbeque Sauce and serve immediately with plenty of sauce for dipping. Serves 4.

For Sauce: Heat a large stockpot over high heat. Add all ingredients and stir. Bring to a boil. Reduce heat to medium-low and simmer for 1-2 hours. Strain sauce and serve immediately or keep warm until ready to use.

Chris & Suzie Smith

One year I had my ear pierced to wear a Celtic cross. (The other earring was with my late wife.) I found Father Pesci before he found me and told him why I wore it. He just said he didn't think he could stand the pain of having an ear pierced. That was the end of it.

- John McEniry, 1968, RHS Faculty member

Pork Chops and Peppers

2 thick pork chops

Salt and pepper

¼ cup olive oil

1 clove garlic, crushed

3 peppers, sliced (best if one red, one yellow, one green, but any will do)

8 ounces fresh mushrooms, sliced

Garlic salt

Chopped parsley

Sweet basil

¼ cup vermouth

Pat pork chops dry, season with salt and pepper. Heat olive oil in an electric fry pan. Add garlic and pork chops. Remove chops when brown, keep warm. Add peppers and mushrooms to the pan, sauté with garlic salt, chopped parsley and basil until soft. Return pork chops to pan along with vermouth. Cook at 200 degrees for 15 minutes.

Fred Campisano
RHS Faculty member

Italian Sausages and Peppers

8-12 Italian sausage links

1-2 large onions, thinly sliced

2-3 green and red peppers, thinly sliced

2-3 (14.5-ounce) cans Italian-style tomatoes, with juice

Italian seasoning, optional

Parmesan cheese

Hoagie buns or frozen cheese tortellini, prepared according to package directions

Spray large cake or roasting pan with cooking spray. Add sausages, then layer onions and peppers on top. Pour tomatoes over all. Mix slightly with spoon and add Italian seasoning if desired. Cover pan tightly. Bake at 350 degrees for one hour. Remove from oven, keep covered and let sit for 15 more minutes. Remove foil, sprinkle with grated Parmesan cheese. Serve on hoagie buns or combine with prepared cheese tortellini and serve in bowls.

Beverly Hynes
Sons Chris, 1995; David, 1995

Feeds a crowd of hungry boys!

Marinated Ham Steaks

1½ cups pineapple juice

¼ cup packed brown sugar

2 tablespoons butter or margarine, melted

1-2 tablespoons ground mustard

1 garlic clove, minced

¼ teaspoon paprika

2 thick fully cooked ham steaks (about 1 pound each)

In a large resealable plastic bag or shallow glass container, combine first 6 ingredients; mix well. Add ham and turn to coat. Seal or cover and refrigerate for at least 2 hours, turning occasionally. Drain and reserve marinade. Grill ham uncovered over medium-hot heat for 3-4 minutes on each side, basting frequently with reserved marinade. Serves 6.

Sue Dierks
Husband Bernard, 1955; Sons Chris, 1986; Mike, 1991

Cheesy Meat Loaf

1½ pounds lean ground beef

1 cup cubed mild cheddar cheese

1 small onion, diced, optional

2 eggs, beaten

1⅓ cups cracker crumbs

⅔ cup milk

½ teaspoon salt

¼ teaspoon pepper

¼ cup catsup

¼ cup brown sugar

1 teaspoon prepared yellow mustard

Mix beef, cheese, onion, eggs, cracker crumbs, milk, salt and pepper together in a large bowl. Divide into two loaves and place in a baking dish. In a small bowl, mix catsup, brown sugar and mustard, pour over top of meat loaves. Bake at 350 degrees for 1 hour and 15 minutes. Serves 8-10.

Audrey Streib
Son Steven, 2009

First Rockhurst Auction Meatballs

2 eggs, beaten

4 slices fresh bread, torn, or 1½ cups dry breadcrumbs

2 cloves garlic, chopped

2 teaspoons salt

½ teaspoon pepper

1 teaspoon oregano

6 tablespoons fresh parsley, chopped very fine (about 8 sprigs)

2 pounds ground chuck or other lean ground beef

6 ounces grated Romano cheese

¼ cup olive oil

Sauce:

8-ounce can tomato sauce

1 medium onion, chopped

Salt and pepper

Mix eggs with breadcrumbs. Add garlic, salt, pepper, oregano and parsley. Add meat and cheese, mix well. Form rounded tablespoons of meat mixture into balls. Heat olive oil in deep skillet and brown meatballs on all sides. Place browned meatballs in casserole dish.

Mix sauce ingredients in saucepan over medium heat. Bring to slight boil. Pour over meatballs. Cover dish, bake at 300 degrees for 45 minutes. Enjoy!

Gene Vandenboom, 1970
Son Joe, 2008

These were served at the first RHS auction in 1971.

The first RHS Auction on November 13, 1971 was a much smaller affair compared to what we are used to now. It consisted of the auction items, a cash bar and appetizers made by members of the Mothers' Club. Several of us recent 1970 graduates volunteered to check coats and hats. It was such a warm night that no one wore coats. Al Paradise was the VP of the Fathers Club. He sent my mom a meatball recipe to use at the auction. She kept the letter with the recipe, so we have the recipe for the First RHS Auction Meatballs!

- Gene VandenBoom, 1970

Italian Grinder Meatballs

4 English muffins

1 pound ground beef

½ pound ground pork

½ pound Italian sausage, crumbled

3 eggs, lightly beaten

½ cup freshly grated Parmesan cheese

3 cloves garlic, minced

Italian parsley, chopped

Salt and pepper to taste

Spaghetti sauce

Wet muffins and squeeze the water out. Crumble and add to meats and other ingredients. Mix well and form meatballs, about golf ball size. Put on a greased baking sheet and bake at 350 degrees until about half done. (They should hold together and have shed some of the grease.) At this point, either add to the sauce and continue cooking to add flavor to the sauce, or freeze meatballs for later use.

Marianne Damon
Sons Paul, 2002; Quinn, 2008

I usually triple the recipe and freeze the partially cooked meatballs in ziplock bags, six in a bag. I pull them out later and finish cooking in a small amount of sauce and make grinders, with mozzarella cheese.

Sarma (Croatian Cabbage Rolls)

2 pounds lean ground beef

1 pound ground pork

¾ cup uncooked rice

2 eggs, beaten

1 small onion, chopped

Salt to taste (if using fresh cabbage)

Pepper to taste

1 large sour cabbage head, or fresh cabbage head

1 pound kraut

1 ring smoked sausage, sliced

1 small can tomato sauce

Thoroughly combine beef, pork, rice, eggs, onion, salt and pepper in large bowl. Remove cabbage leaves and rinse in cool water to remove some of the brine. Use fresh cabbage if sour cabbage is not available. Just add more kraut on top of rolls in pan.

Begin making rolls by putting ½-¾ cup meat mixture on stem end of cabbage leaf. Roll and tuck in sides of leaf, secure with a toothpick. Repeat until all meat and cabbage are used. Any remaining unusable small pieces of sour cabbage can be chopped and added to top of cabbage rolls.

Put a layer of kraut in a large roasting pan. Next place cabbage rolls on top of kraut and sausage slices over cabbage. Pour small can of tomato sauce over all rolls and sausage. Cover with water just to the top of rolls. Cover roasting pan tightly with foil. Bake at 450 degrees for about 1 hour, then lower temperature to 350 degrees for about 2 hours.

Dottie Ruby
Husband Larry, RHS Principal

This is traditionally a holiday dish we would make for Christmas. It is usually served with mashed potatoes and green beans seasoned with bacon and green onions. The sour cabbage, homemade kraut and smoked sausage can all be found at House of Sausage, a family-owned and run business in the Strawberry Hill neighborhood of Kansas City. Joe Krizman is a Rockhurst graduate and helps with the family business.

Named to the Kansas City All-Metro soccer team in 1971 were Jim Clarke, Jim Flanagan, John Lawless, Mark Nobrega, Paul DeBacco, Gus Jiminez and David Chartrand. New Head Coach was Jim Salter. The team won the Kansas City Metro Soccer Trophy for the 3rd year in a row.

- 1971 yearbook

Beef and Green Chili Quesadillas

1 pound ground chuck

1 medium onion, chopped

½ teaspoon salt

¾ cup chunky salsa

4 ounce can chopped green chilies, drained

10-12 medium flour tortillas

2 cups shredded cheddar cheese

Cooking spray

Preheat oven to 450 degrees. In large skillet, brown ground beef and onion until no longer pink. Pour off drippings. Season with salt. Add salsa and chilies to beef, mix well. Spoon about ¼ cup beef mixture on top of each tortilla. Sprinkle each with about 2 tablespoons of cheese. Fold tortillas like an envelope, enclosing beef mixture. Arrange on greased baking sheet. Lightly spray tops of tortillas with cooking spray. Bake 8-10 minutes or until lightly browned. Serve with shredded lettuce, sour cream, guacamole, salsa and cheese. Makes 10-12.

Pam Cowan
Son Alex, 2008

Tortilla Pie

1 pound ground beef

1 onion, diced

1 dozen corn tortillas

15½-ounce can pinto beans, undrained

1 pound longhorn cheese, sliced

10-ounce can tomatoes and green chilies (Rotel)

10½-ounce can cream of chicken soup

Sliced jalapeno peppers, optional, for garnish

Brown meat with onion, drain. In a 9x13-inch baking dish, layer 6 tortillas, then meat mixture, beans and cheese. Top with remaining 6 tortillas. Combine tomato and chili sauce with soup. Pour mixture over tortillas. Bake at 350 degrees for one hour or until cooked through and bubby. Garnish with jalapenos.

Karen Miller
Husband Sean, 1977; Son Ryan, 2008

Ultimate Lamb Burger

24 ounces ground lamb

2 cloves garlic, minced

2 teaspoons chopped fresh rosemary

1 red onion, thickly sliced

½ pint kalamata olives

1 cup mayonnaise

2 large pita bread rounds, cut in half, toasted

⅓ cup sundried tomatoes

½ cup crumbled feta cheese

Mix lamb, garlic and rosemary together and form into 4 patties. Grill patties and red onion to desired doneness. Meanwhile, pureé olives and mayonnaise in food processor or blender. Assemble burger patty on pita with olive pureé, grilled onions, sundried tomatoes and feta. Serves 4.

Pam Cowan
Son Alex, 2008

Martini Lamb

½ medium onion, chopped

10 garlic cloves

Juice and zest of 1 lemon

3 tablespoons gin

2 teaspoons kosher salt

¼ cup olive oil

5-6 pound leg of lamb, preferably boned and butterflied

A day ahead, prepare martini paste: In a food processor, combine onion, garlic, lemon juice and zest, gin and salt. Process to combine. Continue processing, pouring in oil until a thin paste forms. Generously spread paste on lamb. Place lamb in a plastic bag and refrigerate overnight.

Remove lamb from refrigerator and let sit at room temperature for 30 minutes. Grill over medium heat until internal temperature reaches 145 degrees for rare to medium-rare. Remove lamb from grill and let sit for 10 minutes before slicing.

Firmin & Antoinette Snodell
Sons Thomas, 1977; Steve, 1978; Grandson Alex VanMaren, 2007

This is also awesome cooked in a smoker. We often have this at Easter.

Osso Bucco

4 meaty veal shanks, sawed into pieces 2 inches long

Flour

Salt and freshly ground black pepper

¼ cup butter or margarine

2 tablespoons olive oil

1 medium onion, finely chopped

1 carrot, finely chopped

1 leek, finely chopped

2 ribs celery, finely chopped

2 cloves garlic, minced

1 cup dry white wine or dry white vermouth

½ cup tomato purée

1 cup veal stock or chicken or beef broth

Bouquet Garni (4 sprigs parsley and 1 bay leaf tied together in cheesecloth bag)

½ teaspoon basil

Gremolata:

Zest of 1 orange

Zest of 1 lemon

1 clove garlic, minced

1 anchovy fillet, optional

Dredge veal shanks in flour, then season with salt and pepper. If possible, select a heavy casserole dish large enough to hold meat in one layer. In it, heat butter and oil, and brown meat. Add remaining ingredients except gremolata, cover and simmer gently over low heat or bake at 325 degrees until tender, about 1½ hours. Taste for seasoning and discard bouquet garni. Skim fat. Mix gremolata ingredients and sprinkle evenly over meat. Serve from the casserole. Serves 4.

James Flanagan, 1937
Sons Jim, 1971; Terry, 1975
Grandsons Bryan, 2002; Sean, 2004; Kevin, 2007
Grandson Nick Vaughn, RHS Faculty member

Cookies AND Bars

1990s

National:

With the fall of the Soviet Union in 1991, the U.S. turned its attention to Iraq, as operation Desert Storm began that same year. On home soil, the nation was rocked by a couple of major bombings: New York City's World Trade Center in 1993 and Oklahoma City's Alfred P. Murrah Federal Building in 1995. Computer technology advanced at the speed of Pentium processor, released by Intel in 1993. Instant messaging, chat rooms and even online shopping became part of the typical Rockhurst student's routine - and a source of consternation for many Rockhurst parents. Hip-hop music and boy bands came to the forefront of the American entertainment conscience at the close of the 20th century, and Mark McGwire and Sammy Sosa captivated the nation with their chase for Major League baseball's single-season home run record in 1998. Even in the face of such fearsome power hitting, some pitchers prospered; Rockhurst High graduate David Cone threw the 16th perfect game in Major League history in 1999.

Local:

Kansas City saw a couple of firsts in civic leadership in the 1990s. The city elected its first African American mayor, Emanuel Cleaver, in 1990, and its first woman mayor, Kay Waldo Barnes, in 1998. Kansas City and the rest of the Midwest weathered the flood of the Missouri River in 1993. This all came, somewhat ironically, on the heels of a vote in support of the legalization of riverboat gambling in 1992. Kansas City voters also approved the renovation of Union Station, which was completed in 1999. Major League Soccer kicked off in 1996, with Kansas City's Wizards enjoying early success.

Chipper Cookies

1 cup unsalted butter, softened

¾ cup sugar

¾ cup brown sugar

1 tablespoon vanilla

1 tablespoon Frangelico liqueur

1 tablespoon Kaluha liqueur

2 eggs

2½ cups flour

1 teaspoon baking soda

½ teaspoon salt

2 (11½-ounce) packages milk chocolate chips

1 cup chopped walnuts

1 cup chopped pecans

1 cup chopped macadamia nuts

Preheat oven to 325 degrees. Mix butter, sugars, vanilla and liqueurs until fluffy. Add eggs and mix well. Add flour, baking soda and salt, mix again. Fold in chips and nuts. Drop by ¼-cupfuls onto a greased cookie sheet, spacing well apart. Bake for 13-16 minutes or until golden brown. Makes 3 dozen.

Pam Cowan
Son Alex, 2008

Liqueurs and nuts make this cookie anything but ordinary.

Country Club Cookies

1 cup butter

1 cup sugar

1 cup brown sugar

2 eggs

1 teaspoon vanilla

2½ cups flour

1 teaspoon baking soda

1 teaspoon baking powder

½ teaspoon salt

1½ cups rolled oats

1 large Hershey's Symphony bar with almonds and toffee, coarsely chopped

4 (2-ounce) Butterfinger bars, coarsely chopped

Preheat oven to 350 degrees. Cream butter and sugars until light and fluffy. Add eggs and vanilla, beat well. Stir in flour, baking soda, baking powder and salt. Add oats and candy pieces. Drop by rounded teaspoons onto cookie sheets. Bake 10 minutes or until set and light brown. Cool on wire racks. Makes 5 dozen.

Michelle Nemmers
Son John, 2008

Foothill House Sweet Dreams

1 cup butter	1 teaspoon cinnamon
1½ cups brown sugar	1 teaspoon ginger
1 egg	½ teaspoon salt
1 teaspoon vanilla	12 ounces chocolate chips
2 cups flour	1 cup chopped walnuts
1 teaspoon baking soda	1 cup powdered sugar

Cream butter, add brown sugar, egg and vanilla. Beat until light and fluffy. Combine flour, baking soda, spices and salt. Blend into butter mixture. Fold in chocolate chips and walnuts. Refrigerate until firm. Preheat oven to 375 degrees. Lightly grease baking sheets. Roll dough into 1-inch balls and dredge in powdered sugar. Place on baking sheets 2 inches apart, bake 10 minutes. Cool 5 minutes then transfer to wire racks. Makes 6 dozen.

Kate Brown
Husband Peter, 1976
Sons Chris, 2000; Kevin, 2003; Scott, 2010

Although the Lacrosse team technically got started in the spring of 1995, the first "competitive" season was actually the following year, 1996.
Since most of the games were played in St. Louis, Maureen McInerney (sons Sean, 1996; Kieran, 1998) began sending along homemade chocolate chip cookies for the long bus rides.
After 3 years of baking for the boys, she passed on the tradition to a new set of lacrosse moms, who then turned it into an entire committee. The program had grown to 3 teams - freshmen, JV and varsity - with over 75 members! Ten years and 2 state championships later, the cookie tradition continues.

- Cyd Jokisch
Sons Craig Hakes, 1998;
Pete Jokisch, 2002

Lacrosse Chip Cookies

1 cup unsalted butter, softened	1 teaspoon baking soda
½ cup sugar	¼ teaspoon kosher salt
1 cup brown sugar	2½ cups flour
2 teaspoons vanilla	18 ounces semisweet chocolate chunks or chips
2 eggs	

Preheat oven to 325 degrees. Beat butter and sugars until creamy. Add vanilla and eggs, beat. Add baking soda, salt and flour in small amounts at a time. Beat in flour just until mixed. Stir in chocolate chunks. Bake on ungreased cookie sheets or on parchment paper for 12-15 minutes. Edges will be brown and middles a little soft. Leave on cookie sheet a few minutes and then transfer to a wire rack to cool. Makes about 3 dozen.

Maureen McInerney
Sons Sean, 1996; Kieran, 1998

Chocolate Krispies

1½ cups sugar	1 teaspoon salt
1½ cups packed brown sugar	1 teaspoon baking soda
1½ cups butter	1 teaspoon cream of tartar
1 cup vegetable oil	1 cup crispy rice cereal
1 egg plus one egg white	1 cup oats
1 teaspoon vanilla	1 cup coconut
3½ cups flour	½ cup chopped pecans
¾ cup cocoa	Powdered sugar

Preheat oven to 350 degrees. Cream together sugars, butter and oil. Add egg, egg white and vanilla. In separate bowl, combine flour, cocoa, salt, baking soda and cream of tartar. Add dry mix a bit at a time to creamed mixture, blending well. Add rice cereal, oats, coconut and pecans. Drop by large teaspoonfuls onto ungreased baking sheets, press with a fork. Bake about 10 minutes. Cool slightly then sprinkle with powdered sugar. Makes about 10 dozen cookies.

Andrea Noth
Sons George, 2007; Henry, 2009

Jam Thumbprint Cookies

1 cup butter, softened	3 cups flour
½ cup packed brown sugar	½ teaspoon salt
1 egg	Sugar
1 teaspoon vanilla	½ cup jam or preserves

Cream butter and brown sugar until smooth. Stir in egg and vanilla. Gradually stir in flour and salt. Cover and refrigerate 1-2 hours or until firm enough to roll into balls. Preheat oven to 350 degrees. Roll dough into 1-inch balls, roll balls in sugar. Place on ungreased cookie sheets, 2 inches apart. Make indentation in center of each cookie. Fill center with about ½ teaspoon jam or preserves. Bake 10-12 minutes or until lightly browned. Cool on baking sheets for 2 minutes, then transfer to wire racks. Makes 4 dozen. Doubles easily.

Catherine Moussa
Son Alex VanMaren, 2007

Rockhurst cross country came of age in 1973, taking the 1st place championship at St. Mary's, 3rd place trophies at Miege and Savior, and convincing wins over Southwest, Schlagle, and O'Hara. The coach was Len McCabe. The team's final record was 33 wins and 11 losses.

Hidden Chocolate Cookies

1 cup sugar

½ cup brown sugar

½ cup shortening

½ cup butter, softened

2 eggs

1 teaspoon vanilla

3⅓ cups flour

1 teaspoon baking soda

½ teaspoon salt

2½ dozen chocolate mint candies (such as York Peppermint Patties)

frosting:

2 cups powdered sugar

3 tablespoons milk

½ teaspoon vanilla or almond extract

Familiar names and memories to treasure. Some Rockhurst grads from the 1920s: Joseph Earnshaw, 1923; Omer Kimpler, 1922; Martin Ryan, 1926; Anthony Christ, 1925; T. Galvin Scanlon, 1925; Marvin Paulin, 1927; Byrne Deam, 1925; Bernard Craig, Sr., 1927; Harry Morris, 1927; Robert Dierks, 1929; Thomas Newton, 1929; Arthur McDonald, 1924, Al VanHee, 1922; Gerald Fling, 1923.

Heat oven to 400 degrees. Mix sugars, shortening, butter, egg and vanilla. Stir in flour, baking soda and salt. Mold some dough carefully around a candy, sealing all edges. Place 2 inches apart on ungreased baking sheets. Bake 9-10 minutes or until light brown, cool. Mix frosting ingredients together until smooth, frost cookies. Makes about 2½ dozen.

Nancy Cowing
Son Nick, 2007

These were devoured by parents and sons alike at the 2006 National Honor Society induction reception.

Donald Duck's Peanut Butter Cookies

1 cup peanut butter

1 cup sugar

1 egg

Preheat oven to 350 degrees. Mix all ingredients until well blended. Roll into walnut-sized balls. Place on cookie sheet, press each with a floured fork. Bake 10 minutes. Makes 3 dozen.

Ann Marie Scahill
Son Michael, 2009

My dear friend Betty Calcara's uncle was the voice of Donald Duck. The little Donald Duck stamp he used to "sign" his name was stamped on this recipe card and he wrote "My favorite recipe" next to it.

Pistachio Thumbprints

Cookies:

⅓ cup powdered sugar

1 cup butter

1 teaspoon vanilla

¾ teaspoon almond extract

3½-ounce package instant pistachio pudding

1 egg

2 cups flour

½ cup mini chocolate chips

Filling:

1½ cups powdered sugar

2 tablespoons butter

½ teaspoon almond extract

½ teaspoon vanilla

1-3 tablespoons milk or cream

¼ cup mini chocolate chips

Preheat oven to 350 degrees. Cream powdered sugar, butter, vanilla, almond extract, pudding mix and egg together in a mixing bowl. Stir in flour and add chocolate chips. Shape into 1-inch balls and place 2 inches apart on greased cookie sheets. With thumb or knuckle, make an indentation in center of each cookie. Bake 10-14 minutes or until edges are just beginning to turn golden. Cool and remove to wire racks.

In small bowl combine all filling ingredients except chocolate chips. Beat until light and well blended. Using a small spoon, scoop filling into the well in the cooled cookies and sprinkle with a few mini chips. Makes about 60 cookies.

Kate Brown
Husband Peter, 1976
Sons Chris, 2000; Kevin, 2003; Scott, 2010

I developed this recipe years ago and they have become a mainstay both at our home and at each of our children's schools. Whenever asked to bring cookies to an event, these are the requested favorites! The delicate green color adds to the cookie's intrigue, but flavor is the reason behind their popularity.

My husband Hal Reno (1959) was an avid Rockhurst supporter. He believed his education at Rockhurst paved his way into a successful business, marriage, family life and spiritual life. He dedicated himself to the Rockhurst mantra "a man for others" and was very proud that his two sons Jay and Michael are also Rockhurst MEN.

- Joan Reno

Banana Cookies

Cookies:

¾ cup butter, softened

¾ cup brown sugar

1 egg

½ teaspoon vanilla

3 ripe bananas, mashed

2 cups flour

1 teaspoon baking soda

Caramel Icing:

4 tablespoons butter

4 tablespoons milk

6 tablespoons brown sugar

Powdered sugar, sifted

Preheat oven to 350 degrees. For cookies, mix butter and brown sugar together. Add egg and vanilla and mix thoroughly. Mix in banana and dry ingredients. Drop 1 tablespoon batter on cookie sheet, placing batter about 2 inches apart. Bake 12-14 minutes, until slightly browned around edges. Cool.

For caramel icing, melt butter, milk and brown sugar over medium heat, stirring occasionally. Once boiling, take off heat and add sifted powdered sugar. Mix until smooth. Frost cooled cookies. Makes 3 dozen.

Sarah Jurcyk
Sons Jordan, 2006; Seth, 2008

Almost every kid (and adult) I know loves these cookies.

Lemon Whippersnaps

1 (2 layer) lemon cake mix

2 cups Cool Whip

1 egg

1 cup powdered sugar

Preheat oven to 350 degrees. Mix cake mix, Cool Whip and egg until blended. Roll dough into balls. Batter will be sticky. Roll balls in powdered sugar. Place on greased cookie sheet and bake for 10 minutes. Makes 3 dozen.

Natalie Wolfe
Son Brad, 2007

Cashew-Caramel Cookies

1⅔ cups flour

½ teaspoon salt

2½ cups roasted, salted cashews, divided

2 tablespoons plus 1 teaspoon oil

½ cup butter, softened

¾ cup brown sugar

½ cup sugar

1 egg

1 teaspoon vanilla

24 soft caramel squares, unwrapped (about 7 ounces)

¼ cup heavy cream

Preheat oven to 350 degrees. Sift flour and salt together, set aside. Coarsely chop 1 cup cashews and set aside. Process remaining cashews in a food processor until finely chopped. Pour in oil and process until mixture is creamy, about 2 minutes. Put cashew mixture, butter and sugars in mixing bowl and beat until fluffy, about 2 minutes. Mix in egg and vanilla. Reduce speed to low and add gradually add flour mixture. Stir in reserved chopped cashews.

Shape dough into 1½-inch balls and place 2 inches apart on parchment-lined baking sheets. Bake 6 minutes, then gently flatten with spatula and bake until bottoms are just golden, about 6-7 minutes more. Cool and transfer to wire racks.

Melt caramels with cream in a small saucepan over low heat while stirring. Let cool. Using a spoon, drizzle caramel over cookies and let set until dry. Store in single layers. Makes about 3 dozen.

Kate Brown
Husband Peter, 1976
Sons Chris, 2000; Kevin, 2003; Scott, 2010

The unusual deep flavor of these cookies comes from using cashews both ground and chopped.

I spent Rockhurst Prom day waiting to hear news from my date, who was playing tennis in the state tournament. I was all dressed up and ready to go. I even went without Pete to dinner with his best friend Terry Dwyer and Terry's date Nancy! I married him, so he was worth the wait!

- Kate Thompson Brown Husband Peter, 1976 Sons Chris, 2000; Kevin, 2003; Scott, 2010

The Virginia Executive Mansion Gingersnap Cookies

¾ cup shortening

1 cup sugar plus additional for sprinkling

¼ cup molasses

1 egg

2 cups flour

2 teaspoons baking soda

¼ teaspoon salt

1 tablespoon ground ginger

⅓ teaspoon ground cinnamon

Cream shortening, gradually add 1 cup sugar, beating at medium speed with electric mixer until light and fluffy. Add egg and molasses, mix well. Combine flour, soda, salt and spices in a separate bowl, mix well. Add about ¼ dry mixture at a time to creamed mixture, mixing until smooth after each addition. Chill dough at least 1 hour.

Shape dough into 1-inch balls and place 2 inches apart on ungreased cookie sheets. Sprinkle additional sugar on top of dough balls. Bake at 375 degrees for 10 minutes. Cool on wire racks. Makes 4½ dozen.

Tim Kaine, 1976

Governor Kaine sent this recipe from Virginia after his election in 2006.

Gooey Butter Cookies

1 box yellow cake mix

8-ounce package cream cheese

½ cup butter

½ teaspoon vanilla

1 egg

Powdered sugar for rolling

Preheat oven to 350 degrees. Mix all ingredients except powdered sugar and roll into walnut-sized balls. Roll each in powdered sugar and chill. Bake for 12 minutes.

Megan Viviano
Son Joseph, 2009

This very easily made treat is reminiscent of the famous St. Louis Gooey Butter Coffeecake!

Chris (2006) was unexpectedly hospitalized his senior year.
There was a constant flow of boys visiting him. I would guess 30 boys were there at one point. The nurse had to ask them to visit in shifts.
The boys came, sometimes with dates, and brought snacks, sodas, movies and games.
I have never been as touched by the kindness of others as I was by those young men during those stressful days.

- George Fakoury

No-Chill Sugar Cookies with Icing

Cookies:

1 cup butter

1 cup sugar

1 egg

1 teaspoon vanilla

2 teaspoons baking powder

3 cups flour

Icing:

2 cups powdered sugar

½ teaspoon almond extract

⅓ cup (about) milk

Food coloring

Preheat oven to 400 degrees. Cream butter and sugar. Beat in egg and vanilla, add baking powder. Add flour, 1 cup at a time, blending well after each addition. Do not chill. Roll out dough and cut with cookie cutters. Bake on ungreased baking sheets for 8-10 minutes. Cool and transfer to wire racks.

To make icing, sift powdered sugar into a bowl. Gradually add almond extract and enough milk to make consistency of thin glue. Mix in food coloring as desired. To decorate, dip top of cookie into icing. Remove quickly and let icing drip off. Place dipped cookies on racks until completely dry. When dry, cookies may be stacked with wax paper between and kept loosely covered.

Anne O'Flaherty
Husband Vince, 1980; Son Jack, 2008

English Toffee Bars

Saltine crackers

1 cup butter (no substitutes)

1 cup brown sugar

12-ounce bag milk chocolate chips

½ cup toasted sliced almonds

Preheat oven to 375 degrees. Line a jellyroll pan with foil or parchment paper, then line pan with a single layer of saltines. Melt butter and sugar together, boil gently for 3 minutes. Pour mixture over saltines. Bake for 5 minutes, until bubbly. Remove from oven, sprinkle chocolate chips over all, spreading chocolate as it melts. Sprinkle with nuts, cool. Makes 30-48 pieces.

Jennifer Blanck
Husband Paul, 1981

No-Chill Sugar Cookies have made many appearances at Rockhurst Theatre events, compliments of Janet Wagner (Vince, 2004). Patrons of musicals have enjoyed these cookies as fiddles for "Fiddler on the Roof", golden bow ties for "A Chorus Line" and dice for "Guys and Dolls". At a winter choir production the cookies were made in the shape of musical notes and treble clefs only to have the show cancelled at the last minute because of a major ice storm. The yummy treats did not go to waste, as Janet sent her son carefully up and down her street delivering the goodies to their unsuspecting but delighted neighbors. When the show was rescheduled, Janet was ready again with another batch of decorated cookies but Mother Nature struck once more! Heavy snow cancelled the show yet again.

Almond Apricot Biscotti

2 cups flour

¾ cup sugar

1½ teaspoons baking powder

½ teaspoon salt

¼ cup cold, unsalted butter, cut into small pieces

1 whole large egg, lightly beaten

⅓ cup whole milk

½ teaspoon vanilla

¼ teaspoon almond extract

1 cup whole almonds with skins (5½ ounces), toasted, cooled

1 cup dried apricots (6 ounces), quartered

1 large egg yolk

1 tablespoon water

Preheat oven to 350 degrees. Whisk together flour, sugar, baking powder and salt in a bowl. Blend in butter with pastry blender or fingertips until mixture resembles coarse meal. Add whole egg, milk and extracts, stirring with a fork until a soft dough forms, then knead in almonds.

Divide dough between 2 sheets of wax paper. Form into 2 equal mounds and flatten each mound into a 5-inch disk. Put half the apricots in center of 1 disk and fold dough over apricots to enclose them (use wax paper as an aid if necessary.) Transfer to parchment-lined baking sheet. Form into a 14x2½-inch log lengthwise on 1 side of baking sheet, spreading dough with wet hands. Make another log with remaining dough and apricots, arranging it about 4 inches from first log.

Beat egg yolk and water to make egg wash. Brush logs with egg wash and bake in middle of oven until pale golden and firm, about 20 minutes. Cool on baking sheet on a rack 20 minutes. Reduce oven temperature to 300 degrees while logs cool.

Carefully transfer baked logs to a cutting board using 2 wide metal spatulas, then cut logs diagonally into ½-inch-wide slices with a large heavy knife. Line baking sheet with a clean sheet of parchment. Stand slices, curved sides up, ½-inch apart on baking sheet and bake in upper third of oven until biscotti are dry, about 30 minutes. They will become hard as they cool. Transfer biscotti to rack to cool. Makes about 5½ dozen.

Anne Rhoades
Sons Charles, 1998; Chris, 2005; Dan, 2007

I've made these for Christmas gifts for Rockhurst parents. I have to think they are somewhat healthy with the almonds and apricots!

Baklava

Phyllo and Filling:

1 pound phyllo dough, thawed

1 pound walnuts, finely chopped

1½ teaspoons cinnamon

¼ cup sugar

1 cup butter, melted

50-60 whole cloves

Syrup:

2 cups sugar

1 cup water

2 tablespoons honey

1 cinnamon stick

½ lemon

Preheat oven to 350 degrees. When working with phyllo, keep it covered with a damp towel to prevent the sheets from drying out. Mix chopped nuts, cinnamon and sugar in a bowl. Brush a 9x13-inch pan with butter. Place 6 phyllo sheets in bottom of pan, brushing each with butter and sprinkling each with some of the nut mixture as they are layered, using approximately 1 cup nut mixture total.

Continue laying sheets of phyllo down, buttering each. After every two sheets, sprinkle more nut mixture over phyllo. Continue this pattern until there are only 6 sheets of phyllo left. Place last six sheets down, covering each only with melted butter. Using a sharp knife, cut pan of phyllo stacks into 5 long strips, from short end to short end of pan. Next cut across the pan diagonally, creating diamond-shaped pieces. Insert a whole clove onto each diamond. Bake 35-45 minutes, or until golden brown.

While baklava is baking, make syrup. In a medium saucepan, mix sugar, water and honey. Squeeze lemon juice into mixture and then drop squeezed lemon in as well. Add cinnamon stick and boil until sugar dissolves, approximately 7-10 minutes. Be careful mixture does not boil over. Let cool to room temperature. Remove lemon and cinnamon stick and pour cooled syrup over hot baklava. Makes 50-60 pieces.

Susan Jianas
Sons Matt, 2004; Michael, 2007

A delicious traditional Greek treat.

Tim Jantsch is the 1976 Cross Country District Champion with a time of 12:33.

1949 Prep News staff: Leonard Quigley, editor; James Siegfried, Donald Foley, sports editors; Henry Massman, business manager

Pumpkin Bars

Bars:

4 eggs

1⅔ cups sugar

1 cup cooking oil

15-ounce can pumpkin

1 teaspoon baking soda

2 cups flour

2 teaspoons baking powder

1 teaspoon cinnamon

1 teaspoon pumpkin pie spice

1 teaspoon salt

Icing:

3-ounce package cream cheese

½ cup butter, softened

1 teaspoon vanilla

2 cups powdered sugar

Preheat oven to 350 degrees. In mixing bowl beat together eggs, sugar, oil and pumpkin until light and fluffy. Stir together baking soda, flour, baking powder, cinnamon, pumpkin pie spice and salt, then add to pumpkin mixture and mix well. Spread batter in an ungreased 15x10-inch baking pan. Bake 25-30 minutes. Cool, then frost.

For icing, combine cream cheese and butter in a medium bowl and mix until smooth. Add powdered sugar and vanilla, mix until smooth. Spread on cooled pumpkin bars. Cut into bars. Makes 24-48 bars.

Lisa Ledom
Sons Mark 2007; Matthew, 2009

Lisa has made these each year for the Lunch Bunch group in the Fall. Nancy Cowing (son Nick, 2007) adds an extra teaspoon of cinnamon and served these at a Fall Parents Club meeting at Rockhurst. Everyone loved them!

I think Spanish was first taught at Rockhurst in the mid-1940s. Mr. Nash was our Spanish teacher and he was new at it. We practiced trilling our "r's". I can still remember "El burrrro es un animal. El burrrrro es un animal importante!"

- George J. Frye, 1949

Special "R" Bars

½ cup white Karo syrup

½ cup sugar

¾ cup peanut butter

3 cups Special K cereal

1 cup chocolate chips

Heat syrup and sugar over medium-low heat for 5 minutes. Add peanut butter and stir until blended. Pour over 3 cups of cereal and mix. Spread in an 8x8-inch or 9x9-inch pan. Melt chocolate chips and spread on top of bars when cool. Makes 12 bars. Double this recipe to make 24 bars in a 9x13-inch pan.

Mary Thompson
Husband Paul, 1980; Son P.J., 2006

Kit Kat Bars

Bars:

1 cup butter

⅓ cup sugar

1 cup brown sugar

½ cup milk

2 cups graham cracker crumbs

1 box club crackers

Topping:

½ cup butterscotch chips

½ cup semisweet chocolate chips

⅔ cup peanut butter

Melt butter in a saucepan. Add sugars and milk, stir to blend. Add graham cracker crumbs, bring to a boil. Reduce heat and simmer for 5 minutes. Melt topping ingredients in microwave and stir until well blended.

To assemble, line bottom of a lightly greased 9x13-inch pan with crackers. Pour half the boiled mixture over crackers. Place a second layer of crackers on top and pour remaining boiled mixture over. Place third layer of crackers, cover with melted topping. Refrigerate and cut after topping becomes firm, about 1-2 hours. Store in refrigerator. Makes 24 bars.

Patti Gound
Sons Ryan, 2003; Matthew, 2007

"Special R" Bars were brought to the State Soccer Tournament in November 2004. With the combination of chocolate, peanut butter and cereal, they provided much-needed energy for the tough competition at State. Rockhurst won the 8 p.m. game in a shoot-out after playing 40 minutes of overtime! The team lost in triple overtime the very next day and ended the season with a second place finish at State. Probably the person who liked the bars best was Coach Lawson!

- Mary Thompson
Son P.J., 2006

Pay Day Bars

1 (2 layer) box yellow cake mix

⅓ cup margarine or butter

1 egg

3 cups mini marshmallows

⅔ cup light corn syrup

¼ cup margarine or butter

2 teaspoons vanilla

12-ounce package peanut butter chips

2 cups salted peanuts

2 cups crispy rice cereal

Preheat oven to 350 degrees. Combine first three ingredients and press into a 9x13-inch pan. Use wax paper to press down sticky ingredients. Bake 15 minutes. Remove, cover with marshmallows, bake for another 2 minutes. Heat corn syrup, margarine and vanilla until melted. Add peanut butter chips and stir until chips are melted. Stir in peanuts and cereal. Spoon over melted marshmallows, chill until firm. Makes 30-36 bars.

Janelle Stamm
Husband Jeff, 1981; Stepson John, 2009

Caramel Pecan Bars

⅓ cup plus ½ cup butter, divided

20 Oreo cookies, crushed

14-ounce package caramels

2½ cups toasted chopped pecans

Topping:

¾ cup chocolate chips

3 tablespoons butter

3 tablespoons heavy whipping cream

¾ teaspoon vanilla

Melt ⅓ cup butter, mix with Oreos. Press into bottom of ungreased 11x7-inch baking dish. Bake at 325 degrees for 10-12 minutes or until set. Cool on wire rack. On low heat, melt caramels and ½ cup butter together, stirring often. Stir in pecans, pour over crust, cool. Combine chocolate chips, butter and cream in a pan. Stir over low heat until smooth. Remove from heat, stir in vanilla. Pour over caramel layer. Cool on wire rack.

Jan Flanagan
Husband Jim, 1971; Sons Bryan, 2002; Sean, 2004; Kevin, 2007

The Senior Moms (class of 2007) threw diets out the window when I brought these to a gathering in December 2006.

Chocolate Peanut Bars

1 cup butter

1 cup crunchy peanut butter

16 ounces powdered sugar

1½ cups crushed vanilla wafers (about 45 cookies)

12-ounce package semisweet chocolate chips

½ cup whipping cream

Beat butter and peanut butter until blended. Add powdered sugar and wafer crumbs, blend again. Press mixture evenly into a lightly greased 13x9-inch baking pan lined with wax paper.

Stir together chocolate chips and whipping cream in a medium saucepan over low heat until melted and smooth. Spread evenly over peanut butter mixture. Chill 1 hour or until firm. Remove from refrigerator and let stand at room temperature 10 minutes or until slightly softened. Cut into bars. Makes 24 bars.

Lori Keenan
Sons Connor, 2007; Tommy, 2009

Deep Dish Brownies

¾ cup butter, melted

1½ cups sugar

1½ teaspoons vanilla

3 eggs

¾ cup flour

½ cup cocoa

½ teaspoon baking powder

½ teaspoon salt

1 cup chocolate chips

Powdered sugar

Preheat oven to 350 degrees. Blend melted butter, sugar and vanilla. Add eggs, beating well with a spoon. In separate bowl, combine flour, cocoa, baking powder and salt. Gradually add flour mixture to egg mixture, stirring until well blended. Add chocolate chips and pour batter into greased 9x9-inch baking pan. Bake for 35 minutes. Dust with powdered sugar when cool. Makes 12 brownies.

Barb Haden
Husband Jon, 1975; Son Robbie, 2009

Peanut Butter Brownies

12-ounce package chocolate chips

¼ cup butter or margarine

½ cup peanut butter

3 eggs

1 teaspoon vanilla

1½ cups sugar

1¼ cups flour

½ teaspoon baking powder

Frosting:

1½ cups powdered sugar

2 tablespoons peanut butter

½ teaspoon vanilla

2 tablespoons milk

Heat oven to 350 degrees. Put paper liners in muffin tin. Melt chocolate chips and butter in 2-quart saucepan over low heat. Stir in peanut butter until well blended. Beat in eggs one at a time until smooth, add vanilla. Beat in remaining ingredients. Divide batter equally among muffin cups. Bake 18-22 minutes or until tops are dry. Cool. Mix all frosting ingredients together until smooth, spread on brownies. Makes 12.

Nancy Cowing
Son Nick, 2007

Easy Brownies

1 box devil's food cake mix

1 egg

¼ cup water

Chopped pecans, optional

Chocolate chips, optional

Stir all ingredients together. Batter will be very thick. Press into greased 9x13-inch pan. Bake at 350 degrees for 20-25 minutes for a chewy-type brownie, slightly longer for the cake type.

Rose Dorlac & Jim Bevan
Grandson Dennis Ogle, 2009

Half & Half Brownies

Brownies:

1 cup butter, softened

1½ teaspoons vanilla

2 cups sugar

4 eggs

2¼ cups flour

½ teaspoon salt

2 (1-ounce) squares
unsweetened chocolate,
melted

Icing:

2 tablespoons dry cocoa

3 tablespoons butter, melted

1½ cups powdered sugar

2 tablespoons milk

1 teaspoon vanilla

2 cups chopped nuts

Preheat oven to 350 degrees. Thoroughly blend brownie ingredients except chocolate squares in a mixing bowl. Divide mixture in half and add melted chocolate to one half, stirring well to incorporate chocolate. Grease a 9x13-inch pan. Drop light batter by teaspoonfuls into baking pan, leaving spaces to add dark batter. Drop chocolate batter between light batter then gently swirl batters together to create a marbled effect. Bake 45 minutes.

For icing: Stir cocoa and butter until mixed. Add remaining ingredients except nuts and beat until smooth, adding more milk if necessary. Stir in nuts and spread over cooled brownies. Cut into bars. Makes 24 bars.

Kathleen Donnelly
Husband Arthur, 1964
Sons David, 1988; Kevin, 1991; Christopher 2003

The Half & Half Brownie recipe dates from 1994 and was featured at the "Snack-O-Rama" booth at the famous Rockhurst fundraising tradition known as Sale-O-Rama.
This annual event was a huge garage sale held on the Rockhurst campus in the 1970s, '80s and '90s. It generated many thousands of dollars for the school each year. Parents worked in the same Sale-O booth for years, even after their sons had graduated.

- Kathleen Donnelly
Sons David, 1988; Kevin, 1991; Christopher, 2003

Decadent Raspberry Brownies

Brownies:

4 (1-ounce) squares unsweetened baking chocolate

¾ cup butter

2 cups sugar

3 eggs

1 teaspoon vanilla

1 cup flour

Toppings:

¼ cup seedless raspberry jam

6 (1-ounce) squares semi-
sweet chocolate, chopped

¾ cup heavy whipping cream

Fresh raspberries, optional

Preheat oven to 350 degrees. Grease a 9x13-inch baking pan. In a large microwave-safe bowl, microwave 4 squares chocolate and butter on high for 2 minutes, or until butter is melted. Stir until chocolate is completely melted. Blend in sugar, then add eggs and vanilla and mix well. Stir in flour until well blended and spread mixture into prepared pan. Bake 30-35 minutes until toothpick inserted in center comes out with fudgy crumbs. Do not overbake. Cool.

Spread jam over cooled brownies. Microwave 6 squares chocolate and cream in microwave on high for 2 minutes or until simmering. Stir until chocolate is completely melted and mixture is well blended. Spread evenly over jam layer. Refrigerate one hour or until chocolate layer is set. Cut into 32 brownies. Garnish each brownie with a fresh raspberry.

Jan Flanagan
Husband Jim, 1971; Sons Bryan, 2002; Sean, 2004; Kevin, 2007

These are delicious and so easy to make!

I spent 3 different time periods at Rockhurst. From 1963-1966 I was in the first years of Regency as a Jesuit Scholastic. I returned in 1970-1976 as Pastoral Chair and chair of the English Department. Then in 1985 I returned as President (until 1993.) I hope I impressed upon every student that a talent is not a gift until it is given away. Each of you is called through the Ignatian vision to be a gift to the world for the greater glory of God.

- Rev. Thomas Cummings, S.J.

Desserts

DESSERTS

2000s

National:

The new millennium was greeted with celebration and trepidation. Computer users everywhere breathed a collective sigh of relief when Y2K came and passed without any complications. The following year, the world watched in shock as terrorists crashed commercial airliners into the World Trade Centers and Pentagon on September 11, 2001. In the aftermath, the United States deployed troops to Iraq and Afghanistan, where wars still rage today. In 2003, scientists successfully mapped the human genome, and California elected the Terminator, making Arnold Schwarzenegger governor of the Golden State. The world embraced everything from far-fetched fiction to all-too-real television. Harry Potter and his Hogwarts crew put British author J.K. Rowling on the best-seller list time and again, and "reality" shows like "Survivor" and "Big Brother" pulled in big ratings.

Local:

Kansas City's urban core experienced an unprecedented renaissance and construction boom during the first decade of the 21st century. Urban renewal projects including the Sprint Center and Power and Light district sprung up in downtown Kansas City, earning the city a spot among four finalists in the 2006 world competition for the most dramatically improved urban setting. Such growth was not isolated to the city's urban core; many suburban areas experienced considerable development as well. Zona Rosa opened in the Northland, and Village West opened in Wyandotte County, neighboring Kansas City's new NASCAR venue, the Kansas Speedway. In other sports news, the Wizards brought Kansas City its first Major League Soccer championship in 2000.

Sticky Toffee Pudding Cake

Cake:

1 cup plus 1 tablespoon flour

1 teaspoon baking powder

¼ cup finely chopped pitted dates

¾ cup chopped walnuts

4 tablespoons butter

¾ cup sugar

1 large egg

1 teaspoon baking soda

1 teaspoon vanilla

1¼ cups boiling water

Caramel topping:

3 tablespoons butter

¼ cup plus 1 tablespoon brown sugar

2 tablespoons cream

Cake: Preheat oven to 350 degrees. Butter a 9-inch pie dish or oval gratin dish. Sift one cup flour and baking powder and set aside. Toss dates in remaining one tablespoon flour.

Beat butter and sugar until fluffy in a mixer. Beat in egg and flour until smooth. Sprinkle baking soda and vanilla over dates, add boiling water to combine. Add date mixture to batter, mixing well. Pour into prepared dish. Bake until set and browned, 30-40 minutes. Remove from oven and cover with caramel topping.

Caramel topping: Bring butter, brown sugar and cream to a boil. Simmer for 3 minutes and pour over pudding cake. Return cake to oven for 2-3 minutes. Remove from oven and serve hot or reheat later.

Michelle Nemmers
Son John, 2008

I like to make extra sauce and pour more on when serving. I top it all with whipped cream.

Mint Julep Cake

Cake:

3 cups flour

2 cups sugar

1 teaspoon salt

1 teaspoon baking powder

½ teaspoon baking soda

1 cup buttermilk

1 cup butter

2 teaspoons vanilla

4 eggs

Butter sauce:

½ cup powdered sugar

⅓ cup butter

3 tablespoons water

2 teaspoons Kentucky bourbon

Frosting:

2 cups (12-ounce package) white chocolate chips

14-ounce can sweetened condensed milk

1 teaspoon white or green crème de menthe or ½ teaspoon mint extract

Fresh mint leaves to garnish

Preheat oven to 325 degrees. Grease and flour a 10-inch Bundt pan. Whisk together flour, sugar, salt, baking powder and baking soda. Make a well in the center. In a small bowl, combine buttermilk, butter, vanilla and eggs. Add wet ingredients to flour mixture. Beat on low 1 minute, then at medium for 3 more minutes. Pour into Bundt pan, smooth batter. Bake 50 minutes or until toothpick inserted in center comes out clean. Ten minutes before cake is done, begin preparing butter sauce.

Butter sauce: In a small pan heat all ingredients except bourbon. Stir until melted, do not boil. Remove from heat, continue stirring 2 minutes, then stir in bourbon. When cake is done, remove from oven and poke holes around the top with a wooden skewer. Pour sauce evenly over cake and cool completely.

Frosting: Melt white chocolate chips with condensed milk over low heat, stirring constantly until chips are melted. Remove from heat, add crème de menthe. Cool 10 minutes, then spread over cooled cake. Garnish with mint. Chill to set frosting. Remove from refrigerator 30 minutes before cutting. Serves 12-18.

Bryan Flanagan, 2002

Green crème de menthe may be used, but also add a couple drops of green food coloring or the frosting color will be unappealing. Also good without the frosting. I have good college friends from Louisville, Kentucky and this is a favorite, especially at Derby time!

Actor Spencer Tracy attended Rockhurst in 1917. His father John E. Tracy managed the local office of the Sterling Motor Truck Company. Jim Curtis, writing a biography of Spencer, says that Tracy's time at Rockhurst seemed to have a great influence on him. His grades and class load improved terrifically at Rockhurst, leading Mr. Curtis to believe that someone at Rockhurst had a profound influence on the 16-year-old boy. The Tracy family transferred back to Milwaukee later in 1917 and Spencer left school to go to war.

Italian Cream Cake

Cake:

½ cup butter

½ cup shortening

2 cups sugar

5 eggs, separated

2 cups flour

1 teaspoon baking soda

1 cup buttermilk

1 teaspoon vanilla

1 small can coconut

1 cup chopped pecans

Cream Cheese Icing:

8-ounce package cream cheese

¼ cup butter

16-ounce box powdered sugar

1 teaspoon vanilla

1 cup chopped pecans

Cake: Preheat oven to 350 degrees. Cream butter and shortening, add sugar, beat until smooth. Add egg yolks and beat well. Combine flour and baking soda and add to creamed mixture alternately with buttermilk. Stir in vanilla, add coconut and chopped pecans. Beat egg whites until stiff, fold into batter. Pour into 3 greased and floured 8-inch round cake pans. Bake for 25 minutes or until tested done.

Icing: Beat cream cheese and butter until smooth. Add sugar and mix well. Add vanilla and beat until smooth. Spread on cake and then sprinkle with chopped pecans.

Martie Eftink
Son Jim, 2003

My husband Gerry's family has lived on the same farm in southeast Missouri for 100 years. Every year my mother-in-law sends me a big box of pecans gathered from trees planted by Gerry's great-grandfather. They are the best pecans I've ever tasted and I enjoy making desserts such as this one using the delicious nuts.

Ron Geldhof not only introduced us to Honors and AP Chemistry but also spent every winter in the ice and snow, coaching some of us in soccer. Come spring he laid the foundation for our emerging tennis program with the first State Championships in 1975 and 1976. When I think of the discipline for science, and time and energy outside of the classroom that he shared with us as a young man himself, I surely think of him as one of Rockhurst's "Men for Others."

- Keith Connor, 1976

Banana Cake

My mom told me before
freshman year that
she was done packing
lunches and that I could
buy mine in high school.
So that first day I bought
a hearty meal that
included coconut cream
pie for dessert.
I can't remember what
the bill was,
but it was high.
I was trying out for
freshman football
and in the August heat
that afternoon,
lunch all came back up,
particularly the pie.
After I told Mom how
much lunch cost and what
eventually happened to it,
she packed my lunch
every day for the
next 4 years!

- Mark Fitzpatrick, 1974
Sons Tim, 2002;
John, 2008

Cake:

1 cup butter, room temperature

3 cups sugar

4 eggs

6 very ripe bananas, peeled, mashed

2 teaspoons baking soda

½ cup sour cream

3 cups flour

Butter Frosting:

½ cup butter, room temperature

3 cups sifted powdered sugar

3-4 tablespoons whipping cream

1 teaspoon vanilla

Cake: Grease and flour 3 (8-inch) cake pans and set aside. Preheat oven to 325 degrees. Cream together butter and sugar in a large bowl. Add eggs, one at a time, beating thoroughly after each addition. Beat in mashed bananas. Mix baking soda and sour cream together and add to mixture. Add flour and mix well. Pour batter into prepared cake pans. Bake 25-35 minutes, or until a toothpick inserted in the center comes out clean. Let cake cool before frosting.

Butter frosting: Cream butter and powdered sugar. Beat in whipping cream and vanilla until frosting is smooth and creamy. Frost cooled cake. Serves 8-10.

Marie Neenan
Husband Bob, 1977; Sons Matthew, 2002; Ben, 2004

Blueberry Cake

2 eggs, separated

1 cup sugar

½ cup butter

1½ cups flour

1 teaspoon baking powder

½ teaspoon salt

⅓ cup milk

1 teaspoon vanilla

1½ cups fresh blueberries, tossed with flour to coat

Sugar for topping

Preheat oven to 350 degrees. Beat egg whites until stiff; set aside. Cream sugar and butter. Beat egg yolks well and add to butter mixture. Sift flour, baking powder and salt.

Add flour mixture to creamed mixture alternating with milk. Gently fold in egg whites and vanilla. Add floured blueberries. Pour into a greased and floured 9-inch square pan. Sprinkle lightly with sugar. Bake 35-40 minutes or until a toothpick comes out clean. Cake will be lightly brown on top. Don't overbake. Serves 9.

Rosemary Cunningham
Husband Bob, 1943; Son Kevin, 1974
Grandsons Jordan Jurcyk, 2006; Seth, 2008

During senior year, our lunch table decided to make Cake Day a weekly tradition. Each of us took turns bringing in a cake to share with everyone at the table. Some were homemade, some were store-bought. We looked forward to all of them. One member of our table, Nick Liddeke, is a vegan, though, so he didn't eat our cakes. Others at the table were Michael Jianas, John Shealy, Stuart McCausland, Michael Sizemore, Andrew Robinson, Timmy Trabon, Jack Connealy and me. We declared our last week of school Cake Week, and we brought a cake in every day. Then, on the last lunch of our last year, someone (Jack) forgot to bring the cake!

- Kevin Flanagan, 2007

Rhubarb Cake

About 100 students started in our freshman class. We were divided into A, B, C or D class according to test scores. By sophomore year, the class size was down to about 75. D class was eliminated, but the students continued to be reshuffled quarterly among the A, B, and C classes based on overall class rank at the end of each quarter. Junior year the reshuffling stopped, and those who ended their sophomore year in C went to the Spanish class. This meant that they stopped taking Latin and started taking Spanish. Everything else was the same. Those in A and B classes were then allowed the one curriculum choice they had the entire four years of high school. They could choose the Honors class and take Greek (in addition to Latin and everything else), or they could choose the Latin Scientific class and take advanced math. I finished my sophomore year in B class. Having barely survived algebra and geometry, I figured that Greek had to be easier than advanced math, so I chose the Honors class. Compared to Rockhurst High School, college was a lark.

- Ken Fligg, 1951

Cake:

2 cups flour

1 teaspoon baking soda

1 teaspoon cinnamon

¼ teaspoon allspice

¼ teaspoon ground cloves

1 teaspoon salt

½ cup butter

1¼ cups sugar

2 eggs

⅓ cup milk

2 cups chopped rhubarb or apples

Topping:

⅔ cup flour

½ cup brown sugar

½ teaspoon cinnamon

4 tablespoons butter, softened

Cake: Sift together flour, baking soda, cinnamon, allspice, cloves and salt; set aside. Blend butter, sugar, eggs and milk. Add dry ingredients and mix well. Stir in chopped rhubarb. Spread batter in a greased 9x13-inch pan.

Topping: In a small bowl mix all topping ingredients with fingers until well mixed and crumbly. Place topping over batter and pat down. Bake at 350 degrees for 40 minutes or until knife inserted in center comes out clean. The cake will be very moist.

Tonja Kernell
Son Tate, 2009

Piña Colada Cake

Cake:

4 eggs, separated

2 egg whites

1½ cups sugar, divided

½ cup vegetable oil

½ cup water

1 teaspoon vanilla

1½ cups flour

1 tablespoon baking powder

⅛ teaspoon salt

Tropical flavors:

¼ cup pineapple juice (drained from pineapple for frosting)

¼ cream of coconut

2 tablespoons light rum

Frostings:

6 tablespoons butter, softened

1 pound powdered sugar

⅓ cup whipping cream

1 teaspoon vanilla

¼ cup drained, crushed pineapple, juice reserved

1 tablespoon dark rum

Finale:

2 cups shredded coconut, toasted

Cake: Beat 6 egg whites until foamy. Add ½ cup sugar, one tablespoon at a time, beating until stiff peaks form and sugar is dissolved, 2-4 minutes. In a separate bowl, whisk 4 egg yolks, oil, water and vanilla, set aside. Stir together remaining 1 cup sugar, flour, baking powder and salt in a large bowl. Fold in egg yolk mixture until blended. Fold in egg white mixture. Pour batter into 2 lightly greased, wax paper-lined 9-inch round cake pans. Bake at 350 degrees 25-30 minutes. Cool in pan on wire racks for 10 minutes, remove from pans and cool on racks.

Tropical flavors: Stir together pineapple juice, cream of coconut and light rum. Brush over cooled cake layers.

Frostings: Beat butter at medium speed until creamy. Gradually beat in powdered sugar and whipping cream until smooth. Stir in vanilla. Remove ½ cup frosting, reserve remaining frosting. Stir pineapple into ½ cup frosting. Spread between layers. Stir dark rum into reserved frosting. Spread on top and sides of cake.

Finale: Press toasted coconut onto top and sides of cake.

Jan Flanagan
Husband Jim, 1971; Sons Bryan, 2002; Sean, 2004; Kevin, 2007

Although this requires some time and effort, the result is quite impressive and is really delicious.

I took over the Rock Shop when Father Paul Stark decided to give it up. What a job! How he did it alone I will never know. I ran it for 10 years and the best part of the job was getting to know all the young men. It was great when they would come up and say hello no matter where I was.

- Donna Raydo
Sons Shawn, 1993; David, 1999

The beautiful RHS campus does not stay that way without serious behind the scenes effort year-round. Director Delbert Conrad, supervisor Artie Vielhauer and their crews have been a big part of Rockhurst for many years. Their skills keep RHS humming and their ever-present smiles are a wonderful bonus.

Chocolate and Peanut Butter Cake

Cake:

1 cup butter

¼ cup cocoa

1 cup water

½ cup buttermilk

2 eggs, well beaten

2 cups sugar

2 cups flour

1 teaspoon baking soda

1 teaspoon vanilla

2 cups creamy peanut butter

Icing:

½ cup butter

¼ cup cocoa

6 tablespoons buttermilk

16 ounces powdered sugar

½ teaspoon vanilla

Cake: Mix butter, cocoa, water and buttermilk over medium heat until bubbly. In a bowl, mix sugar, flour and baking soda. Pour butter mixture over flour mixture, stir until blended. Add eggs and vanilla, stir until combined. Pour batter into a greased 9x13-inch baking pan. Bake at 350 degrees about 25 minutes. Let cake cool completely, then spread cooled cake with peanut butter.

Icing: Heat butter, cocoa and buttermilk in a saucepan over medium heat until bubbly. Add powdered sugar and vanilla, beat until smooth. Pour over peanut butter layer.

Kris Balderston
Son Blaine, 2007

Father Tom Pesci was from the east coast and in the beginning of his time here he thought we Midwestern folks were too casual. He was fearful that our casual attitude would not allow him to accomplish all that he wanted to do. He quickly learned to appreciate our work ethic and more fun-loving spirit. I will always admire the fact that he made an enormous effort to understand the Rockhurst community that was so different from his own and to fit in with us and our Midwestern ways. A bouncy start turned out to be a smooth ride.

- Judie Scanlon, RHS Special Events Coordinator Sons Steve, 1988; Kerry, 1994

Hershey Bar Pie

6 (1.5-ounce) Hershey bars, with or without almonds

½ cup milk

16 large marshmallows, cut in half to speed melting

8-ounce tub Cool Whip (not lite)

Graham cracker or Oreo piecrust

Over low heat, melt Hershey bars with milk and marshmallows, stirring continuously. Cool, then fold in Cool Whip. Pour into crust and put in freezer for 2-3 hours before serving. Serves 8.

Kathleen Wendland
Son Jack, 2008

Butterscotch Praline Pie

Crust:

9-inch prepared pie crust

¼ cup butter

¼ cup brown sugar

¾ cup chopped pecans

Filling:

2 (3.5-ounce) boxes cook and serve butterscotch pudding mix

1½ cups milk

1 cup whipped cream

Crust: Place prepared crust into 9-inch pie plate. Bake at 450 degrees for 5-6 minutes until partially baked but not brown. Remove from oven. Heat butter and brown sugar, stirring until bubbly, add pecans. Pour mixture into crust and place back in oven until crust is brown, about 5-7 more minutes. Remove from oven and cool.

Filling: Prepare butterscotch pudding with milk according to package. Pour into cooled crust. Cover with waxed paper and chill. Just before serving, top with whipped cream. Serves 8.

Sheri Cook Cunningham
Son Daniel, 2009

Sour Cream Lemon Pie

1 cup sugar

¼ cup butter

4 tablespoons cornstarch

1 tablespoon lemon zest

¼ cup lemon juice

1 cup milk

3 egg yolks, slightly beaten

1 cup sour cream

9-inch baked pie crust

Whipped cream for garnish

Stir together sugar, butter, cornstarch, lemon zest, juice, milk and egg yolks in a medium saucepan. Cook over medium heat until thickened. Cool slightly and fold in sour cream. Pour into a baked pie crust and refrigerate for several hours. Serve with whipped cream.

Kathleen Clement
Sons Chris, 1999; Andrew, 2003

Creamy Blueberry Pie

9-inch unbaked pie crust

3-4 cups blueberries, rinsed, drained well

1 cup sour cream

¾ cup sugar

⅓ cup flour

2 eggs

1 teaspoon vanilla

Topping:

¼ cup butter, softened

½ cup sugar

½ cup flour

Place crust in pie pan. Pour in blueberries (fresh or frozen). Mix sour cream, sugar, flour, eggs and vanilla until smooth. Pour evenly over berries. Mix topping ingredients until crumbly. Sprinkle evenly over filling. Bake at 350 degrees 55-60 minutes. If berries were frozen, an additional 5 minutes of baking time may be needed.

Marie Neenan
Husband Bob, 1977; Sons Matthew, 2002; Ben, 2004

During baseball season, Ryan Bennett and I would text message each other in whichever class we were in and both ask our teachers to use the restroom. We would skip over the restroom and meet each other at the indoor batting cage for a quick round of batting practice.

- Brandon Doherty, 2004 [editor: And now we know one reason cell phones are banned in the classrooms!]

Raspberry Custard Pie

9-inch pie crust

3 eggs

2 cups sugar

½ cup flour

⅓ cup evaporated milk

2 teaspoons vanilla

Dash salt

5½ cups fresh or frozen raspberries or other berries

Topping:

½ cup flour

¼ cup brown sugar

¼ cup cold butter

Line a 9-inch pie plate with crust. In a large bowl, beat eggs, then add sugar, flour, milk, vanilla and salt. Mix well. Gently fold in raspberries. Pour into crust. For topping, combine flour and brown sugar in a small bowl; cut in butter until crumbly. Sprinkle over pie filling. Bake at 400 degrees for 10 minutes, reduce heat to 350 degrees and bake 45-50 minutes longer, until knife inserted near center comes out clean. Cool on wire rack. Refrigerate leftovers.

Marjie Bergman
Grandsons Bryan Flanagan, 2002; Sean, 2004; Kevin, 2007

Chocolate Silk Pie

1 cup semisweet chocolate chips

½ cup butter

Pinch of salt

1 tablespoon unsweetened cocoa

1 cup sugar

3 eggs

⅔ cup evaporated milk

1 teaspoon vanilla

9-inch unbaked pie crust

Whipped cream and chocolate shavings for garnish

Preheat over to 350 degrees. In a large microwave-safe bowl, melt chocolate chips and butter at 50% power for 2 minutes, or until butter is melted. Stir until smooth. Whisk in salt, cocoa, sugar, eggs, evaporated milk and vanilla. Whisk until well blended. Pour chocolate mixture into crust. Bake for 30 minutes or until filling has puffed but center still wiggles. Cool completely. Refrigerate until ready to serve. Garnish with whipped cream and chocolate shavings.

Barb Haden
Husband Jon, 1975; Son Robbie, 2009

Impossible Pumpkin Pie

¾ cup Bisquick baking mix

2 tablespoons butter or margarine

13-ounce can evaporated milk

2 eggs

16-ounce can pumpkin

2½ teaspoons pumpkin pie spice

2 teaspoons vanilla

Whipped cream for garnish

Preheat oven to 350 degrees. Grease a 9- or 10-inch pie plate. Beat all ingredients until smooth. Pour into pie plate. Bake until knife inserted in center comes out clean, 50-55 minutes. Top with whipped cream.

Rev. Terrence A. Baum, S.J.
RHS President

After hearing a commotion outside her home on Westover one day, Laura Bluhm (son Scott, 2007) looked out to see a trolley full of men, gawking at her home. Seems Laura and her husband Mark had unknowingly purchased "Club 630" a popular party hangout when it was the Lawler residence. Rockhurst alums in town for a reunion wanted a look at their former gathering spot.

Key Lime Pie

3 egg whites

2 teaspoons Key lime zest

14-ounce can sweetened condensed milk

⅔ cup freshly squeezed Key lime juice (about 2 dozen Key limes)

9-inch prepared graham cracker crust

1 cup heavy whipping cream

1 tablespoon powdered sugar

Preheat oven to 350 degrees. Mix egg whites and lime zest with a hand mixer for about 5 minutes, until very foamy. Slowly add condensed milk and continue to mix for another 3-4 minutes until mixture thickens. Slowly add lime juice and mix briefly until just combined. Pour mixture into pie crust and bake 10-15 minutes until it just begins to set. Remove to a wire rack to cool. When cool, place in refrigerator. Place in freezer 20-30 minutes before serving. Meanwhile, beat cream and powdered sugar to desired consistency to make topping. Top pie with whipped cream and serve.

Joellen Messerli
Sons Robbie, 2007; Kyle, 2009

Oyster House Chocolate Chip Peanut Butter Pie

8 ounces cream cheese

1 cup smooth peanut butter

8 ounces powdered sugar

8 ounces Cool Whip topping, room temperature

1 ounce Chapala or other coffee liqueur, optional

¾ cup mini chocolate chips

Oreo cookie prepared pie crust

Refrigerate or freeze bowl and beater until ice cold. Mix cream cheese, peanut butter and sugar together. Add Cool Whip and Chapala, blend well. Fold in chocolate chips. Pour into pie crust, mounding high in the middle. Refrigerate.

Jim Flanagan, 1971
Sons Bryan, 2002; Sean, 2004; Kevin, 2007

I ate this at a restaurant on the Gulf Coast and had to ask for the recipe. It is very rich!

Lemon Blueberry Citrus Tart

1 cup butter, room temperature

¾ cup sifted powdered sugar

2¼ cups flour, divided

4 eggs

1½ cups sugar

⅓ cup lemon juice

2 tablespoons lemon zest

1 teaspoon baking powder

1½ cups fresh or frozen blueberries

Powdered sugar for garnish

Orange or lemon zest for garnish

Preheat oven to 350 degrees. Lightly grease a 9x13-inch baking pan. With electric mixer, cream butter and powdered sugar until smooth. Add 2 cups flour and mix until well blended. Press mixture into baking pan and bake for 20 minutes until golden. In a mixing bowl combine eggs, sugar, lemon juice, zest, remaining ¼ cup flour and baking powder. Beat for 2 minutes. Sprinkle berries over cooked crust. Pour egg mixture over berries, arranging berries with a spoon. Bake for 30-35 minutes until light brown and set. Cool thoroughly in pan on wire rack. Cut into triangles or bars and sprinkle with powdered sugar just before serving. Garnish with orange or lemon zest. Serves 12-16.

Laura O'Rourke
The Culinary Center of Kansas City
Husband Kevin, 1972; Sons Delaney, 2008; Devin, 2010

Lemon Curd

4 medium lemons, juice and zest

1¼ cups sugar

4 tablespoons butter

4 eggs, lightly beaten

In a double boiler or heavy pan, melt together lemon juice and zest, sugar and butter. Stir in eggs. Cook, stirring constantly until mixture coats back of a spoon. Pour into clean jars. Cool a bit, then put on lids and refrigerate.

Sarah Jurcyk
Sons Jordan, 2006; Seth, 2008

Banana Split Dessert

2 cups graham cracker crumbs

1½ cups margarine, divided

2 eggs

2 cups powdered sugar

5 bananas

15-ounce can crushed pineapple, drained well

1½ cups miniature marshmallows

1 cup coconut

16-ounce tub Cool Whip

½ cup pecans

1 small jar maraschino cherries

Mix crumbs with ½ cup margarine. Press into 9x13-inch pan. Mix eggs, powdered sugar and 1 cup margarine. Beat 5 minutes and spread over crumbs. Layer sliced bananas over mixture, pour drained pineapple over bananas. Layer marshmallows and coconut over pineapple. Spread Cool Whip on top. Garnish with pecans and cherries. Refrigerate at least 8 hours.

Katy O'Dowd
Sons Nolen, 1999; Clark, 2009

Lemon Crème Anglaise

1 quart cream

1 cup sugar

1 teaspoon vanilla

10 egg yolks

1¾ cups lemon curd

Heat cream, sugar and vanilla. Temper in egg yolks. Heat just enough to slightly thicken. Strain and cool. Gently fold in lemon curd.

Marcia & Lon Lane
The Catering Company
Sons Lon 2002; Stewart, 2004

Lemon Cream

½ cup lemon curd (homemade or purchased)

½ cup sour cream

Mix together, cover and chill. Delicious on warm berry cobbler!

Diane Frese
Nephews Bryan Flanagan, 2002; Sean, 2004; Kevin, 2007

Frozen Lemon Mousse

4 egg yolks

½ cup fresh lemon juice

1½ tablespoons lemon zest

1 cup sugar, divided

4 egg whites

⅛ teaspoon cream of tartar

⅛ teaspoon salt

1½ cups whipping cream

Raspberries, blueberries, mint sprigs for garnish

Combine egg yolks, lemon juice, zest and ¼ cup sugar in large bowl and mix well. Separately beat egg whites until foamy. Add cream of tartar and salt and beat until soft peak forms. Add ¾ cup sugar gradually and beat until stiff. Whip cream in a separate bowl until stiff. Fold egg whites and whipped cream gently into egg yolk mixture, spoon into bowl. Freeze, covered with foil, for 8 hours or more. Let mousse stand in refrigerator for 1-2 hours before serving. Spoon into 12 dessert dishes. Garnish with berries and mint.

Michelle Nemmers
Son John, 2008

Chocolate Raspberry
Frozen Dessert

3 squares semisweet chocolate

¼ cup water plus 2 tablespoons, divided

8 ounces light cream cheese

½ cup raspberry jam or spread, divided

8 ounces lite Cool Whip, divided

36 fresh raspberries

2 chocolate wafer cookies, crushed

Microwave chocolate and ¼ cup water for 1-1½ minutes. Stir until smooth. Beat chocolate mixture with cream cheese and ¼ cup raspberry jam. Stir until smooth. Add 2½ cups Cool Whip and blend until smooth. Spread in springform pan. Freeze 3-4 hours or overnight.

Remove from freezer 10-15 minutes before serving. Briefly heat remaining jam and water, stir until blended. Drizzle over dessert. Top with Cool Whip, raspberries and crushed chocolate wafers.

Cathy Toth
Husband Robert, 1979 ; Son Kyle, 2009

After Mom Prom my senior year, my mom Jacque arranged for EBT restaurant to open for a large group of us to enjoy desserts and coffee. It was a wonderful way to relax and wind down a special evening.

- Nick Solsburg, 2002

Chocolate Fondue

9 ounces milk chocolate

7 ounces semi-sweet chocolate

14 ounces Eagle brand condensed milk

½ cup heavy whipping cream

⅓ cup milk

Melt all ingredients in microwave 1-2 minutes at a time, stirring in between. Serve with strawberries, bananas, cherries, angel food cake, pretzels, etc.

Mary Jo Barton
Sons Brett, 2005; Scott, 2007

Boca Negro Torte

6 ounces unsweetened baking chocolate, broken

6 ounces semisweet chocolate chips

½ cup Grand Marnier or other orange-flavored liqueur

1½ cups sugar

8 ounces butter, unsalted, softened

5 large eggs

1½ tablespoons flour

Sauce:

12-ounce package frozen raspberries

2 tablespoons sugar

2 tablespoons Grand Marnier

Grease a 9-inch springform pan or torte pan and line with parchment or wax paper. Chop unsweetened chocolate in food processor. Add chocolate chips. Heat Grand Marnier and add sugar. Stir until sugar is mostly melted. With food processor running, pour hot Grand Marnier mix over chocolate and whirl until melted. Add butter in small pieces until all is incorporated. Begin adding eggs to processor one at a time, mixing well after each addition. Sprinkle on flour and process until well mixed. Scrape batter into prepared pan.

Bake in a water bath at 350 degrees about 1 hour and 20-30 minutes, or until cake tester comes out clean and top looks dry. Remove from water bath and cool completely in pan. Cake will deflate as it cools. Slice and serve on a chilled plate with fresh raspberry sauce.

Sauce: Cook raspberries, sugar and Grand Marnier in small saucepan until thoroughly blended.

Ann Marie Scahill
Son Michael, 2009

Chocolate Soufflés with White Chocolate Cream

3 tablespoons water

1 tablespoon instant espresso powder

5 ounces semisweet chocolate, chopped

1 tablespoon brandy

3 large egg yolks

4 large egg whites

2½ tablespoons sugar, plus additional for soufflé dishes

Powdered sugar

<u>White Chocolate Cream:</u>

1 cup heavy cream

9 ounces Tobler Narcisse or white chocolate coating, cut into small bits

½ cup Kahlua

Stir water and espresso powder over low heat in small pan until powder dissolves. Add chocolate and brandy. Stir until smooth and remove from heat. Whisk in egg yolks. Cool to room temperature. Grease four ⅔-cup soufflé dishes, coat with sugar.

Beat egg whites until foamy. Gradually add 2½ tablespoons sugar and beat until medium-firm peaks form. Fold chocolate mixture into whites. Divide among dishes, place on baking sheets. Preheat oven to 400 degrees. Bake soufflés until puffed but still moist, about 14 minutes. Dust with powdered sugar. Serve immediately. Pass white chocolate cream separately.

<u>For white chocolate cream:</u> Scald cream and remove from heat. Add white chocolate and process briefly in food processor until smooth. Add Kahlua, stir.

Mary Porto
Sons Tony, 1994; Nicholas, 1996; Tom, 2000

I remember watching the terrorist attacks on the United States unfold on September 11, 2001. I was a senior in Mr. Alvey's 2nd hour theology class. Everyone watched in disbelief and uncertainty. It is a day that none of us will ever forget.

- Chris Constant, 2002

Cashew-Coconut Tart

Crust:

1¼ cups flour

⅔ cup sugar

½ cup unsweetened cocoa powder

¼ teaspoon (generous) salt

10 tablespoons (1¼ sticks) chilled unsalted butter, diced

1½ tablespoons ice water

4 ounces bittersweet (not unsweetened) or semisweet chocolate, chopped

Filling:

1 cup packed dark brown sugar

1 cup heavy whipping cream

⅓ cup pure maple syrup

1½ tablespoons finely chopped peeled fresh ginger

9.25-ounce can (about 2 cups) lightly salted roasted cashews

1 cup flaked sweetened coconut

For crust: Spray 11-inch tart pan with removable bottom with cooking spray. Blend flour, sugar, cocoa and salt in processor 5 seconds. Add butter and blend until moist sandy texture forms. Add ice water and blend until dough comes together. Press dough evenly onto bottom and up sides of prepared pan. Chill crust 30 minutes.

Preheat oven to 350 degrees. Place crust on baking sheet, bake until dry-looking and slightly puffed, about 18 minutes. Maintain oven temperature. Cool crust completely on rack. Place chopped chocolate in small microwave-safe bowl. Cook at medium setting in 15-second intervals until soft and beginning to melt. Stir until completely melted and smooth. Brush enough chocolate over inside of crust to coat completely. Freeze crust until chocolate is cold and hard, about 15 minutes. Reserve remaining melted chocolate for garnish.

For filling: Bring brown sugar, cream, maple syrup and ginger to boil in heavy medium saucepan, whisking gently until sugar dissolves. Cook until candy thermometer registers 222 degrees, whisking occasionally, about 8 minutes. Mix in cashews and coconut. Cool 20 minutes.

Pour filling into crust. Place on rimmed baking sheet. Bake until filling is beginning to darken on top and is thick and bubbly, about 35 minutes. Transfer to wire rack, cool completely. Re-melt reserved chocolate, drizzle over tart in lacy patter. Can be made day ahead. Cover, store at room temperature.

Lori Keenan
Sons Connor, 2007; Tommy, 2009

Rockhurst has a grand cookbook tradition. Hungry Boys was the name of the first volume in the 1970s. Its success paved the way for Hungry Boys II in the 1980s and Hungry Boys III in the 1990s. All were filled with recipes for great food for hungry boys and their families. Cooking Up Memories follows in their great tradition with hopes for the same success!

Swim Coach Paul Winkeler has always said "The parents and families may not swim a lap all year, but no race is ever won without their support."

- Debra Webster
Sons William, 2005; Kevin, 2007; David, 2009

Fresh Peach Cobbler

½ cup butter or margarine

5 cups fresh peaches, sliced

Cinnamon sugar

1½ cups sugar

1½ cups flour

3 teaspoons baking powder

1½ cups milk

Melt butter in bottom of 9x13-inch pan. Arrange sliced peaches in pan, sprinkle with a little cinnamon sugar. Combine other ingredients and pour over peaches. Bake at 350 degrees for 35-40 minutes, until golden brown. Enjoy with ice cream!

Patty McMahon
Husband Mike, 1967; Sons Conor, 1997; Kelly, 2000

This recipe is from Grandma Mary McMahon whose husband went to Rockhurst, as well as their four sons and many grandsons. It was always a favorite of Rockhurst boys!

Simple Cobbler

10 ripe but firm peaches or nectarines, peeled, cut into ¼-inch wedges

2 tablespoons fresh lemon juice

1⅔ cups sugar, divided

1 cup flour

1 tablespoon baking powder

¼ teaspoon salt

1 cup whole milk

½ cup unsalted butter, melted

Cinnamon

Put peaches in 4-quart pot with lemon juice and ⅔ cup sugar. Bring to a boil, stirring. Continue to boil and stir for 4 minutes. Remove from heat. In medium bowl, whisk together flour, 1 cup sugar, baking powder, salt. Add ½ cup milk, stir well, then add remaining milk and stir until well blended.

Pour butter into 9x13-inch baking pan. Pour batter over butter, do not stir or mix. Pour peach mixture over batter, do not stir. It will look messy but mixes together as the batter rises. Sprinkle a little cinnamon on top. Bake 40-45 minutes until top is golden brown. Serves 6-8.

Edward Sandridge, 1977
Sons Michael, 2006; Phillip, 2008

According to the Chancellor yearbook, in 1946, there were 11 Jesuit faculty, 8 scholastics and 4 lay teachers. There were 55 seniors.

In 1999, senior Michael Miller helped at the Gillis Center for his senior project. Matt Euston and Kyle Ehman were at Bryant School. David Raydo assisted at The Children's Place. Daniel Curry read stories to children at St. Francis Xavier. Chris Jennings was at the Niles Home. The Senior Service projects program began in 1972.

Apple Crisp

Apple mixture:

5 Granny Smith apples, peeled, cored, sliced

5 tablespoons sugar

2 teaspoons cinnamon

2 teaspoons lemon juice

Topping:

1¾ cups flour

1¼ cups oats

2¼ cups sugar

⅛ teaspoon allspice

1 teaspoon nutmeg

1 cup cold butter

Preheat oven to 350 degrees. Grease a 9x13-inch pan. Toss apples with sugar, cinnamon and lemon juice, spoon into baking pan. For topping, mix flour, oats, sugar and spices. Using large holes of grater, grate butter into topping. Blend until mixture just begins to come together, don't overmix. Sprinkle topping over fruit. Bake 45-60 minutes or until apples are tender and topping is browned and crisp. Serve warm with ice cream!

Joellen Messerli
Sons Robbie, 2007; Kyle, 2009

Cookbook committee members gave this a big "thumbs up" at a committee tasting meeting!

Pear-Cranberry Crisp

5 cups peeled, sliced pears

1½ cups cranberries

1 cup sugar

⅓ cup plus 2 tablespoons flour

2 tablespoons flour

2 teaspoons orange zest

1 cup rolled oats

½ cup packed brown sugar

¼ margarine or butter

½ cup chopped nuts

Heat oven to 375 degrees. Grease 2-quart baking dish. Combine pears, cranberries, sugar, 2 tablespoons flour and orange zest, toss to coat. Spoon into baking dish. Combine oats, brown sugar and ⅓ cup flour, cut in margarine with pastry blender or fork, stir in nuts. Sprinkle over fruit. Bake 30-40 minutes or until golden.

Mary Porto
Sons Tony, 1994; Nick, 1996; Tom, 2000

Spot any familiar names among these Rockhurst grads? Dave Crooks, 1934; Donald Kable, 1934; Victor Panus, 1935; Joseph Simms, 1935; Herman Hermelink, 1935; Thomas Pendergast, Jr., 1930; William R. Flynn, 1931; Hugh Cahill, 1937; Robert O'Dell, 1931; Richard Ong, 1932; Walter Meiners, 1935; Eugene Mitchell, 1936; Joseph Luby, 1938; John Killiger, 1933; James Kring, 1939; William McGrath, 1931; Edward Reardon, 1933; John Hill, 1937; Dave Crooks, 1934; Robert Muehlebach, 1936.

Cranberry Kuchen with Warm Butter Sauce

1 cup granulated sugar

2 tablespoons butter, room temperature

2 cups flour

1 tablespoon baking powder

Dash salt

1 cup milk, room temperature

1 teaspoon vanilla

3 cups whole fresh cranberries

Powdered sugar

Butter Sauce:

½ cup butter

1 cup granulated sugar

¾ cup heavy cream

Grease and flour an 8- or 9-inch square pan. In large mixing bowl, cream together sugar and butter. In separate bowl, sift together flour, baking powder and salt. Combine milk and vanilla. Add dry ingredients, milk mixture and cranberries to creamed sugar-butter mixture, alternately folding over with spatula. Do not overmix, batter can be lumpy. Pour batter into prepared pan. Bake in preheated 350 degree oven 25-30 minutes. Cool cake in pan; sprinkle with powdered sugar. Ladle sauce over each serving.

Butter Sauce: In small saucepan, brown butter slightly, until not quite golden brown. Add sugar and cream, stir. Bring to boil and remove from heat. Cool to room temperature. Re-warm slightly in microwave before serving.

Michelle Nemmers
Son John, 2008

Blueberry Cobbler

⅔ cup plus 2 teaspoons sugar

2 tablespoons cornstarch

¼ teaspoon plus ⅛ teaspoon ground nutmeg

6 cups fresh blueberries (2½ pints)

2 teaspoons lemon zest

2 tablespoons fresh lemon juice

Biscuits:

2 cups flour

3 tablespoons sugar

2 teaspoons baking powder

½ teaspoon salt

2 cups heavy whipping cream

2 teaspoons lemon zest

Heat oven to 400 degrees. In a shallow 2-quart baking dish, mix ⅔ cup sugar, cornstarch and ¼ teaspoon nutmeg. Add blueberries, lemon zest and juice. Stir gently with a spoon. Cover tightly, bake 20 minutes.

Meanwhile, prepare biscuits. In a medium bowl, whisk together flour, sugar, baking powder and salt until well blended. Add cream and lemon zest, stir just until soft dough forms.

Remove dish from oven. Uncover and gently stir. Drop 8 mounds of dough, not touching (they spread), on filling. Mix remaining 2 teaspoons sugar and ⅛ teaspoon nutmeg, sprinkle evenly over dough. Place baking dish onto baking sheet or foil to catch any drips. Bake uncovered 35 minutes, until biscuits are golden and filling bubbles. Cool on a wire rack. Serve warm or at room temperature.

Sean Flanagan, 2004

Best eaten freshly-made. There won't be leftovers if I'm around, but store at room temperature if there are any.

Tennis doubles champs were Mr. Sticelber and Mr. Connor.

- 1947 yearbook

The 1969 Winter Dance featured a student-constructed Chinese Dragon presiding over the festivity. The musical group was The Next Exit.

Easy Blueberry Dessert

20-ounce can crushed pineapple, undrained

3 cups blueberries, fresh or frozen

1 box yellow cake mix

1 cup butter, melted

2 tablespoons light brown sugar, packed

1 cup chopped pecans

Preheat oven to 350 degrees. Spray 9x13-inch baking pan with cooking spray. Layer, don't mix, pineapple, then blueberries and cake mix. Drizzle melted butter over all, sprinkle with brown sugar, top with pecans. Bake 40-45 minutes until bubbly and cake topping is cooked through.

Dorothy Flanagan
Husband James, 1937, Sons Jim, 1971; Terry, 1974
Grandsons Bryan, 2002; Sean, 2004; Kevin, 2007
Grandson Nick Vaughn, RHS Faculty member

This was served at a Rockette (alumni moms) potluck and enjoyed by all. Since then, the Flanagan grandchildren all the way from Santa Clara, California to Saint Louis have voted it their favorite dessert. It even made its way to Ireland with visiting cousins from Galway!

Bananas Foster

2 tablespoons butter

6 tablespoons brown sugar

1½ ounces banana liqueur

1 banana, quartered

1½ ounces Bacardi 151

Dash cinnamon

2 scoops vanilla ice cream

Melt butter over medium heat, add brown sugar and banana liqueur. Cook slowly for several minutes until sugar dissolves, making a caramel sauce. Add bananas, pour in Bacardi close to the edge and flame. Lightly sprinkle cinnamon over flame for sparkle effect. Sauté for 1 minute and spoon over ice cream. Serves 2.

Ed Holland, 1971
EBT Restaurant
Son Kevin, 1997

March, 1932.
Eight members of the 1932 Hawklet basketball team and Coach Ed Halpin piled into a Hudson Touring Car, hung their basketballs and equipment on the outside of the car, and with $50 donated by Thomas McGee for expenses, took off for Columbia and the State Championship Tournament.
"We were the Cinderella team," recalled E.J. Reardon. "We didn't have anything, but we won it all."
Team members included Bob Reiter, Warren McCanles, Bill Mason, John Prather, Owen Murphy, Jerry Spurck, Ed Reardon and Tom Rooney. The final score? Rockhurst 17, Joplin, 15.

- RHS newsletter, 1982

Cannoli Shells and Filling

Filling:

2 pounds ricotta cheese

1 cup sugar

Pinch of salt

1 teaspoon vanilla

1 tablespoon citron, finely minced

½ cup finely chopped Hershey's chocolate bar

1 cup whipping cream, beaten stiff

Shells:

4 cups or more flour

3 tablespoons sugar

¾ cup milk

1 egg white, slightly beaten

1 tablespoon water

¾ cup lard or 1 quart oil

Powdered sugar

Filling: Beat ricotta in a large bowl for 1 minute, adding sugar and salt gradually. Beat until very light and creamy, about 5 minutes. Add vanilla, citron and chocolate until blended. Fold in whipped cream. Refrigerate overnight.

Shells: Sift flour and sugar together onto bread board or table top. Using a fork, slowly blend in milk. Knead dough until smooth and stiff, about 15 minutes. If dough feels wet and sticky, add more flour. Cover dough and let stand in a cool place for about 2 hours. Roll out very thin and cut into 5-inch circles, then wrap around a metal cannoli tube (5-inches long, 1-inch diameter.) Fold dough around tube loosely so that ¼-inch of form sticks out on the ends. Beat egg white with water. Seal ends of dough by brushing with egg white. Deep fry in hot lard or oil until brown on both sides. Lift out gently with slotted spoon or tongs, drain on paper towels.

Just before serving, fill shells with ricotta filling, sprinkle tops with powdered sugar. Makes about 24.

Antionette Ishmael
Sons Patrick, 2002; Anthony, 2005; Dominic, 2008

The 1983 Bike Club reached new goals. Four members of the club rode across the state of Missouri.

CACHE 1982 changed formats this year with a sit-down dinner served by student waiters. Over 420 attended the auction, raising $60,000.

Italian Bread Pudding

¼ cup butter, melted

1 cup cream

3 eggs, beaten

1½ cups sugar

1 teaspoon nutmeg

1 teaspoon Amaretto

1-pound loaf Italian bread, cut into cubes

3 cups milk

1 cup dried figs, chopped

1 cup sliced almonds

Sauce:

1 cup powdered sugar

1 egg, beaten

½ cup butter, melted

2 ounces Amaretto

Mix butter, cream and eggs together. Mix in sugar, nutmeg, Amaretto. Add bread and milk. Fold in figs and almonds. Put into greased loaf pan or 9x9-inch pan. Bake at 350 degrees for 45 minutes.

For sauce, mix sugar and egg into melted butter. Cook in double boiler until sauce thickens. Add Amaretto. Pour over bread pudding.

Debbie Campbell
Son Andrew, 2007

This recipe comes from a cooking class taught by J.J. Mirabile, RHS class of 1980.

O'Neill's Bread Pudding

⅓ cup sugar

2 teaspoons cinnamon

1 teaspoon nutmeg

¾ cup milk

2¾ cups heavy whipping cream

3 eggs

½ cup butter

10 cups diced (¼-inch) baguette bread, divided

½ cup raisins

Topping:

1¼ cups flour

½ cup sugar

¾ cup brown sugar

1½ teaspoons cinnamon

½ teaspoon nutmeg

½ cup butter, room temperature

Banana Caramel Rum Sauce:

2 cups prepared caramel sauce

2 tablespoons rum (dark or light)

2 tablespoons crème de banana

¼ cup orange juice

Powdered sugar

Combine sugar, spices, milk, cream and eggs, whisk together. Slowly whisk melted butter into mixture. Grease 9x13-inch pan. Put 7 cups bread in pan, top with raisins, then remaining bread. Add cream mixture and let sit for 10 minutes.

Measure topping ingredients except butter into bowl, blend by hand. Cut butter into small pieces and slowly add to dry ingredients, mixing by hand until butter is evenly blended and mix can be formed into a ball. Crumble over top of bread mixture. Bake at 325 degrees for 60 minutes. Cool 20 minutes.

Whisk caramel sauce, rum, crème de banana and orange juice together. Cut bread pudding into portions and transfer to plates. Pour sauce over each portion, sprinkle with powdered sugar, serve.

Brian Schorgl, 1987
O'Neill's Restaurant

This is a well known, much-requested dish at O'Neill's.

Under the direction of Fathers Club President Michael Haughton, a monthly father-son Mass was begun in 1981. Mass was held at 7 am in the Sacred Heart Chapel and followed by coffee and doughnuts in the school cafeteria. The Fathers Club also sponsored a traditional Father-Son dinner and fun nights for each class.

White Chocolate and Raspberry Bread Pudding

10-12 ounces French bread, cut into 1-inch pieces

3 cups whipping cream

1 cup milk

½ cup sugar

10 ounces white chocolate

7 egg yolks

2 eggs

½ pint raspberries

Preheat oven to 275 degrees. Arrange bread cubes on baking sheet. Bake until light golden and dry, about 10 minutes. Cool completely. Increase oven temperature to 350 degrees.

Combine whipping cream, milk and sugar in large saucepan. Simmer over medium heat, stirring until sugar dissolves. Remove from heat. Add white chocolate and stir until melted.

Whisk yolks and eggs into warm chocolate mixture. Place bread in bowl and pour chocolate mixture over. Let stand 15 minutes. Gently stir in raspberries. Place in pans and cover with foil coated with cooking spray. Bake 45 minutes. Uncover and bake until golden, about 15 more minutes.

Marcia & Lon Lane
The Catering Company
Sons Lon, 2002; Stewart, 2004

On a windy spring day in 1973, young first year tennis coach Ron Geldhof was leading the junior varsity team in a dual match at Shawnee Mission North. With the skies quickly darkening, senior Lonnie Taylor stopped by to check up on the young team. He leaned out of his Jeep and said, "Good luck, fellas! I hope you don't get blown away, Coach!" The opposing coach came up and said, "Coach, with the weather blowing in, I think we ought to go to a Pro 8 set." Coach Geldhof heartily agreed, turned to me and said, "Charlie, what the heck is a Pro 8?" From that cold, windy day 37 years ago to today, Coach Geldhof is believed to hold the most state titles in RHS history.

- Charlie Murphy, 1976

Toffee Crunch Caramel Cheesecake

Crust:

1½ cups ground gingersnap cookies (about 7¼ ounces)

5 tablespoons unsalted butter, melted

2 tablespoons packed brown sugar

Cheesecake:

4 (8-ounce) packages cream cheese, room temperature

1 cup packed brown sugar

2 tablespoons butter, melted

5 large eggs

1 teaspoon vanilla extract

Caramel Topping:

1½ cups sugar

¼ cup water

½ teaspoon fresh lemon juice

1 cup heavy whipping cream

4 (1.4-ounce) English toffee candy bars (such as Heath or Skor), chopped

Crust: Preheat oven to 350 degrees. Spray bottom of 9-inch springform pan with cooking spray. Stir ground cookies, butter, and sugar in medium bowl until moist clumps form. Press firmly onto bottom of pan. Wrap outside of pan with 3 layers of heavy-duty foil. Bake crust until firm, about 14 minutes. Cool.

Cheesecake: Beat cream cheese and sugar in large bowl until smooth. Beat in butter, then eggs, one at a time, until blended. Add vanilla. Pour batter over crust in pan. Place foil-wrapped springform pan in large roasting pan. Add enough hot water to come halfway up sides of springform pan. Bake uncovered until filling is puffed around edges and moves slightly in center when pan is gently shaken, about 1 hour and 10 minutes. Remove pan from water, remove foil. Place hot cheesecake uncovered in refrigerator overnight.

Caramel Topping: Stir sugar, water and lemon juice in large saucepan over medium heat until sugar dissolves. Increase heat. Boil without stirring until mixture turns deep amber, occasionally swirling pan and brushing down sides with wet pastry brush, about 9 minutes. Add cream (mixture will bubble). Reduce heat to medium-low. Simmer until reduced to 1¼ cups, stirring occasionally, about 8 minutes. Chill until thickened but still pourable, about 15 minutes.

Spoon caramel over top of cake just to edges. Do not drip down sides. Garnish top edges with chopped English toffee. Chill at least 2 hours.

Patti Gound
Sons Ryan, 2003; Matthew, 2007

Winning the annual Blue-White Mixer Air Band competition in 2003 were seniors Mike Adkins, Jimmy Chalmers and Seamus McLaughlin. With their big fro hair and jump suits, the trio was cheered loudly and won a decisive victory.

Blueberry Cheesecake

Crust:

30 vanilla wafers, crushed
(about 1 cup crumbs)

3 tablespoons sugar

3 tablespoons butter, melted

Filling:

3 (8-ounce) packages cream
cheese, room temperature

14-ounce can sweetened
condensed milk

4 eggs

1 teaspoon vanilla

1 tablespoon lemon juice

1 teaspoon lemon zest

2 cups fresh or frozen
blueberries

1 teaspoon sugar

Blueberry jam, optional

Preheat oven to 350 degrees. Combine crust ingredients, press onto bottom and slightly up sides of 10-inch springform pan. Bake 5 minutes. Set aside.

For filling, beat cream cheese and sweetened condensed milk until well combined. Add eggs, vanilla, lemon juice and lemon zest, beat until just combined. Toss blueberries with sugar and gently stir in batter. Pour into crust.

Bake about 50 minutes, until center is set. Cool on wire rack 15 minutes, then run a knife around sides of pan to loosen. Cool 30 minutes more, then remove sides of pan. Chill overnight or at least 4 hours. If desired, spoon blueberry jam over top of cake.

Jan Flanagan
Husband Jim, 1971; Sons Bryan, 2002; Sean, 2004; Kevin, 2007

A complete Bavarian Village arose in the Rec Room for the 1970 Winter Dance. Over 200 couples admired the decorations and enjoyed the evening, including Jim Benoit and Bob Hughes and their dates. Chris Davis, Ron East, Ron Paradise, Hugh Kelly, Bob Peterschmidt, Jim Petrie, Jim Glynn, John Spence, Chris Turner, John McManus, Brian O'Malley, Terry Houlton, Mark Thornhill, Steve Kelly, Dave McManus and Ed Cotter were among those decorating for the event.

Key Lime Cheesecake

2 cups graham cracker crumbs

1½ cups sugar, divided

½ cup butter, melted

3 (8-ounce) packages cream cheese

8 ounces sour cream

1½ teaspoons lime zest

½ cup Key lime juice

Whites from 6 large eggs

Combine crumbs, ¼ cup sugar and melted butter in a small bowl, stirring well. Firmly press mixture in bottom and 1-inch up sides of a buttered 9-inch springform pan. Bake crust at 350 degrees for 8 minutes. Cool in pan on a wire rack.

Beat cream cheese until creamy. Gradually add 1¼ cups sugar, beating after each addition. Stir in sour cream, lime zest and Key lime juice. Beat egg whites at high speed until stiff peaks form, gently fold into cream cheese mixture. Pour batter into crust.

Bake at 350 degrees for 1 hour and 5 minutes, then turn oven off, partially open oven door and let cheesecake cool in oven 15 minutes. Remove and cool to room temperature. Refrigerate until serving.

Cindy Schultz

As a brand new freshman at summer football camp, I felt very special, being a part of history. Maybe even a little grown up… or so I thought. I found myself walking next to Al Davis as we headed outside. "Al, how long have you been teaching here?" I asked, not realizing my blunder which probably seems obvious to you already. Just then I slipped on a wet spot and he caught me. The very next day, I again found myself walking next to this important figure in Rockhurst history. And very casually, I asked another question, "Al, how does the varsity team look this year?" I don't remember exactly what he said. It might be my memory or the trauma, but if you knew "Coach Davis" as I quickly learned to call him, you can imagine what he might have said. I'm sure I'm not the only over-confident freshman to come into Rockhurst, but not many can say they called Coach Davis "Al" to his face, not once, but twice!

- Cary Brewer, 1991

Many moms have helped in the cafeteria over the years. I was one of them for 9 straight years. Marcia Lane (Lon, 2002; Stewart, 2004) and I started in 1998. We sold snack items and drinks.
I remember one freshman coming up to me saying "I forgot my lunch. Can I have a Coke and 2 Snickers?" I didn't know the boy, but I gave him a "mom" look and said, "Well, it's okay with me, but what would your mother say?" He gave me a startled glance but took them anyway. Jan Stacy joined our lunch crew when her son Michael (2003) started at the Rock. Susie Jianas (Matt, 2004; Michael, 2007) became part of our crew next. Finally, Pat Shealy (John, 2007; West, 2010) became the last of our revolving snack lady group. We enjoyed watching the lunch room moderators interact with the boys. John Morris, Bernie Kreikemeier, Bert Roney and Pete Campbell kept everyone in line. We knew who needed a haircut, who forgot a belt and who was washing tables for their infractions. It was a fun and fast 9 years!

- Jan Flanagan
Sons Bryan, 2002;
Sean, 2004; Kevin, 2007

Pan Cheesecake

30 Oreo cookies, crushed

½ cup butter, melted

¼ cup chopped pecans

¼ cup flaked coconut

4 (8-ounce) packages cream cheese, softened

1 cup sugar

4 eggs

½ cup whipping cream

6 ounces chocolate chips

Preheat oven to 350 degrees. Mix cookies, butter, pecans and coconut. Press into bottom of 9x13-inch pan. Refrigerate while preparing filling. Beat cream cheese and sugar until well blended. Add eggs one at a time, mixing after each addition just until blended. Pour over crust. Bake 40 minutes, until center is almost set. Cool. Refrigerate 3 hours or overnight.

Melt cream and chocolate together in small pan over low heat. Stir to blend well. Pour over cheesecake. Refrigerate 15 minutes or until chocolate is firm. Cut and serve. Store leftovers in refrigerator. Serves 16.

Carrie McCausland
Son Stuart, 2007

Hamlet Highlights

HAWKLET HIGHLIGHTS

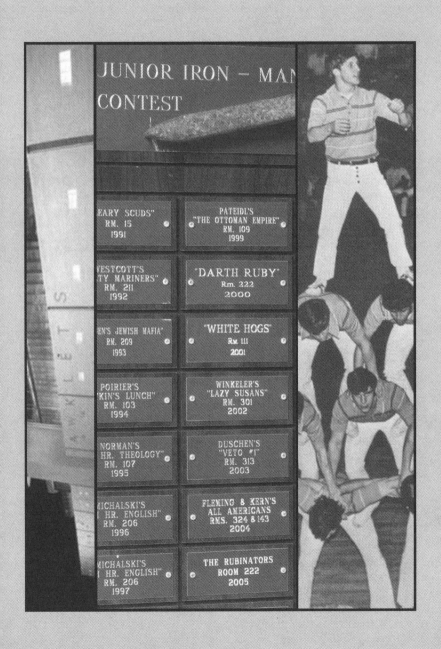

JUNIOR IRON – MAN CONTEST

EARY SCUDS" RM. 15 1991	PATEIDL'S "THE OTTOMAN EMPIRE" RM. 109 1999
VESTCOTT'S TY MARINERS" RM. 211 1992	"DARTH RUBY" Rm. 222 2000
EN'S JEWISH MAFIA" RM. 209 1993	"WHITE HOGS" Rm. 111 2001
POIRIER'S KIN'S LUNCH" RM. 103 1994	WINKELER'S "LAZY SUSANS" RM. 301 2002
NORMAN'S HR. THEOLOGY" RM. 107 1995	DUSCHEN'S "VETO #1" RM. 313 2003
MICHALSKI'S HR. ENGLISH" RM. 206 1996	FLEMING & KERN'S ALL AMERICANS RMS. 324 & 143 2004
MICHALSKI'S HR. ENGLISH" RM. 206 1997	THE RUBINATORS ROOM 222 2005

Committee

This book involved the dedication and hard work of a number of current and former students and parents. Sincere thanks to all who shared their time and talents to produce this salute to Rockhurst High School.

Project Chair: Jan Bergman Flanagan
Business Manager: Carolyn Tuccillo Sturgeon
Design Chair: Joellen O'Byrne Messerli

Design assistance and lettering: Peter Noth

Photography: Keith Gard, Joe Fleming

Writers/Researchers: Jan Flanagan, Matt Keenan, Michael Stacy

Editing: Jan Flanagan, Kevin Flanagan

Recipe Committees:

Appetizers: Kate Link, chair; Laura Connealy, Joan Jones, Mimi O'Laughlin, Mary Ring, Karen Stacy, Mary Pat Williams; *Brunch:* Marcia Sabates, chair; Donna Allred, Sherri Burke, Marianne Damon, Linda Dro, Linda Gentile, Georgeanne Kelly, Suzanne Orscheln, Patty Parsons, Ann Renne, Julie Rieck, Debby Schloegel, Vicki Springs, Mary Ann Welsh; *Breads:* Anne Rhoades, chair; Tonja Kernell, Jackie Miller; *Salads:* Annie Osborn, chair; Karen Miyawaki; *Soups & Stews:* Martie Eftink, chair; Cyd Jokisch, Beth Selanders, Jane Sorrentino; *Vegetables & Grains:* Maraline Hayob, chair; Patty Crutchfield, Kathy Fallon, Cathy Janish, Laura Murphy, Sandy Pummill, Suzanne Orscheln, Karen VanDyke, Betsy Vossman; *Pasta & Pizza:* Pat Shealy, chair; *Poultry & Game:* Wendy Zecy, chair; Diane Bradshaw, Laura Fitzpatrick, Carol Fryer, Joy Blake-Krug, Mary Reintjes, Alison Ward; *Meats:* Catherine Moussa, chair; Mary Jane Sirna, Linda Sizemore, Suzie Smith; *Fish & Seafood:* Laura Bluhm, chair; Mary Campbell, Patti Gound, Lynn Knott, Maryanne Roepke; *Cookies & Bars:* Kate Brown, chair; *Cakes & Pies:* Sarah Jurcyk, chair; *Desserts:* Michelle Nemmers, chair

Heritage Committee: Jan Flanagan, chair; Debbie Campbell, Dorothy Flanagan, Katherine Gierster, Mary Elizabeth Heiman, Sue Sabaugh, Karen VanDyke, Maryhelen Van Dyke, Debra Webster

Heritage Committee

Cookbook Committee

Special thanks to RHS staff members for their assistance with various aspects of the project:
Dana Brack, Kevin Campbell, Joanne Comiskey; Laurence Freeman, Julie Koppen;
Michael Nigro, Kelli Reidy, Judie Scanlon;
and enormous love and gratitude to our families for their patience and support!

Contributors

Thanks to all those who sent in recipes, shared a story or information, assisted with mailings or PR or were helpful in other ways. Space limitations required cutting some contributions, but we appreciated every submission. We regret any inadvertent omission from this list of contributors.

Able, Barb
Adair, Mary
Adler, Karen
Aldrich, Ann
Allred, Donna
Bailey, Betty
Bailey, Laura
Balderston, Kris
Barth, Grace
Barnhart, Jean
Barton, Mary Jo
Baum, Terrence, Fr.
Becker, Jack
Bergman, Marjie
Bergman, Tom
Bessenbacher, Jean
Best, Debbie
Bevan, Jim
Bishop, Rick
Blake-Krug, Joy
Blanck, Jennifer
Bluhm, Laura
Bly, Terri
Bradshaw, Diane
Brain, Charleen
Brewer, Cary
Broski, Jim
Brown, Kate
Brown, Peter
Burke, Sherri
Busenbark, Brandon
Byrne, S.J., Fr. Luke
Caffrey, Mark
Caffrey, Raymond
Caffrey, Valerie
Callahan, Kathleen
Campbell, Debbie
Campbell, Kevin
Campisano, Fred
Cappo, Mary Ann
Carter, Jan
Christian, Patti

Cicchetti, Mary Beth
Clement, Kathleen
Coleman, Jean
Comiskey, Joanne
Connealy, Laura
Connell, Nancy
Connelly, Robin
Connor, Keith
Constant, Chris
Conway, Betty
Cooke, Tom
Cowan, Pam
Cowing, Nancy
Cummings, Jean
Cummings, Sean
Cummings, S.J., Fr. Tom
Cunningham,
    Rosemary
Cunningham,
    Sherri Cook
Cusick, Dr. Michael
Damon, Marianne
Davidson, Pam
Davis, Cathy
Davis, Valerie
Davison, Sharon
Dehaemers, Barbara
Dierks, Mike
Dierks, Sue
Dix, Dr.
Doherty, Brandon
Donnelly, Kathleen
Dorlac, Rose
Dorman, Jennifer
Doyle, Joe
Dro, Linda
Eckert, Shanthi
Eftink, Martie
Elmore, Chris
Estes, Sondra
Euston, Kathy
Fakoury, George

Fakoury, Jan
Fallon, Kathy
Fendler, Ellen
Fitzgerald, Leabby
FitzPatrick, Bernadette
Fitzpatrick, Mark
Fitzpatrick, Nancy
Flake-Gerhardt, Gloria
Flanagan, Bryan
Flanagan, Dorothy
Flanagan, James
Flanagan, Jan
Flanagan, Jim
Flanagan, Julie
Flanagan, Kevin
Flanagan, Sean
Flanagan, Terry
Fligg, Ken
Foley, Laura
Fowler-Swartz,
    RoseMarie
Franke, Francis S.& Co.
Freeman, Laurence
Frese, Diane
Friedman, Lois
Frye, George
Fryer, Carol
Gallo, Rosemary
Gard, Keith
Gaughan, Tina
Gentile, Linda
Gierster, Katherine
Gorman , Mike
Gotschall, Loretta
Gound, Patti
Gutek, Donna
Haden, Barb
Haden, Jon
Hake, Lorraine
Hamid, Mohamed
Hamline, Lori
Harding, Frances

Harris, Matthew
Hart, Katie
Hayob, Maraline
Heiman, Harold
Heiman, Mary
    Elizabeth
Hire, Lynne
Hodes, Ann
Hodes, Deedy
Hogan, JoMarie
Holland, Ed
Howell, John S., Sr
Hudnall, Roseann
Hudson, Debi
Huerter, Daniel
Huerter, Katherine
Hunthausen, S.J.,
    Fr. John
Hynes, Beverly
Ishmael, Antionette
Ishmael, Phil
Janish, Cathy
Jianas, Susan
Jokisch, Cyd
Jones, Bill
Jones, Joan
Jones, Maryan Hake
Jurcyk, Sarah
Kaine, Tim
Kampfe, Sally
Kane, Kathy
Keenan, Lori
Keenan, Matt
Kelly, Mike "Kyle"
Kernell, Tonja
Knott, Lynne
Kokjer, Harriet
Koons, Laura
Koppen, Julie
Korth, Christopher
Krizman, Joe
Lane, Lon

Contributors

Lane, Marcia
Laughlin, David
LeCluyse, Mary Knaus
Ledom, Lisa
Leone, Elvie
Lillis, John
Link, Kate
Long, Mary
Looby, Shelley
Lucas, Cyndi
Mahoney, Kate
Mandl, Donna
Mandl, Polly
Mashburn, Barbara
McCausland, Carolyn
McCracken, Karen
McEniry, John
McGahan, Charlotte
McGannon, Jessica
McGonigle, Mike
McInerney, Maureen
McLeese, Karen
   Reintjes
McMahon, Patty
McManus, Julie
Menendez, Chico
Menendez, Sharon
Messerli, Joellen
Messerli, Rob
Miceli, Yvette
Miller, Christy
Miller, Jackie
Miller, Karen
Miyawaki, Karen
Montgomery, Connor
Montgomery, Tina
Moore, Joe
Moussa, Catherine
Mumford, Alice
Mura, Thomas R.
Murphy, Charlie
Murphy, Laura
Murphy-Marx,
   Kathleen
Myers, Joe

Neenan, Marie
Nemmers, Michelle
Neuner, Joe
Nigro, Josephine
Nigro, Michael
Noth, Andrea
Noth, Peter
Novick, Sande
O'Brien, Melinda
O'Brien, Tim
O'Byrne, Diane
O'Byrne, Mary Jo
O'Byrne, Pat
O'Byrne, Rob
O'Dowd, Katy
O'Flaherty, Anne
O'Flaherty, Barbara
Ogle, Dennis
O'Laughlin, Mimi
O'Leary, Michael
O'Neill, Sally
Orndorff, Mary
   Coppinger
O'Rourke, Kevin
O'Rourke, Laura
Orscheln, Suzanne
Osborn, Annie
Pesci, S.J., Fr. Thomas
Pinne, S.J., Fr. Chris
Porto, Mary
Prater, Laurie
Prater, Michael
Ptasnik, Paul
Pummill, Sandy
Quinn, Laurel
Rastorfer, Rob
Rau, Jeanne Gorman
Rauschelbach, Jerry
Rauschelbach, Diane
Raydo, Donna
Reidy, Kelli
Reintjes, Carolyn
Reintjes, Jeannette
Reintjes, Mary
Renne, Ann

Reno, Harold J.
Reno, Joan
Rhoades, Anne
Richter, Victoria
Rieck, Julie
Riesmeyer, Carol
Ring, Mary
Rockhold, Jeneen
Rodriguez, Amy
Romine, Joyce
Ruby, Dottie
Ruby, Larry
Runyan, Jack
Russell, Jim
Ryan, Heather
Ryan, Steve
Sabates, Marcia
Sabaugh, Sue
Sandridge, Edward
Sauder, Molly
Scahill, AnnMarie
Scanlon, Judie
Scarbrough, Chely
Schleicher, Julie
Schloegel, Debbie
Schmiedeler, Peggy
Schorgl, Brian
Schorgl, Julie
Schorgl, Katherine
Schulte, Barbara
Schust, Mary
Selanders, Beth
Shealy, Pat
Sirna, Mary Jane
Smith, Chris
Smith, Suzie
Snodell, Firmin
Snodell, Steve
Solsburg, Nick
Sondergaard, Beverly
Soher, Brian
Sopyla, Gerri
Sorrentino, Jane
Spink, Andrea
Spink, Tom

Springs, Vicki
Stablein, King
Stabler, Cece
Stacy, Karen
Stacy, Michael
Stacy, Patrick
Stamm, Janelle
Strauss, Mary Jo
Streib, Audrey
Sturgeon, Carolyn
Taylor, John
Thedinger, Bradley
Thompson, Mary
Thompson, P.J.
Thorne, Bridget
Toth, Cathy
Toth, Margo
Toth, Robert
Trakas, Ellen
Tulipana, Donna
Useldinger, Clint
Useldinger, Sina
VandenBoom, Gene
VanDyke, Karen
VanDyke, Maryhelen
VanDyke, Peggy
Veach, Lois
Veltrie, S.J., Fr. Jim
Viviano, Megan
Vossman, Betsy
Wagner, Janet
Walsh, Pat
Walsworth, Shea
Ward, Allison
Webb, Shari
Webster, Debra
Wells, Pat
Welsh, Mary Ann
Wendland, Kathleen
Wiest, Deloris
Wikiera, Rich
Winget, Bridget
Wirken, Jim
Wolfe, Natalie
Zecy, Wendy

Recipe Index

285